Faith

The Reach of an Empty Hand

James Schuppe

SHENANDOAH PRESS

SHENANDOAH JCT, WV

Library of Congress Control Number: 2021922778

ISBN: 978-1-7369334-6-6

Printed in the United States of America

DEDICATION

This book is dedicated to the memory of the beautiful woman who so fully completed my life for fifty years and eleven months, *Martha Jo.*

CONTENTS

Acknowledgments

This book owes its origin to wonderful times I had as a professor in the classroom with students at the Washington Bible College in Lanham MD. Their penetrating questions caused me to dig deeper to find answers that weren't in the standard answer book collection. I'm grateful for all the students at WBC and sad that the school is no more.

I owe a large debt of gratitude to my beautiful wife who put up with a rather flaky, sometimes blind-to-what's-important husband for fifty plus years, and then left for a better place as we were working on Chapter 15. She will be remembered as an amazing woman of God, joyful in the Lord, faithful in service, compassionate toward those in need, wise in counsel, and most of all, humble as a quiet servant of her God. I am the better man for her fifty years of companionship and sad that she is no longer with me.

I also owe a debt of gratitude to three people who have read and made very insightful comments on this manuscript. Many thanks to Wayne Ferguson, Rebecca Villafane, and E. James Bos.

Introduction

This book is intended to be an introduction to the subject of faith. It is not an argument or a theological tome answering all the questions, of which there are many. Rather it's designed to investigate some of the difficulties in the way we define faith today. I will use the words *faith* and *believe* interchangeably, viewing the word *believe* as the verb and *faith* as the noun. Both words portray the same process of human interaction with God, which I have entitled, "the reach of an empty hand." My desire is simply to help readers understand faith: what it is and how to live it out.

My plan is to briefly explain the faith process in the first two chapters and then interrupt the explanation in chapter three to discuss the phrase "not of works." It's an issue I feel has to be answered before I can continue.

Chapters 4 through 6 talk about the first step of faith; *listening*. Chapter 7 is another "wait a minute" chapter that answers the question of whether people who are dead in trespasses and sins can actually listen and believe.

Chapters 8 and 9 deal with the second step of faith, *believing*. Chapter 10 explains the third step, *obeying*.

Then chapters 11 through 15 connect the definition of faith with the Christian life. How does a Christian live by faith? What happens if people quit believing? And what's the goal of all this?

I trust that you will be encouraged, even excited over the amazingly beautiful way that God has designed for humans to come to know and fellowship with Him by the simple reach of an empty hand.

Chapter 1

My first thoughts about faith

It's not hard to get people to agree that this thing called *faith* is important. People accept that without question, but what's more difficult is to get a handle on what faith is.

Some say, "Just believe," as if it doesn't need a definition because it is as normal as breathing.

Others view it as a mysterious leap into the dark, or even something more ambiguous like Tertullian, the father of Latin theology, who defined it with, "I believe because it is impossible,"[1] or the little boy who said, "faith is believin' what you know ain't true."

"Does the Bible give us a clear definition of faith?" After all, the Bible warns us that without faith it is impossible to please God (Hebrews 11:6), and salvation is only by grace through faith (Ephesians 2:8-9).

Does our future promise of heaven depend on exercising an unclear concept? If faith is one of the most important aspects of our relationship with God, does God fully explain what it is?

I wasn't very sure for several years. I bounced around between definitions, sometimes thinking that faith was a gift that God gave out. Other times I was quite certain that faith was a response that I initiated, and still other times I wondered if I needed to declare what I believed, or even if I had lost it. Let me start with a little personal history.

1. My first experience with faith

It was a late summer afternoon when a man down the street from our house in Arlington, Virginia drove up in a new car. It was a 1949 Ford. It was red. I don't know if you remember those post-war Fords, but they were groundbreaking in their design. Most cars up to that time had hoods that went to a point in the front. You could call it the "nose" of the car because it looked like a nose. And usually at the very tip of the nose was some sort of chrome emblem that set the car apart: a flying lady, a lurching lion, or a circle of some sort.

But the Fords broke with all that history and came out with a hood that was essentially flat all the way across. And as you sat in the car, or stood behind the driver, as was in my case, it looked like you were going down the street behind a plow that seemed like it was every bit of ten feet wide and threatened to push away all the parked cars.

The owner of the car was a family friend, George Miles. He offered to give several of us kids in the neighborhood a ride in the car that evening. We had to get permission and after dinner, we piled into the car for a ride.

It wasn't just a ride around the block; we were going a considerable distance. I don't know where we went, but it was somewhere downtown, Washington, DC, to a church. It was a young peoples' meeting and George Miles the driver, the President of the Washington Bible Institute, was speaking. I don't remember if there was any singing, but I do remember Mr. Miles explaining the "good news." He made it very clear that

Jesus died on a cross to pay for my sin, and that I was a sinner headed for Hell at the age of seven. He asked those who wanted to trust in Christ as Savior to raise a hand and come forward. I raised my hand, went forward and joined in a circle of five or six others.

Mr. Miles went around the circle individually and led each one of us in a prayer inviting Jesus into our heart. I prayed, admitting I was a sinner, requesting Jesus to forgive me and come into my life. I'm not sure I felt anything, but I was pretty sure that God had heard my prayer and had come into my life.

My life became different. In subsequent days I had a new peace, a new joy, a new attitude toward the Bible. I announced to my mother that evening that I had trusted Christ as my Savior. She was excited. The next morning I announced that I had trusted Christ to some men on a garbage truck as it stopped in front of our house. They weren't as excited.

2. My first clue as to a definition of faith

I was ten years old when my friend, Wendell, invited me to attend a revival meeting at a small Baptist church about five miles away. As soon as the speaker got up he held out his hand with fist clenched, and said, "I have something valuable in my hand and will give it to the first person who comes to get it." There was a pause as fifty to sixty people looked around at each other without moving, so I went up and got what was in his hand. It was a dollar bill.

As I stood there, a visitor knowing no one, a little embarrassed over my boldness and quite happy with my gift, the speaker made an example of me by pointing out what I had done. I had heard what he promised and responded to it by coming up and getting it. He described my response as a move of *faith*. He said to the rest of the folks, "as you sat there in your pew, you may have thought to yourself, 'I believe the preacher has something valuable in his hand,' but you didn't actually believe that because you didn't move. This lad believed me. You may have thought you believed, but you didn't."

I thought about that example for a much longer period than the dollar lasted. He said that faith is a response to a promise. That was a new concept to me. I wouldn't have had the dollar except for the fact that I moved. Yet the preacher called my action, "faith."

3. My quest for a Biblical definition of faith

It wasn't long after I entered Bible College at seventeen that I was introduced to some of the confusion over the definition of faith.

There was an active definition of faith, which I knew from the dollar I had received in that church. But then I was introduced to a definition which contradicted what I thought. It seemed to be more passive and developed its authority by the word, "works" in the Bible. Since the Bible states that salvation is "not of works, lest anyone should boast" (Ephesians 2:8-9), faith needs to contain little or no effort.

I remember walking home from the bus stop one afternoon debating with myself over the meaning of faith. "How can faith be apart from works when I have to do something?" "How can doing something be *believing?*" "How can faith be commanded? Doesn't a command expect a response, something that would be categorized as *works?*" "Can faith still be faith when you do something?"

And of course, the bottom line always came to my personal relationship with God:

"Have I really believed?"

"Did I really get saved?"

"Did I believe enough?"

"Did I pray enough?"

"Maybe I was really trying to save myself?"

It was all so confusing. The prayer I prayed back at the age of seven was a very simple request. Was that faith? Was that enough? I didn't cry and I didn't plead; it was just a very simple request.

At the end of my first year in Bible College I was invited to travel for the summer with a quartet, moving from church to church and camp to camp, packing into and out of a 1956 Ford station wagon with four other fellows. I took five books, all on the subject of faith. I had prayed that God would give me an understanding of this most important issue since my eternal salvation depended on it. Strangely, He didn't seem to answer, and my confusion remained, even after digesting as much of the content of the five books as I could.

It was discouraging. I thought, "If this many people who know this much about the Bible present this much confusion over such an essential part of my relationship with God, what hope is there for me?" And even more so, "Does God make the subject clear?" "Why does He tolerate such confusion? Why doesn't He explain faith simply?"

One thing stood out from my reading: I needed to pray that God would show me the answer from His Word. I realized that I had taken the books with me partly because I really didn't believe that God had explained Himself very clearly in the Bible. I thought the books would help explain what He meant. They didn't and that left me back at square one.

So I began praying that God would both show and convince me from His Word. I can remember asking, "Have You made the definition of faith clear in Your revelation of Yourself?" "You've said, 'without faith it is impossible to please You,' but where have You explained what it is that pleases You?" "Can You show me a verse that makes it clear?"

I didn't pray all night or for long periods of time. It was just something that kept bugging me by reminding me of my inability to piece things together.

4. The answer to my prayer – perhaps

I don't remember how long it took before the answer took shape, but one day two verses suggested an answer to my prayer. Sometime during my second summer of quartet travel I began looking at a couple of verses differently because I began to see that they suggested a process. Here's the passage:

> For "whoever calls on the name of the LORD shall be saved." How then shall they call on Him in whom they have not believed? And how shall they believe in Him of whom they have not heard? And how shall they hear without a preacher? And how shall they preach unless they are sent? As it is written: "How beautiful are the feet of those who preach the gospel of peace, Who bring glad tidings of good things!" But they have not all obeyed the gospel. For Isaiah says, "Lord, who has believed our report?" So then faith comes by hearing, and hearing by the word of God. (Romans 10:13-17)

I was struck with the way Paul asked the questions in verses 14-15: "How shall they call on Him in whom they have not believed?" *as if believing preceded calling on Him.* And "how shall they believe in Him of whom they have not heard?" *as if hearing preceded believing.* And "how shall they hear without a preacher?" *as if preaching the gospel preceded hearing.* And "how shall they preach unless they are sent?" *as if sending preceded preaching.* In other words, each one seemed to result from the other. And if they are sequential, then maybe verse 17 is a sort of summary statement of the process: "faith comes by hearing and hearing by the Word of God."

If Paul is giving us the process of faith in this passage, it looked to me like it would develop this way:

Step one: Faith begins with someone who announces the "good news" (the gospel) that Jesus died for our sins and that "whoever calls on the name of the Lord will be saved." Step one begins with God, who not only provided for our salvation, but sent out preachers to broadcast the amazing truth that forgiveness of sins and eternal life in heaven is a gift. In my case that was George Miles at a youth service in Washington DC.

Step two: Someone has to listen to the message, "hearing" the announcement of God's wonderful provision of salvation in Christ. Since I grew up in a Christian family I had heard the gospel many times. But that night as I listened, the Holy Spirit convicted me of my sin and my need of Christ. I heard the message in a fresh way and knew it was addressed to me.

Step three: Hearing has to lead to "believing." Believing acknowledges that you accept the message as true, that God meant what He said and stated it accurately. I can remember hearing the gospel earlier, and viewing it as something other people needed. But that evening I realized and believed that the promise was for me, was true, and that I needed to call on the name of the Lord.

Step four: Believing needs to result in a response of "calling" for salvation to occur. "Whoever calls on the name of the LORD shall be saved." I wasn't saved because I believed the message was factual. I wasn't saved because I believed there was a God, or even that Jesus died for me. I was saved when I responded, when I called. Mr. Miles led me in a simple prayer requesting God's forgiveness and the salvation offered in Christ.

What Paul outlined is a four-step process that is clearly spelled out: It has to start with someone announcing, then someone listening, then believing, and then calling on the name of the Lord. Could it be that faith is that simple? Could it be that God has actually defined the process for us? I was excited. That's easy enough for a child to understand and follow.

In the past sixty years since that summer day, I have come to realize that, *yes, faith is that simple*. However, the questions which arise from these four steps are not as easy to answer. The simplicity of the process seems to generate an amazing number of problems. For example:

1. Is faith passive? "Passive" would suggest that faith is a gift which God gives to certain ones He chooses. Since it is the work of God, there is nothing a person can do to get or exercise faith. It only comes from God and when He gives it to you, you know you have it.

2. **Is faith active?** Does it include some sort of human responsibility, like listening, choosing, moving, committing? If it does, is that "works?" Can faith be faith when you have to do something? And how can God's work expect a response from humans? Isn't that "synergism" where humans help God? Wouldn't that idea detract from the sovereignty of God by giving more responsibility –and ability– to humans than they have?

3. Is it even possible for those who are "dead in trespasses and sins" to believe? If faith is the exercise of a human responsibility, how is that accomplished by someone who is dead? It would be like expecting a response in a mortuary. Does the directive from God presuppose a work by God to make obedience possible?

4. How long does faith have to continue believing to be genuine? Is real faith continuous trust, or is it more a momentary thing where one believes someone at a point in time? Why did Jesus address His disciples as having "no faith?" Did they have faith when they came to Him? Had they lost it?

5. If a person stops believing and turns away from God, does that indicate that his initial belief wasn't genuine? Is it possible to believe God at one time and not at another?

6. What's the difference between faith and faithfulness? Is faithfulness continuous faith? Or repeated faith? Or faith that has accompanying works? Is there a conflict between Paul and James? Paul claims that "to him who does not work but believes on Him who justifies the ungodly, his faith is accounted for righteousness" (Romans 4:5). On the other hand James says, "You see then that a man is justified by works, and not by faith only," and "For as the body without the spirit is dead, so faith without works is dead also" (James 2:24, 26).

Paul states that genuine faith excludes works, while James states what looks like the opposite, that faith has to include works to be faith. How are we to reconcile these statements?

By the time I was ready to graduate from Capital Bible Seminary I had pretty well decided that Romans 10:13-17 contained the definition of faith I was looking for. I was grateful for God's kindness in showing me the basis of my responsibility to Him. When I began teaching at the Washington Bible College in 1966 this definition of faith became part of my lesson plans.

In 1988 John MacArthur published a book entitled, *The Gospel of Jesus Christ*. That set off a round of controversy and arguments over the definition of faith, which surprised me. How could brothers and sisters in Christ disagree so widely over what is so essential in their spiritual lives? It made me question whether I had the correct definition of faith. One thing that surprised me was that much of the argument was carried on with little or no reference to Romans 10:13-17. So here I am, sixty or more years after that first answer to my prayerful question asking for God's definition of faith. I am more convinced than ever that Romans 10:13-17 holds the key to understanding our responsibility in our relationship with God. But how does it all work out? Read on.

Chapter 2

The simple definition of the faith process

I can still remember my emotions that day when I was convinced that God had revealed to me the definition of the word "faith." It was like discovering gold – from the Bible. God had actually answered my prayer! Over the years I have had dozens of questions and challenges to that definition. In the rest of this book I want to show how God has answered some of them through His Word. But first of all I'd like to clarify the definition of faith as presented in Romans 10:13-17.

What does it mean for someone to "believe," or exercise "faith?" What are the *human responsibilities?* How is it like "the reach of an empty hand," as the title suggests? Let me explain the way it unfolds in this passage:

> For "whoever calls on the name of the LORD shall be saved." How then shall they call on Him in whom they have not believed? And how shall they believe in Him of whom they have not heard? And how shall they hear without a preacher? And how shall they preach unless they are sent? As it is written: "How beautiful are the feet of those who preach the gospel of peace, Who bring glad tidings of good things!" But they have not all obeyed the gospel. For

Isaiah says, "Lord, who has believed our report?" So then faith comes by hearing, and hearing by the word of God (Romans 10:13-17).

As mentioned in the last chapter we can see at least four parts or steps to this explanation of faith: (a) it begins with God; (b) it continues when someone listens; (c) it continues when the listener accepts the message as true and (d) it culminates when the listener obeys by calling on the name of the Lord.

I. Faith *begins* with God's provision

God initiated the entire plan of salvation by His marvelous work that has made faith possible. Let me point out three wonderful actions of God that kick-started the faith process.

A. God reconciled the world. Salvation centers on the fact that Christ died on a cross and rose again. His sacrifice paid the penalty for our sins making forgiveness possible. Faith begins with a preacher from God announcing the amazing news that Jesus Christ has finished paying the incredible debt our sins created.

The preacher announces that "God has reconciled the world unto Himself," and "the work of reconciliation is already finished!" As sinners we don't contribute to our salvation. God has already provided all that is needed! Here's Paul's description of the event:

> "Now all things are of God, who has reconciled us to Himself through Jesus Christ, and has given us the ministry of reconciliation, that is, that God was in Christ reconciling the world to Himself, not imputing their trespasses to

them, and has committed to us the word of reconciliation.
Now then, we are ambassadors for Christ, as though God
were pleading through us: we implore you on Christ's be-
half, be reconciled to God" (2 Corinthians 5:18-20).

The amazing work which is *already finished* is expressed by, "reconciled us to Himself through Jesus Christ" (v. 18), and "God was in Christ reconciling the world to Himself" (v. 19). Reconciliation is needed for enemies to become friends. It's what needs to happen when your bank statement doesn't match the checks you have written. You bring them into harmony so both agree.

Enemies won't be reconciled until there is a response from both sides. If one forgives but the other one doesn't, there is no reconciliation. A similar thing is true with God and humanity. God took the first step by reconciling the world to Himself at the cross. That's the most important step, because if God's wrath remained on our sin, we would have no hope, no matter what we did. But God has reconciled the world to Himself! Step number one is finished!

B. God sent out preachers to announce the fact. How do we know that God has put away His wrath and reconciled the world to Himself? There is one clear way: *by the appearance of preachers announcing reconciliation!* Who are these preachers? Paul says that He "gave us the ministry of reconciliation" (v. 18), and that "He has committed to us the word of reconciliation" (v. 19). Those who have received Christ's reconciliation are, in fact, the designated preachers!

The Creator of the universe has sent out preachers to knock on doors of tiny dust specks on planet Earth and announce peace! Why? *Because God has been reconciled with the world!* Pastor James Denny said, "Enemies do not send such messages."[2] Faith begins with an announcement from God.

C. God the Holy Spirit convicts and calls the world to repentance. Before He died on the cross Jesus announced that He would send the Holy Spirit to accomplish a specific ministry in the world:

> And when He has come, He will convict the world of sin, and of righteousness, and of judgment: of sin, because they do not believe in Me; of righteousness, because I go to My Father and you see Me no more; of judgment, because the ruler of this world is judged (John 16:8-11).

The Holy Spirit is even now using the words He wrote to convict unbelievers of their sin, Christ's righteousness, and the Father's judgment. He opens human eyes to the truth, showing them their sinfulness and helpless state. He points them to the answer, the cross of Christ where reconciliation for sin was marvelously accomplished. This ministry is world-wide; He convicts "the world." Everyone receives the blessing of His ministry.

II. Faith comes from *hearing* what God says

"And how shall they believe in Him of whom they have not heard?

. . . So then faith comes by hearing" (Romans 10:14, 17).

No one can believe or reject a message without knowing what it says. More than a leap into the dark, faith is a conscious response to a word that someone else has spoken.

A. There is no faith until God's Word appears. Someone says to you, "loan me $100 and I will give you $20,000 tomorrow," but you didn't hear them. How could you respond? There would be zero response, even though you would expect an instant reaction to a promise like that.

That's the point of verse 17; all faith begins with "hearing." We can't believe something we know nothing about. There's a strange notion that people can find God by searching their inner selves or by some intense introspective investigation. Rather than listening to Him, they are seeking their own way. It's like trying to find out what it's like to live in North Korea by searching your inner being. The differences between God and humans are infinitely beyond the differences between Americans and North Koreans. It's a gap that is impossible to bridge without God taking the initiative to introduce Himself.

This doesn't mean that someone needs to actually, physically hear a preacher to believe. Some read the good news in a book or tract; others may receive God's promise from the testimony of a friend. But the point is that faith begins from the outside rather than from the inside. It begins with an announcement from God. Without that announcement there would be no faith, because faith is simply our response to God's message.

B. Listening is not automatic. Every parent knows that there are huge differences between listening and *Listening!* Just because your child looks like he is listening, or just because he says he is listening, doesn't mean he gets what you have said. Obviously listening is more than simply hearing words.

What makes God's words more difficult to attend to are things like: (1) they introduce us to something radically new (what God is like), or (2) they tell us something hard to hear (what we are like and that we need to repent), or (3) that we can't do anything to fix the problem because the answer is a gift from God (and we can't do anything to earn God's Grace). Each of these truths make the listening process more challenging because they are strange to our normal thought patterns.

Thus for faith to come by hearing means effort and work. Effort sometimes involves physical activity, like concentration, to collect and assemble the pieces of the message, to remember it, to evaluate and decide what to do with it. Many times, listening is simply too much work, so we opt for the easier road, non-listening or pretend-listening.

The point is that listening is a prerequisite to faith. "Listen" is a command in Scripture (Luke 8:8). It's active, it's our responsibility, and it's the beginning human response that opens the door to a relationship with God.

III. Faith is *believing* God's promise to be true

"How then shall they call on Him in whom they have not believed? And how shall they believe in Him of whom they have not heard?" (Romans 10:14).

Oxford's first definition of "believe" is, "accept as true or as conveying the truth."[3] This definition implies a process of evaluation.

If I said to you, "loan me $100 and I'll pay you back tomorrow," you would first want to check your catalog of information about me. Can I be trusted to pay you back tomorrow? Have I paid you back in the past? Is my word trustworthy? Only as you believe my promise do you give yourself permission to obey my request.

A. The *object of faith* is what makes it valid. One of the strange concepts in American religious experience today is the notion that faith by itself is valuable. Bumper stickers proclaim: "JUST BELIEVE." The implication is that your life will be better if you just have more faith. That's ridiculous. People don't need to be told to believe; they have great amounts of faith, but usually in the wrong thing. They may believe in their invincibility, in their wisdom, in their ability to captain their own ship. They may believe in some financial guru who is taking them for a ride; they may believe in some religious guru who has "gone to heaven and back." Finding believers is no problem. Everybody believes. The question is who they believe in, or what they believe.

Picture two men standing on the deck of the sinking Titanic having this conversation. One man says to the other, "it is in an hour like this that one must exercise faith." The other replies, "faith in what? We put our faith in this ship, and it's now going down. We were told by an employee of the White Star Line that even God in Heaven couldn't sink this ship, and we trusted that word. Now who do you want to have faith in?"

Great faith in the wrong person, the wrong promise, is worthless, and it can be deadly. The greatness of one's faith makes no difference, it's the truthfulness of faith's object. That White Star Line employee didn't know what he was talking about. But Jesus does.

B. The credibility of a person, the truthfulness of a statement is what makes faith valid. If I were to say to you, "I want you to believe in Gastric," your response would probably be, "who is Gastric, what did he say or do for me to believe in? Is Gastric powerful? Wise? Loving?" "I heard that he was a thief." And I say, "It doesn't matter who Gastric is, or what he did, just believe in Gastric. Just believe."

Do you see the problem? What I'd be asking for is not faith as much as it is blind acceptance of my will. But you can't believe until there is some satisfactory fact, truth, statement, or promise about the person to believe.

Who is Jesus Christ? Well, He is the One who said, "I am the bread of life;" "I am the light of the world;" "I am the door. If anyone enters by Me, he will be saved." He also said, "I am the way, the truth, and the life; no one comes to the Father except through Me." Are these statements true? If they are, we should come and eat of the bread and walk in the light and enter through the door and come to the Father by Christ. That would be faith in action.

Perhaps you were cruising through life without thinking much about God until a word from Christ somehow got to you. It said something like, "You are a sinner, and because of that are heading for Hell." That word caused you to slow down and say, "wait a minute, how do you know that? Is that true? That can't be true, because I'm not a bad person. Who said that?" Listening leads to the question of believing: "Can I accept Christ's words as true?" Faith is a response to Jesus Christ Himself, by trusting His words.

IV. Faith is *obeying* God's direction

For there is no distinction between Jew and Greek, for the same Lord over all is rich to all who call upon Him. For "whoever calls on the name of the LORD shall be saved."

How then shall they call on Him in whom they have not believed? And how shall they believe in Him of whom they have not heard? And how shall they hear without a preacher? (Romans 10:12-14).

A. Faith is personal action. God's promise is that He will save "whoever calls on the name of the LORD." I puzzled for some time over the word "calls." "Why didn't Paul say, 'whoever believes on the name of the Lord shall be saved'?" "Why does he specify *calls* here when John 3:16 assures us that salvation comes by believing? Calling implies a response.

Then I noticed other gospel invitations that expect a personal response. Jesus for example said, "I am the bread of life. He who *comes* to Me shall never hunger, and he who believes in Me shall never thirst" (John 6:35).

Does He provide this bread for everyone? No, there's an expected response. "Comes to Me," and "believes in Me" are synonymous and express the condition for receiving bread. Believing Him is done by obeying His call and coming to Him.

I noticed other gospel invitations that actually *command us to respond.* For example, when God sent out messengers with the announcement that He had reconciled the world to Himself they arrived with a command: "Be reconciled to God" (2 Corinthians 5:20). Similarly, the apostle Paul commanded the jailer in Philippi, "Believe on the Lord Jesus Christ, and you will be saved, you and your household" (Acts 16:31).

B. The response of faith is specific. There is a distinction between obeying God's direction and "doing something religious" like keeping the Ten Commandments or helping the poor. If I tell you to loan me $100 promising to pay you back tomorrow, how do you show that you believe my promise? Could you do it by mowing my lawn? Telling others that I am an honest Joe? No, only by producing $100.

Faith is a specific response to a specific promise with specific instructions. People can do all kinds of good, nice, religious things, feel better and think that they have impressed God – all without ever obeying God's command.

My dad recorded the testimony of a woman he heard who said that she was praying in agony of heart, wondering whether her sins were forgiven. Suddenly a white form appeared before her with pierced hands. A drop of blood fell from one hand. Instantly she knew her sins were forgiven!

Were they? Is that what the Bible says? "When you see a drop of blood you will know?" You might counter "Well, that is spectacular; that must be of God." But in contrast, God says, "whoever calls on the name of the LORD shall be saved." Did she call?

I know a man who was in agony over his sins and prayed about his sins for more than a week, and then, one afternoon, peace came over him and he "knew that his sins were forgiven." Were they? Does the Bible say to "pray about your sins until you get peace?" Then you will be saved? Perhaps he was saved. But the assurance that the Bible gives comes from exact obedience, in this case, from calling on the name of the Lord. Did the man actually call upon the name of the Lord for forgiveness?

In summary, Romans 10:13-14 describes faith as *a process with four aspects:* a *message*, along with one who *listens, believes* the message, and *obeys* the directions.

Additionally Paul makes the point that these steps are *progressive:* people have to hear the good news *before* they can process and believe it. And people aren't going to respond and call upon the name of the Lord *until* they really believe the message.

We can condense these four steps into three human responsibilities: to *hear what God says,* to *believe it to be true,* and to *obey the specific directions.* Perhaps a good, summary definition of faith in light of Romans 10:13-21 is: Faith is *Hearing God's promise and Believing it enough to Obey it.*

So that's where it all started. I was excited to have a Bible based definition of faith. But I wasn't too sure about it. I felt like I had just chipped a golf ball up onto a severely tilted green and wondered if it would *hold.* Does the entire Bible clearly demonstrate that faith should be understood this way?

Chapter 3

Is this a "works-for-salvation" system?

One of the first questions I had was with the "obedience" step. How can a response of obedience be a part of faith without salvation being accomplished by my effort? *Doing something* in order to receive salvation makes it seem like salvation might not be as much a gift from God as it is God's blessing on my response, or His approval of my obedience.

One of my key questions was: "Does salvation depend on the sinner making a move?" In other words, does one have to engage his or her will in order to have faith? Or is believing something, accepting something (eternal life from Jesus Christ) action-less and passive, perhaps only mental? At the same time I was asking, "Why would anyone even think about associating faith with action or obedience when Scripture clearly declares that it is 'not of works?'" Let me explain how faith can be "not of works" and yet expect a response from the listener.

I. Faith and works seem to compete in Scripture

The question bothered me for some time, "How can God promise salvation to those who *call* (Romans 10:13) while at the same time declaring that faith is *not of works?*" How can God command us to respond without the response being in the category of *works?*

In discussing this with others over the years, it seemed like almost everyone had a similar question concerning the part that works plays in the definition of faith. The problem is that Scripture presents faith as "without works," and "not of yourself" (Ephesians 2:8-9) while at the same time making it a command (Acts 16:30-31) and describing it as obedience (Hebrews 5:9). How can something that is "without works" be *commanded?* A command is something I do or should do. How can God give me a gift as a result of my *obedience to His command* without that gift being *earned?*

I sensed this tension in the first chapter of John's gospel:

> He came to His own, and His own did not receive Him. But as many as received Him, to them He gave the right to become children of God, to those who believe in His name: who were born, not of blood, nor of the will of the flesh, nor of the will of man, but of God (John 1:11-13).

Notice "nor of the will of the flesh, nor of the will of man." Salvation is not of the will of man. It can't be accomplished by anything human, not "blood," or the will of the "flesh" or the will of "man," because it's God's work. Does that mean an unbeliever's *will* can have no part in his salvation, that salvation has to be *will-less*, or *passive?*

Some take that position on this issue. They claim that there can be no human participation in our salvation. From the start (with election) to the work of the Holy Spirit in an unbeliever's heart (irresistible grace) to regeneration, it is all of God. All a person does is wake up one day and realize that God has saved him.

But if that's true, how does the earlier part fit, where Jesus came to His own nation, and His own people *would not* receive Him? They exercised their wills and collectively responded with "no, we don't want Him." Their response wasn't *will-less*. It was *will-full*.

You might say, "Well, that's the normal response of an unregenerate person." And that's very true. But remember that these people were the *elect*, the nation of Israel, God's chosen people. They possessed blessings from God that no other nation possessed. They should have responded positively.

And remember that if a willful "no" is the response of every unregenerate person, why the positive response in verse 12? There were some *who did receive Him* by believing in His name. In spite of the large national "NO," there were individuals, Jewish and others, who said, "YES," and received/believed in Him.

In this context where some were willing "no" and others willing "yes," verse 13 appears declaring that: "nor" was it "of the will of man." How can we fit, "not of the will of man" with "as many as received Him?" The two seem contradictory. People in verse 11 were exercising their wills to refuse salvation in Jesus, in verse 12 some were exercising their wills to receive Him, and verse 13 declares that salvation is apart from the will of man. How can salvation be "not of the will of man" when the two previous verses expressed the will of man?

II. Faith sometimes clearly involves a response

I grew up in a culture that taught an action-less faith, and I came to believe that as soon as one made any kind of effort, faith became works. Thus I was searching for a clear definition of faith that did not involve personal effort. It might be okay to have mental activity, even a sinner making a choice, although that was pretty close to the edge of "works."

At the same time I was bothered by Romans 10:13 which tells us that "whoever calls on the name of the LORD shall be saved." The word *calls* suggested to me that a sinner had to make up his or her mind and do something. And the word "call" is a fairly strong word, meaning "to cry out upon the name of someone." I wondered why the verse wasn't written, "whoever believes on the name of the Lord shall be saved." That would have made my theology simpler. But *call*, even *cry out*, as if the person is in trouble and realizes that the only help is in the Lord, didn't fit my categories for faith very well.

Then I found other intentional actions in this passage: "that if you confess with your mouth the Lord Jesus and believe in your heart that God has raised Him from the dead, you will be saved" (Romans 10:9). "Confess" sounds like one has to make up one's mind and go public with a decision to acknowledge that Jesus is Lord.

And in the same chapter verse 16 reminds us: "But they have not all obeyed the gospel. For Isaiah says, 'Lord, who has believed our report'?" I saw that Paul connected Isaiah's question, "who has believed our report?" with the negative response of Israel and called it *disobedience*. He equated believing with obeying. He said in effect, *you can see that the nation of Israel has not believed the gospel because they have not obeyed it*. That to me was a major statement: *a person doesn't believe the gospel until he or she obeys it.* Knowing it and accepting it as true would not necessarily be faith.

That raised another question: "what kind of obedience was Paul expecting in v. 16?" Verse 13 says, "whoever calls on the name of the LORD shall be saved." "Call" is the obedience word. Salvation by faith is defined as "calling on the name of the Lord."

That thought made a lot of sense in light of other commands in Scripture that required a response. "Come" for example, in John 6:35: "I am the bread of life. He who comes to Me shall never hunger, and he who believes in Me shall never thirst." The correlation between *comes* and *believes* suggests that believing is coming to Christ which implies that one doesn't believe until one comes.

All of a sudden many verses made sense: "But as many as received Him, to them He gave the right to become children of God, to those who believe in His name" (John 1:12). The obedience part here is to *receive* Christ, which most of the Israelites refused to do in the previous verse. Believing is *receiving*.

"If you knew the gift of God, and who it is who says to you, 'Give Me a drink,' you would have asked Him, and He would have given you living water" (John 4:10). The obedience part was for the woman at the well to *ask* Christ for living water. *Asking* for living water is believing in Christ.

These verses suggested that faith was not passive but an active response. It involves listening to God's Word, *becoming convinced* by it and *coming* to Christ or *receiving* Him, or *asking* for living water. Faith is not action-less. It is willful, purposeful *obedience* to God's Word.

III. The word "works" can be defined in different ways

Bible authors don't use the word "works" with exactly the same definition each time. Sometimes works are negative in God's sight (Titus 3:5) and other times they are positive (Jonah 3:10). Is it possible that Scripture uses the word *works* in different ways? Yes, dictionaries give us that permission. For our purposes, there are at least two important, distinguishable, meanings of the word *work*. One points to what we can accomplish and get credit for, while the other refers to basic human effort, like simply lifting a pen.

A. Work is something you produce or accomplish. The first two definitions in Thayer's lexicon equate work with, "that which is accomplished by hand, art, industry, or mind." It can mean a business, or employment ("that with which any one is occupied.")[4] Or it can refer to a thing accomplished ("a good night's work"). A good example of this kind of work is where Hebrews says, "You, LORD, in the beginning laid the foundation of the earth, And the heavens are the work of Your hands" (1:10). The heavens are the product of His awesome creative ability.

This kind of work is used in the sense of "accomplishment" or "earnings," what one achieves by personal creativity, whether God or humans. It can be something a sinner tries to accomplish to impress God so that God owes him a blessing. That's the definition in Romans 4:4: "Now to him who works, the wages are not counted as grace but as debt." Paul uses the word *works* to mean something earned so that the wages are a *debt*. An unbeliever who works according to this definition is attempting to make God his debtor. God would owe him righteousness or salvation

because of all the goodness he has generated. I call this type activity
WORKS^{earnings}.

Salvation is a gift, and everyone knows that a gift can never be earned.
Perhaps you've had the experience of suddenly realizing that one of your
friends is trying to pay you back for an expensive gift you gave him. What
does that do to you? Do you thank him for trying to pay you back? No,
you are insulted, because you intended he accept it as a gift. "Thank you"
would be the appropriate response.

The same is true with God's gifts. They are all "of grace." Grace describes a gift from God that we don't deserve. He has given each of us
countless gifts of grace, such as a body, and food to feed it, and air to
breathe, and temperature boundaries so we don't freeze or boil. How
much have we contributed for these blessings? Nothing. They are all
grace gifts from God. We should live in thankfulness.

But many believe that "you have to work for everything you get,"
and find it difficult to accept forgiveness of sins and eternal life as a gift.
They attempt to pay for it by turning over a new leaf or getting baptized
or joining a church. The problem is that once there's an attempt to pay,
it is no longer a gift.

That's the point of Romans 4:4: "Now to him who works, the wages
are not counted as grace but as debt." Once God detects that a sinner is
attempting to *earn His favor*, He can no longer give him a gift. He must
instead *pay him what he is due*. And all his righteous acts are filthy in God's
sight (Isaiah 64:6). The sinner's due payment is the lake of fire.

No one can do enough of anything to deserve salvation. God's blessings don't come because of our works^{earnings} to make ourselves acceptable
in His sight. Our rebellion has made us deserving of God's wrath and
judgment (Romans 1:18-32). Grace does not come from God because
we deserve it or because God is indebted to us and paying what He owes.

This is why Ephesians 2:8-9 emphasizes that nothing in salvation comes from us: "For by grace you have been saved through faith, and that not of yourselves; it is the gift of God, not of works, lest anyone should boast." Works[earnings] produces zero in God's sight.

B. Work is any kind of effort. There's another way to read the word "works." This is the third definition in Thayer's lexicon: "an act, deed, thing done: the idea of working."[5] This defines work in the physics sense, the mechanical sense, as *anything that takes effort.* Work is "the application of mental or physical effort to a purpose; the use of energy."[6]

Think of Noah building a boat. He was putting out effort day after day for years, yet Hebrews 11:7 says that all his work was *by faith.* What made it faith was that Noah was simply obeying God's directions rather than earning credit. I call this **WORKS**[effort].

Paul said to Timothy, "do the work of an evangelist" (2 Timothy 4:5). He said to the Corinthians, "that you also submit to such, and to everyone who works and labors with us" (1 Corinthians 16:16). Luke says, "At Joppa there was a certain disciple named Tabitha, which is translated Dorcas. This woman was full of good works and charitable deeds which she did" (Acts 9:36).

These verses present works as *obedience* to what God directs, not as an attempt to *earn* something in God's sight. Such obedience was displayed by the Ninevites: "Then God saw their works, that they turned from their evil way; and God relented from the disaster that He had said He would bring upon them, and He did not do it" (Jonah 3:10).

Here the Ninevites received from God the *opposite* of what Romans 4:4 promises. Instead of giving these sinners what they deserved, God responded positively to their works and relented. Why? Because what they did was works^{effort}. They weren't doing anything to earn credit from God. Their works were simply humble repentance.

Thus the word, "work," is used in at least two different ways: (1) that which someone produces, accomplishes, creates by his own effort and ability, and (2) that which expends energy to get a job done. The word can mean either *earnings* or *effort*.

That's a significant difference. If Paul is saying that *salvation cannot be earned by works that we generate* (and he is), he may not necessarily be saying that s*alvation can have no movement or effort in it*. Simply putting out *effort* is not the same as working to *earn God's favor.*

Think of an example. A homeless person is sitting on the side of the road, and you want to give him a nice meal. But does he want it? He looks hungry, but is he really hungry? So you devise a test. You say to him, "come over here to my car and I will give you a steak dinner." He walks over and you present him an enormous, tasty meal. Was your meal a gift? Yes. But how could it be a gift when he had to walk over to your car to get it? The poor man worked for that gift. Let's suppose he needed to cross a four-lane city street where the traffic was moving quickly, and by coming over he may have put his life in danger. He could have been killed trying to obey you. But the question is, "did his action *earn* your steak dinner or was the meal still a gift?"

It was a total gift. You came up with the idea; you spent the time and money to cook the great meal, drive downtown and make the offer. Nothing would have happened unless you caused it. All he did was respond in faith. He first had to *hear* your promise. And if there were four lanes of traffic, he may have had to concentrate to hear you, which would take effort. Secondly, he had to *believe* that what you promised was true, and believe it enough to *act in obedience* to your instruction by getting up and coming to receive your gift.

What *title* do we give to the move he made in response to your offer of grace – WORKS^{earnings} or WORKS^{effort}? He may have danced around cars in coming to you. He may have been scared by a near-death experience with a tractor-trailer truck. It was work. But did he *earn* your grace? No, the meal was completely your creation. He said "yes" to your offer by WORKS^{effort} which we call "faith." *He believed you enough to obey your command to come over.* His response was simply the reach of an empty hand.

God's infinite Grace comes along similar paths. The message comes to helpless (and maybe homeless) people. If the message didn't come, there would be no way they could ever figure it out themselves. As they listen the message brings light, to open their eyes to the awesome glories of a gracious God. And that new light introduces them to a new responsibility — to respond to the light by believing the promise and obeying by coming to Jesus to receive His forgiveness and salvation.

The fact that the homeless man responded with obedience by crossing the street in no way made your gift less of a gift. You may have even commanded him to come over. Still your meal was total grace. He had no part in thinking up the meal, creating it, preparing everything, bringing it to him, and announcing the good news that a wonderful meal was available. His response of coming was faith, which could have included effort, obedience, perhaps even placing his life in jeopardy.

In a similar way God's gifts can never be earned by our efforts. But the fact that we can't earn them doesn't mean that there is no response on our part. The truth is, *faith is hearing a promise and believing the person making the promise enough to obey what the promise commands.*

IV. Scripture consistently connects faith with WORKS^{effort}

"By faith Noah, being divinely warned of things not yet seen, moved with godly fear, prepared an ark for the saving of his household, by which he condemned the world and became heir of the righteousness which is according to faith" (Hebrews 11:7).

How could Noah's eighty to one hundred years of effort be characterized as "by faith?" Would it be more correct to say, "by faith and works Noah built an ark?" Did he really build the ark by faith, or was faith only the initiator and everything afterward was works?

Observe that the writer doesn't even talk about the "good works" that Noah did. Suppose that he held prayer meetings and conducted Bible classes and improved church doctrinal statements to include the flood promise while neglecting to work on the ark. Would his efforts have been good works? Could they have been done by faith? No. What made his work faith was his obedience to a specific command from God, the command to "build."

As he built, probably every day brought new challenges to his faith. Imagine him thinking: "Should I interrupt building this ark to fix our house which collapsed yesterday?" Or "I've been working on the ark and preaching for thirty years now, and no one in town has listened to my message and placed their trust in God." Or "We're getting pretty close to bankruptcy and the boat is only twenty-five percent complete. I'm beginning to wonder what the sense is in all this effort."

Noah probably had to re-play God's original command day after day and determine to do each day what he had chosen to do the first day, *go to work on the ark*.

Do you see the faith? We can surmise that Noah had to remind himself of what God said and review God's promise of rain as he man-handled each enormous beam. What made it faith was that he repeatedly believed and responded to a Person by obeying His directions. Eighty plus years of effort was all done because Noah believed his God.

Hebrews 11 consistently connects faith with specific acts of obedience. Consider these examples:

"By faith Abel offered to God a more excellent sacrifice than Cain" (11:4). Abel's sacrifice was "more excellent" because Abel listened to and obeyed God's directions.

"By faith Abraham obeyed when he was called to go out to the place which he would receive as an inheritance. And he went out, not knowing where he was going" (11:8). Moving his family seven hundred miles took an enormous amount of effort. Living in tents for one hundred years was probably quite difficult for someone raised in Ur of the Chaldees with its two-story houses and running water (as archaeologists have discovered).

Additionally, by faith Abraham "offered up Isaac" (11:17) and Isaac "blessed Jacob and Esau" (11:20). These examples were of a faith that included effort. Faith in the promise included obedience to the command.

One of the most famous examples in ordinary life that shows the connection between faith and works[effort] is the story of Charles Blondin. He developed his fame by tight-rope walking in strange places. In 1859 he stretched a cable across Niagara Falls and walked across. He did the same feat several other times, once blindfolded, once on stilts, once pushing a wheelbarrow, and once with a man on his back.

But according to myth, he once came back to the Canadian side after pushing a wheelbarrow across and asked a young girl if she believed that he could carry a person across in the wheelbarrow. She replied, "Sure."

He asked, "Do you believe I could carry someone as big as you across in my wheelbarrow? She answered, "Yes, I believe." He commanded, "OK, get in."

The command put her claim of faith to the test. Did she *really* believe that he could carry someone like her across? A response of faith would have been getting in. But could she have done something else to show her faith? Could she have done "good works?" Could she have sung "praise Blondin" songs, or produced a radio show and "confessed" his name? Could she have encouraged others to get in the wheelbarrow?

After Blondin's command to "get in," everything else that she did apart from getting in the wheelbarrow would have been *unbelief,* and/or *disobedience.* Faith involved *believing his promise enough to respond* by getting in the wheelbarrow.

Jesus said, "I am the bread of life. He who comes to Me . . . ." The command is to "come." It's not a command to obey the Ten Commandments, but to "come to Me." Those who come, come in faith. They have heard His promise and invitation, they believe that He really is the Bread of Life which they desperately need, and they respond by coming to Him.

Are they saved because they have "worked" and "earned" their salvation? Did they do enough "coming" to earn anything? No. They are saved by the gracious gift of God, which is given to anyone who will listen to His promise and believe it enough to respond.

V. Scripture affirms that *faith without WORKS*^{effort} *is not faith*

This is the opposite side of the coin. Not only is it true that works^{effort} is an integral part of faith, but the Bible makes clear that apart from a response of obedience, faith is not faith.

We see this in Jonah's situation: "Then God saw their works, that they turned from their evil way; and God relented from the disaster that He had said He would bring upon them, and He did not do it" (Jonah 3:10).

How should we define the word "works" in this sentence? What did God *see?* He saw the efforts of sinners who seriously wanted to repent. Were they attempting to earn anything? No, they believed that Jonah's promise of judgment came from God, and turned to Him to make their passionate appeal.

The apostle Paul used the word in a similar way when he said to King Agrippa that he was declaring God's heavenly vision ". . . first to those in Damascus and in Jerusalem, and throughout all the region of Judea, and then to the Gentiles, that they should repent, turn to God, and do works befitting repentance" (Acts 26:20). What are "works befitting repentance?" It's obvious that they are not the same thing as works^{earnings} because they please God.

Another indication of the contrast between works^{earnings} and works^{effort} is in Peter's statement to Cornelius: "But in every nation whoever fears Him and works righteousness is accepted by Him" (Acts 10:35). Question: "how does someone *work righteousness* when righteousness can't come by works?" Titus 3:5 tells us, "not by works of righteousness which we have done, but according to His mercy He saved us . . . ." But Peter declared that certain people are "accepted by God" on the basis of working righteousness.

These verses show us that "works" has at least two different definitions. One is acceptable to God. Jonah 3 and Acts 26 speak of the works associated with repentance and Acts 10 speaks of works that come out of a proper fear of God. I call these works^{effort}.

Thus faith defined as *hearing*, *believing*, and *obeying* does not constitute a works-for-salvation system. Calling upon the name of the Lord is not works/earnings because it is simply a response to God's grace. He prepared the meal. He brought it to our homeless world. He offers it to us with the invitation, "come." Trusting Him may involve effort, but not the kind that merits His grace.

Have you ever called on the name of the Lord for salvation? You may have joined a church or been confirmed or baptized or turned over a new leaf, but have you ever actually called out to Jesus Christ and asked Him to save you?

You have to first realize your danger—eternal punishment in hell because you are a sinner. But then you need to realize the amazing news that God has reconciled the world unto Himself because Jesus paid sin's debt on the cross. That means that when you ask Him to forgive your sin and save you, He will!

Chapter 4

Does the Bible emphasize the importance of listening?

I f faith is a process of *hearing, believing* and *obeying*, then step number one is of immense importance because everything in our relationship with God begins there.

The implication of Paul's statement that "faith comes by hearing" (Romans 10:17) is that faith involves personal effort to *listen*. It's an effort to capture Someone's word.

Now if that statement is true (and it is), then there ought to be a large red flag waving in the Bible to caution everyone about the importance of listening.

Is there such a flag? Where in the Bible does it say, *"Hey folks, do you understand that everything in your relationship with God begins with your ears?"* Have you found such an emphasis?

In the next three chapters I would like to show that the Bible does have such a waving flag which proclaims, "everything begins with your ears!" I want to answer three questions:

(a) Is hearing clearly emphasized in Scripture as the source of faith?

(b) Does Scripture clearly show that God responds differently to listeners than to those who don't listen?

45

(c) Does the Scripture explain what kind of listening pleases God? In this chapter I want to answer the first question: "is hearing clearly emphasized in Scripture as the source of faith?"

I. The Apostle Paul states that listening is the source of faith

Let's start with this striking verse, "So then faith comes by hearing, and hearing by the word of God." Is Paul actually saying that our faith begins with our personal effort to focus on what God is saying? Did he actually mean to say, "the source of faith is listening to God's Word," or am I putting words into his mouth? Did he mean that it's not a gift from God to certain people? Did he mean that it's available to anyone who will pay attention to the gospel message?

Almost all of the different translations for this verse use the phrase, "faith comes from" or "faith comes by." In addition, most commentators agree that the word *comes* refers to the *source of faith*.

For example, Douglas Moo uses the phrase, "awaken faith."[7] Zane Hodges says, "a report was needed to produce faith."[8] C. E. B. Cranfield says, "faith results from hearing the message."[9] The words, "awaken," "produce," and "results" all suggest that listening is the *source of faith*. Faith is created when someone pays attention to the preaching or communication of the amazingly powerful, life-giving Word of God.

Paul quotes the prophet Isaiah as he cried against the weak response of his nation: "But they have not all obeyed the gospel. For Isaiah says, 'Lord, who has believed our report?' So then faith comes by hearing, and hearing by the word of God" (Romans 10:16-17). Israel didn't obey the gospel because she didn't believe the gospel because she didn't *listen to it.*

The normal process would develop in the reverse order: a report or word from God produces faith when someone listens to it. But because Israel didn't listen, the process never got started.

Thus it is clear from Romans 10:13-17 that faith begins with listening. But does anyone or anything in the rest of the Bible corroborate this claim that listening is the most important element in our relationship with God?

II. Jesus emphasized listening

When I have publicly asked the question, "did Jesus emphasize listening?" it has usually been met with fifteen or twenty seconds of silence as people process the question. Then someone will usually remember that Jesus said, "He who has ears to hear, let him hear." When I ask, "how many times did Jesus repeat it?" the normal answer is, "maybe two or three times." Here's the list:

> "He who has ears to hear, let him hear!" (Matthew 11:15).
>
> "He who has ears to hear, let him hear!" (Matthew 13:9; Mark 4:9; Luke 8:8).
>
> "He who has ears to hear, let him hear!" (Matthew 13:43).
>
> "If anyone has ears to hear, let him hear" (Mark 4:23).
>
> "If anyone has ears to hear, let him hear!" (Mark 7: 16).
>
> "He who has ears to hear, let him hear!" (Luke 14:35).
>
> "He who has an ear, let him hear what the Spirit says to the churches" (Revelation 2:7).
>
> "He who has an ear, let him hear what the Spirit says to the churches" (Revelation 2:11).

"He who has an ear, let him hear what the Spirit says to the churches" (Revelation 2:17).

"He who has an ear, let him hear what the Spirit says to the churches" (Revelation 2:29).

"He who has an ear, let him hear what the Spirit says to the churches" (Revelation 3:6).

"He who has an ear, let him hear what the Spirit says to the churches" (Revelation 3:13).

"He who has an ear, let him hear what the Spirit says to the churches" (Revelation 3:22).

"If anyone has an ear, let him hear" (Revelation 13:9).

Jesus the Creator gave people ears so they *can hear*. The question is whether they *will hear*. "Let him hear" is a command to put in the work necessary to actually concentrate. The quotes above are only the beginning of Jesus' emphasis. He also said things like "having eyes, do you not see? And having ears, do you not hear? And do you not remember?" (Mark 8:18).

I find that the whole concept of listening slides underneath our radar of important items. Perhaps the command "hear" isn't as compelling as the word "listen." And who, other than our parents, or perhaps our boss, has ever commanded us to *listen*? It's usually not a prominent part of our lives.

But Jesus said, "Therefore take heed how you hear. For whoever has, to him more will be given; and whoever does not have, even what he seems to have will be taken from him" (Luke 8:18). And the Father said, "This is My beloved Son, in whom I am well pleased. Hear Him!" (Matthew 17:5).

A. "Let him hear" is a command. It's not merely an accessory that would improve the quality of our lives. It's a necessity. Here is what Jesus loudly cried out in Luke 8:8:

> He (anyone) who has ears (present active participle, emphasizing the continuous gift of *hearing*) to hear (present active infinitive, emphasizing our continuous *ability*), let him hear (present active imperative, emphasizing a continuous *requirement*).

An *imperative* makes the activity mandatory. It cannot be neglected. How many other commands did Jesus repeat as often as this command? Even though He repeatedly said to "love your enemies" and "love one another," or "fear not," none of His other commands match the repetition of commands to listen in the identical way more than a dozen times. It's a blinking, buzzing neon sign that says, "red flag this as essential!"

B. The command assumes that we don't normally listen very well. People assume that since we can hear, we pick up everything. If that were true, Christ's command would be unnecessary. The truth is that people have unused ears, especially when it comes to God's Word. Jesus was talking to the nation of Israel which had the complete Old Testament. They largely ignored it or misread it in their haste (John 5:39-40) for other things. The truth is that we often only hear what takes minimal work. That's why TV or media are so popular; they're effortless. Listening to God often takes more effort and concentration than we want to give.

III. The New Testament emphasizes listening

To my surprise, I found many familiar passages which I could even quote but had never put them into the category of "the source of faith." Such as, "Behold, I stand at the door and knock. If anyone hears My voice and opens the door, I will come in to him and dine with him, and he with Me" (Revelation 3:20).

"And the Spirit and the bride say, 'Come!' And let him who hears say, 'Come!' And let him who thirsts come. Whoever desires, let him take the water of life freely" (Revelation 22:17).

"Most assuredly, I say to you, he who hears My word and believes in Him who sent Me has everlasting life, and shall not come into judgment, but has passed from death into life" (John 5:24).

"Take heed what you hear. With the same measure you use, it will be measured to you; and to you who hear, more will be given" (Mark 4:24).

"And it was told Him by some, who said, 'Your mother and Your brothers are standing outside, desiring to see You.' But He answered and said to them, 'My mother and My brothers are these who hear the word of God and do it'" (Luke 8:20).

"He who hears you hears Me, he who rejects you rejects Me, and he who rejects Me rejects Him who sent Me" (Mark 6:11; Luke 10:16).

> Therefore whoever hears these sayings of Mine, and does them, I will liken him to a wise man who built his house on the rock . . . But everyone who hears these sayings of Mine, and does not do them, will be like a foolish man who built his house on the sand (Matthew 7:24-26, also Luke 6:47-49).

Do you see the point? The consistent emphasis in the New Testament is that we need to listen. The apostles repeatedly commanded everyone to put in the work. It didn't matter if they were believers or unbelievers or Gentiles, or baseball players; since they had ears the command was to concentrate on God's Words.

IV. Israel commanded herself to listen every day

Initially I wondered if I would find any emphasis in the Old Testament on the importance of listening. I remembered that the nation of Israel had a history of not listening.

But I thought that perhaps she didn't listen very well because she didn't understand how important it was. Maybe listening wasn't emphasized in her schools; maybe Israeli children weren't taught to listen. Maybe God had not made listening an important part of her education. No, I found the opposite to be true. *God made listening a central feature in the life of every Israelite.* In fact Israel announced her primary task to listen every day. Even today Jewish people repeat the "Great Shema" when they get up and when they go to bed.

What is the Great Shema? Here it is in its context:

> O Israel, you should listen and be careful to do it, that it may be well with you and that you may multiply greatly, just as the LORD, the God of your fathers, has promised you, in a land flowing with milk and honey. Hear, O Israel! The LORD is our God, the LORD is one! You shall love the LORD your God with all your heart and with all your soul and with all your might. These words, which I am commanding you today, shall be on your heart. You shall teach them diligently to your sons and shall talk of them when you sit in your house and when you walk by the way and

when you lie down and when you rise up. (Deuteronomy
6:3-7 NASB).

Notice that the emphasis is on listening and obeying and teaching
words so sons and daughters will learn to listen. Even today, the Shema
is often the first part of Scripture that a Jewish child learns. It comprises
the central prayer in the Jewish prayer book. As a Jewish person quotes
Deuteronomy 6:4, he pronounces each word carefully with his right hand
covering his eyes. It's a tradition to recite it at least twice daily to fulfill
verse 7 which directs them to remember these words, "when you lie
down, and when you rise up." These words are the first words their children hear in the morning and the last words they hear before they go to
sleep.

So what does "Shema" mean? I quote from a website written by Avi-
Yah Byers:[10]

> The word Sh'ma (H8085) from the Brown-Driver-Briggs
> Hebrew Lexicon is pronounced Sha-ma (with a breath
> sound on the end) and is a verb which means in its simplest
> term 'to hear,' but in its fullest literal meaning is: to hear,
> listen to, obey (verb) that is why it is a verb; it is clearly an
> action word. The interesting thing about the word Sh'ma is
> that it also means to understand, yield, grant a request, to
> give heed to, to summon and to proclaim. So when you say
> 'Shema' to a Hebrew believer you are saying much more
> than listen to me, you are saying: "*Listen to me and after you
> hear what I've said please reiterate it to me so that I know that you
> understand what I am asking of you and then think about it, and
> after you have thought about it, and if you make a decision to accept
> what I have said then I expect for you to do it or follow through and
> complete what I have asked you to do.*"

Byers continues:

The Shema is a great example of what I like to call 'One Word Hebrew, Many Words English.' There is no possible way to give you a one word meaning or definition for this word, especially if there is something that has to be done in conjunction with it and if there are consequences if the task is not carried out. This is why the Messiah is so explicit in telling us, 'If any man has an ear let him hear (sh'ma).' The Sh'ma is the bottom line to the entire Scripture; Hear and Obey, that's what Yahweh wants us to do. When the Father tells us to do something we have the choice to listen, decipher intelligently and then to walk it out as He says (not as we want) or the choice to walk in disobedience and reap the repercussions of our actions.

Byers' definition of Shema makes it clear that listening was a huge emphasis in Jewish life. Israel should have recognized that her primary responsibility to God was to listen to Him. Rather than being neglected in family life, she announced this daily to her children and others; it was emblazoned on every wall and in every textbook at school.

Then *how did she miss its importance in her life?* We could answer that question by asking, "How do *we* miss it? Why do *we* not realize that our primary responsibility in life is to listen to God's words?"

Where do we hear of any emphasis on listening? Compare the number of college courses on listening with the number on public speaking. For some reason we teach that speaking is the key to success. That may be true in certain areas, but listening in a marriage, family, church or classroom is much more essential. College catalogs are virtually silent on this issue. Churches are also. Someone has described our problem as, "big egos with little ears." Native Americans have an appropriate proverb that says, "their tongues were keeping them deaf."

Do you see how critical this simple statement is, "faith comes from hearing?" The reverse very clearly is, "no listening, no faith." Faith is not a leap into the dark. It's a response to the light, as one hears the wonderful truth of God's Word.

At the same time listening takes work. It can be very difficult to listen to someone tell you that you're wrong, that you're a sinner and going to Hell forever. It takes submission, a yielding to someone else's word, a concentration on words that may be foreign to your world view. But it's mandatory, *for our own good.* It's the doorway to faith.

Chapter 5

Does God act differently toward those who listen?

The example of Jeremiah

Jeremiah's book shows us the radical difference listening makes in a person (or nation's) life. His ministry called his people to listen. He argued that their response to God's Word determined God's response to them. We miss the primary, foundational emphasis of Jeremiah when we overlook his constantly repeated cries to listen. There are at least three contrasting responses to God's Word in his book: Jeremiah's, the false prophets' and Israel's.

I. Jeremiah treasured God's Words in a way that false prophets didn't

Jeremiah viewed the Word of the Lord as so essential that his life was wrapped up in it. I count seven times that the Word of the Lord came to

Jeremiah in Chapter 1, nine times in Chapter 2, ten times in Chapter 3. That's 26 times in the first three chapters!

It starts in the second verse of the book:

> to whom the word of the LORD came in the days of Josiah the son of Amon, king of Judah, in the thirteenth year of his reign. It came also in the days of Jehoiakim the son of Josiah, king of Judah, until the end of the eleventh year of Zedekiah the son of Josiah, king of Judah, until the carrying away of Jerusalem captive in the fifth month. Then the word of the LORD came to me, saying: (Jeremiah 1:2-4).

Why did the word of the Lord come to Jeremiah? Why not to some of the other brothers or sisters? Was it simply God's choice or did Jeremiah spend his life living in God's Word?

Here's how Jeremiah described it: "Your words were found, and I ate them, And Your word was to me the joy and rejoicing of my heart; For I am called by Your name, O LORD God of hosts" (Jeremiah 15:16).

Jeremiah found God's "words." Someone may say, "I didn't know they were lost." Why did Jeremiah have to *find* them? Because they were lost in the sense that people didn't understand them, didn't see their significance. What did it take to find them? Reading them, digging in, and concentrating on them. Solomon said that it is like searching for silver or hidden treasures (Proverbs 2:4-6), and apparently few people in Jeremiah's day were willing to invest the necessary time and effort.

Throughout this book we see Jeremiah continually interacting with God's Word and obeying the instructions he heard. He bought a "waistband" (13:2). He prayed to the Lord about drought conditions in Israel (14:1). He went down to the potter's house so he could hear God's words (18:2). He also worried over the popularity of false prophets and their lack of genuine interest in God's holy words (23:9).

As a result there are more than fifty messages that came to Jeremiah. They came because the man loved his God and His book.

At the same time we see the contrast between Jeremiah and the false prophets. They tried to speak with authority as from the Lord , but with a different attitude toward His Word. Jeremiah asked, "For who has stood in the counsel of the LORD, and has perceived and heard His word? Who has marked His word and heard it?" (23:18).

The three questions expect three negative answers. The fact is that they didn't *stand* in the counsel of the Lord. They were probably too impatient. They also didn't *perceive* or *hear* His Word. It wasn't important enough to them to actually stop and think about its meaning. Nor did they *mark His Word* in order to hear it. The word *mark* suggests that they needed to give special attention to certain parts in order to understand them. They weren't interested.

Instead, their prophetic messages originated in "their own heart" and made those that listened to them as "worthless" as they were (23:16).

Of these self-centered, self-appointed "ministers," God says "I have not sent these prophets, yet they ran. I have not spoken to them, yet they prophesied" (23:21). They had little time to spend in God's presence listening to His Word because they were too excited to get out and preach their own private heart visions.

A direct result of their preaching was a national loss of interest in God's Word. Other things became more significant: "And the oracle of the LORD you shall mention no more. For every man's word will be his oracle, for you have perverted the words of the living God, the LORD of hosts, our God" (23:36).

"Every man's [own] word" became the standard guide for life because once the false prophets were voted in, what they treasured became the national love. When God is not God, every human becomes sovereign and his or her words "become the oracle!" What was the result of this tragic turn? Nebuchadnezzar came by and made sure that everyone got on the bus to Babylon.

II. Israel treasured something other than God's Word

Jeremiah explained how the false prophets' so-called "ministry" poisoned the entire nation. It wasn't simply that everyone became satisfied with false doctrine; it was that God's Word disappeared from the national consciousness. In contrast to Jeremiah's love for God's Word, Israel *despised it*. Jeremiah preached about their ear problems in at least two ways:

A. He described his listeners much the way Jesus did. He said to them, "Hear this now, O foolish people, Without understanding, Who have eyes and see not, And who have ears and hear not" (Jeremiah 5:21). Jesus made almost the identical pronouncement almost six hundred years later (Luke 8:8; 14:35).

Jeremiah made it clear that Israel's deafness was intentional:

> Thus says the LORD, "Stand by the ways and see and ask for the ancient paths, Where the good way is, and walk in it; And you will find rest for your souls." But they said, "We will not walk in it." "And I set watchmen over you, saying, 'Listen to the sound of the trumpet' But they said, 'We will not listen.' Therefore hear, O nations, And know, O congregation, what is among them. Hear, O earth: behold, I am bringing disaster on this people, The fruit of their plans,

Because they have not listened to My words, And as for My law, they have rejected it also" (Jeremiah 6:16-19 NASB).

The purpose of God's Word was to provide His people with rest for their souls. Their responsibility was to find and walk in the ancient paths. But Israel's response was, *no way.* God sent watchmen to make the warnings loud and blaring like trumpets, which should have made listening easier. They again responded, *no.* As a result, the disaster God promised came not only because they were evil but deaf. They had refused to hear God's law.

Jeremiah reminded them of their original responsibility:

For I did not speak to your fathers, or command them in the day that I brought them out of the land of Egypt, concerning burnt offerings and sacrifices. But this is what I commanded them, saying, "Obey My voice, and I will be your God, and you will be My people; and you will walk in all the way which I command you, that it may be well with you." Yet they did not obey or incline their ear, but walked in their own counsels and in the stubbornness of their evil heart, and went backward and not forward. Since the day that your fathers came out of the land of Egypt until this day, I have sent you all My servants the prophets, daily rising early and sending them. Yet they did not listen to Me or incline their ear, but stiffened their neck; they did more evil than their fathers. You shall speak all these words to them, but they will not listen to you; and you shall call to them, but they will not answer you. You shall say to them, "This is the nation that did not obey the voice of the LORD their God or accept correction; truth has perished and has been cut off from their mouth" (Jeremiah 7:22-28 NASB).

God's original command didn't ask for ritual like sacrifices and offer-ings. Instead her first responsibility when He rescued her from Egyptian bondage was to listen to and obey His voice. Instead "they did not obey or incline their ear." In spite of multiplied prophets who rose early to speak to them, nothing got through and God's truth disappeared from their mouths. So what? Lots of people don't listen. But Jeremiah made clear that the difference between listening and not listening was enor-mous. The end would be Babylonian slavery instead of, "it will be well with you."

Fifty days after God rescued Israel from Egyptian bondage they were at Mount Sinai making a covenant. Jeremiah reminded them of the sig-nificance of that agreement:

> Hear the words of this covenant, and speak to the men of
> Judah and to the inhabitants of Jerusalem; and say to them,
> "Thus says the LORD, the God of Israel, 'Cursed is the
> man who does not heed the words of this covenant which
> I commanded your forefathers in the day that I brought
> them out of the land of Egypt, from the iron furnace, say-
> ing, "Listen to My voice, and do according to all which I
> command you; so you shall be My people, and I will be
> your God,"'" (Jeremiah 11:2-4 NASB).

The word "cursed" puts this covenant into the category of serious business. Who does God promise to curse? Those who won't listen and obey. Again in the next few verses God emphasized how critical their response was:

> And the LORD said to me, "Proclaim all these words in
> the cities of Judah and in the streets of Jerusalem, saying,
> 'Hear the words of this covenant and do them. For I sol-
> emnly warned your fathers in the day that I brought them

up from the land of Egypt, even to this day, warning persistently, saying, "Listen to My voice." Yet they did not
obey or incline their ear, but walked, each one, in the stubbornness of his evil heart; therefore I brought on them all
the words of this covenant, which I commanded them to
do, but they did not'" (Jeremiah 11:6-8).

Can there be any question that God promised to adjust His response
to His people by their response to His Word? It wasn't that the people
hadn't learned the importance of listening in elementary school. They
repeated the Great Shema every day but refused to obey it.

B. He explained how God would respond to their deafness. People respond quite casually to the importance of listening, but Israel's failure meant the loss of everything she held dear: homes, lands, and families. Instead of the peace and freedom that listening promised, she
entered slavery in Nebuchadnezzar's empire. Jeremiah wept as he announced her future:

Listen and give heed, do not be haughty, For the LORD
has spoken. Give glory to the LORD your God, Before He
brings darkness And before your feet stumble On the
dusky mountains, And while you are hoping for light He
makes it into deep darkness, And turns it into gloom. But
if you will not listen to it, My soul will sob in secret for such
pride; And my eyes will bitterly weep And flow down with
tears, Because the flock of the LORD has been taken captive (Jeremiah 13:15-17 NASB).

Nebuchadnezzar attacked Jerusalem three times, with each attack becoming more painful. His third and final arrival lasted eighteen months
and was so brutal that some of the people resorted to cannibalism (19:9).

As he approached Jerusalem for the third and final time (588 B. C.) Zedekiah the king had a private conversation with Jeremiah asking for a word from God. Jeremiah's response was, "if I declare it to you, will you not surely put me to death? And if I give you advice, you will not listen to me" (38:15).

"You will not listen to me" meant "you will not obey me." Zedekiah was listening to him as he spoke, but Jeremiah knew his hardened-heart deafness and lack of faith in God's direction. Everything God promised came upon Zedekiah, even though *it didn't have to occur;* Zedekiah could have listened, believed and obeyed, and God would have judged him differently.

III. Israel went into captivity in spite of God's incredible graciousness

When was Israel's final judgment etched in stone? When did the Babylonian captivity become inevitable? You would think that by the time Nebuchadnezzar started marching toward Jerusalem there was no hope for repentance. Not so. Jeremiah promised that there was still hope if they would listen.

A. Jeremiah announced that Nebuchadnezzar's attack on Jerusalem could be averted. Even though he had been announcing the Babylonian captivity for years, God instructed Jeremiah to make it clear that the announced judgment wasn't inevitable:

> In the beginning of the reign of Jehoiakim the son of Josiah, king of Judah, this word came from the LORD, saying, "Thus says the LORD: 'Stand in the court of the

> LORD's house, and speak to all the cities of Judah, which
> come to worship in the LORD's house, all the words that
> I command you to speak to them. Do not diminish a word.
> Perhaps everyone will listen and turn from his evil way, that
> I may relent concerning the calamity which I purpose to
> bring on them because of the evil of their doings"' (Jere-
> miah 26:1-3).

Think of the graciousness of God's heart when He announced, "perhaps everyone will listen . . . that I may relent." In spite of closed ears,
hard hearts, and disobedient behavior, in spite of the fact that judgment
was promised, it was not *inevitable – if they would only wake up and listen.* This
hopeful promise came in the beginning of Jehoiakim's reign. Nebuchadnezzar arrived in the third year of his reign (2 Kings 24:1).

In the next few verses Jeremiah announced the alternative should
they not listen:

> And you shall say to them, "Thus says the LORD: 'If you
> will not listen to Me, to walk in My law which I have set
> before you, to heed the words of My servants the prophets
> whom I sent to you, both rising up early and sending them
> (but you have not heeded), then I will make this house like
> Shiloh, and will make this city a curse to all the nations of
> the earth"' (Jeremiah 26:4-6).

How did the people who heard God's amazingly gracious promise
respond? They seized Jeremiah and threatened to kill him (26:8)! It wasn't
just a rogue band of druggies and drunkards who threatened him. It was
"the priests and the prophets and all the people." Do you catch the absolute, total, complete disdain these people had for God's Word? It's
mind-boggling! Why had they decided that he was worthy of death? "For
he has prophesied against this city" (26:11).

You would think that God would immediately strike them all dead. But amazingly He again announced that He was willing to relent if they would listen and obey:

> ... The LORD sent me to prophesy against this house and against this city with all the words that you have heard. Now therefore, amend your ways and your doings, and obey the voice of the LORD your God; then the LORD will relent concerning the doom that He has pronounced against you (26:12b-13).

An astounding response! God's desire still was to "relent" of the doom He had promised!

Is there any question that the mercies of our Lord which are new every morning will overlook the worst of human intentions in order to bless? It wasn't long after this that Jeremiah penned "Through the LORD's mercies we are not consumed, Because His compassions fail not. They are new every morning; Great is Your faithfulness" (Lamentations 3:22-23). But *everything depended on Israel's response.* She had to listen and submit. Fast forward twenty years later. Nebuchadnezzar has returned the third time (588 B. C.) and surrounded Jerusalem with his huge army. This word came to king Zedekiah:

> If you surely surrender to the king of Babylon's princes, then your soul shall live; this city shall not be burned with fire, and you and your house shall live. But if you do not surrender to the king of Babylon's princes, then this city shall be given into the hand of the Chaldeans; they shall burn it with fire, and you shall not escape from their hand (38:17b-18).

King Zedekiah was in charge as Nebuchadnezzar approached for the third and final time. He could have saved Jerusalem at the last minute by humbling himself, believing Jeremiah's word, and obeying. Is God gracious to those who will listen even at the last minute? Absolutely! He wanted to bless them even though they had a terrible track record of deafness.

B. Even after sending Israel to Babylon, God's plans for her were gracious. Chapter 29 records a letter Jeremiah wrote to those who were taken captive to Babylon in the 597 B. C. deportation (29:1-3). Prior to that, a false prophet named Hananiah had contradicted Jeremiah by announcing that God had broken the Babylonian yoke and Israel would be free to return in two years (28:3, 10-11).

Jeremiah corrected Hananiah by announcing that the yoke would now be iron instead of wood (28:13-14), and that Hananiah would die (28:17).

In that context Jeremiah wrote a letter to the captives in Babylon and said things like:

> Build houses and dwell in them; plant gardens and eat their fruit. Take wives and beget sons and daughters; and take wives for your sons and give your daughters to husbands, so that they may bear sons and daughters – that you may be increased there, and not diminished. And seek the peace of the city where I have caused you to be carried away captive, and pray to the LORD for it; for in its peace you will have peace (29:5-7).

In other words, "settle down because you are going to be in Babylon for a long time," actually for 70 years (29:10). In the *very next verse* God made this very familiar promise: "For I know the thoughts that I think toward you, says the LORD, thoughts of peace and not of evil, to give you a future and a hope. Then you will call upon Me and go and pray to Me, and I will listen to you" (29:11-12).

The promise is made to slaves who have been dragged to Babylon with no hope of going home for the next 70 years. To them God says, "let Me tell you the thoughts that I think toward you; they are thoughts of peace, not evil, to give you a future and a hope!"

Imagine hearing these verses as a slave in Babylon. Discouraged Americans who are living in the land of plenty find hope in those verses; how much more so would discouraged Israelites living in the land of chains!

What is the *hope* that God saw in the lives of these captives? It's in the next verses:

> And you will seek Me and find Me, when you search for Me with all your heart. I will be found by you, says the LORD, and I will bring you back from your captivity; I will gather you from all the nations and from all the places where I have driven you, says the LORD, and I will bring you to the place from which I cause you to be carried away captive (29:13-14).

In other words, their return from captivity would be accompanied with *searching for God with all their hearts*. Where were they to search? In God's Word, by listening to it and studying it, following the example they had seen in Jeremiah. He was the one who had found God's words and ate them to the joy and rejoicing of his heart (15:16). How amazing is it that the prophet who lived in God's Word would be the one to foretell the day when his people, who had completely rejected that Word in his day, would change! Captivity would open their ears and give them a new, searching heart for the God they had rejected.

The standard that judged them and sent them into Babylon was *the words they had ignored:* "This will be the sign to you," declares the LORD, "that I am going to punish you in this place, so that you may know that My words will surely stand against you for harm" (Jeremiah 44:29 NASB).

The fact that they were the elect of God was not the deciding factor. They were *already chosen.* It was *the elect* who were dragged into Babylon as slaves. Their salvation depended on whether they listened to God's words. They possessed everything necessary for their salvation, for a life of blessing. Their only responsibility was to listen and obey.

C. Even after the nation went into Babylonian captivity the left-behind Israelites refused to listen. You would think that a ruined Jerusalem and the disappearance of Solomon's temple would change the remaining people. But no, the leftover people chose to go down to Egypt and drag Jeremiah with them (43:1-8) even though Jeremiah had announced that they would all die in Egypt. Their only hope was to return to Israel (44:1-14). How did they respond to Jeremiah's warning?

> Then all the men who were aware that their wives were
> burning sacrifices to other gods, along with all the women
> who were standing by, as a large assembly, including all the
> people who were living in Pathros in the land of Egypt,
> responded to Jeremiah, saying, "As for the message that
> you have spoken to us in the name of the LORD, *we are not
> going to listen to you!* But rather we will certainly carry out *every
> word that has proceeded from our mouths,* by burning sacrifices
> to the queen of heaven and pouring out drink offerings to
> her, just as we ourselves, our forefathers, our kings and our
> princes did in the cities of Judah and in the streets of Jeru-
> salem; for then we had plenty of food and were well off

and saw no misfortune" (Jeremiah 44:15-17 NASB emphasis mine).

Can you imagine the gall of saying to the prophet of God, "We are
not going to listen to you," in spite of the fact that they knew he had
spoken "in the name of the LORD?" And then adding, "we will do what
we have said we will do?" They had seen the absolute truthfulness of
God's Word as they watched their parents and brothers and sisters
dragged off into captivity. But nothing changed their hardened deafness.

We started this chapter with the question, "Does God act differently
toward those who listen?" The testimony of Jeremiah bears witness to
the absolute truthfulness of "he who has ears to hear, let him hear." In
spite of the fact that Israel quoted the Great Shema every day, "HEAR
O ISRAEL," in spite of the fact that it was on the lips of her children
when they arose in the morning and when they went to bed at night, she
experienced completely unnecessary, brutal captivity because she never
obeyed three words: *let him hear.*

We face a similar challenge today. Will we actually, seriously, listen?
Or are we in danger of repeating Israel's mistake? **Are you listening –
really?**

Chapter 6

What does it mean to actually "listen?"

W hat's the difference between having "ears to hear" and actually "hearing? What turns ears on so that they actually capture what is being spoken or written?

We saw in Jeremiah that God equated listening with obedience. He said the same thing to Ezekiel: "they hear your words, but they do not do them" (Ezekiel 33:31-32). Their "hearing" did not actually result in hearing. Parents understand this: "Did you hear what I said? Your room is still a mess." Lack of obedience to a command shows lack of listening, no matter how creative the excuse may be.

James says a similar thing in 1:19-25. He promises the blessing of God to those who are "swift to hear" (19), who become doers of the Word, not just casual hearers (22), who continue looking into the Word until they become "a doer of the work" (25).

Does the Bible explain the process of listening? Does it say anywhere, "you know, it's not just taking in information, or understanding a message so you can quote it, but listening is demonstrated when you obey the message?" It does.

Jesus explained the process in three of the gospels (Matthew 13:3-23; Mark 4:2-25, and Luke 8:4-18) using the metaphor of a *seed.* God's Word comes to us like a seed thrown into our yards. What happens to that seed is our responsibility. If we don't properly take care of it, we will lose it and suffer loss by never experiencing the harvest it could produce. If we take care of the seed, God will bless us by making it sprout and bear fruit.

Jesus pointed out four different ways people handle this responsibility. Here's the parable:

> And when a great multitude had gathered, and they had come to Him from every city, He spoke by a parable: "A sower went out to sow his seed. And as he sowed, some fell by the wayside; and it was trampled down, and the birds of the air devoured it. Some fell on rock; and as soon as it sprang up, it withered away because it lacked moisture. And some fell among thorns, and the thorns sprang up with it and choked it. But others fell on good ground, sprang up, and yielded a crop a hundredfold." When He had said these things He cried, "He who has ears to hear, let him hear!" (Luke 8:4-8).

The parable is about *listening.* Jesus repeatedly cried out, "He who has ears to hear, let him hear." The fact is that people who possess the apparatus necessary to hear and obey don't necessarily use it. Each soil represents someone who *heard* the message (Luke 8:12-15). What happened afterwards gave evidence of how they used their auditory assets.

In addition, the parable is specifically about *listening to God's Word.* "The seed is the word of God" (Luke 8:11). God's words work in peoples' lives like tomato seeds grow in the ground. Seeds won't grow on concrete or in below zero weather. They require proper conditions and nurture. The fruitfulness of God's words depends on *listeners providing the right conditions.* Jesus gives four different possible conditions that give four different results.

I. Some listeners are *deaf*

Jesus' interpretation of verse 5 is in verse 12: *"Those by the wayside are the ones who hear; then the devil comes and takes away the word out of their hearts, lest they should believe and be saved."*

"By the wayside" pictures the pathway through or beside the garden. As a result of repeated footsteps, the ground becomes packed and hardened. It pictures a listener who is *uninterested, calloused* or *rejecting,* because they have been beaten down, dried up or hardened by life's traffic. As a result, the words that come from God bounce like hitting concrete. Something in the listener's heart acting as a gatekeeper, decides that the message is *worthless.*

How did this listener arrive at such a state of hardness? R. C. Trench describes it this way: "he has exposed his heart as a common road to every evil influence of the world, till it has become hard as a pavement, till he has laid waste the very soil in which the word of God should have taken root."[11]

A significant change comes with the little word "then." Once a person says, "these words are of no value," *then* the devil comes and takes away the word. The implication is that failure to receive the seed permits or enables Satan to act. Apparently, he can't *automatically* steal the message by blowing away the seed as it comes from the sower's hand (which he would love to do if he could). But the listener grants him some kind of permission by despising or ignoring the seed. As it lays on the hard

surface Satan can readily pick it off. How big is the window of time before Satan steals it? No one knows.

But Jesus' point is that if nothing in a person's heart takes in God's
Word, then *Satan will make sure the word disappears – "lest they should believe
and be saved!"* Faith comes by listening, and a person with a hardened heart
will never believe and be saved because Satan will steal the seed first.

What is it like to listen with a hardened heart? Have you ever had a
calloused attitude toward someone's message and quickly turned it off?
I've asked this question in dozens of college classes, "have you ever listened this way: where you click off the message without ever processing
it?" The most common answer I received was, "Yes, when my parents
start their lecture on how I should behave!"

That's not a good response to one's parents, but how much worse to
respond that way to God's words, because more than anything else faith
depends on getting a hold of God's words.

The parable pictures how fragile the faith-process is. Someone is
poised to steal the words if we are not careful. The end result is that what
God has said disappears from the computer screen of our minds.

Have you ever experienced this on a Sunday morning? You listen to
a sermon from the Word of God, but lose it by dinner time? You watch
and hear someone preach, but have no real reason to listen, you are conscious of no need, you see no value in the message, and in reality you
hear nothing. You may be sitting in a padded chair, smiling, looking at
the preacher, with hands folded humbly in prayer – deaf.

Once a person says "this is not for me," once the gatekeeper in your
heart slams the door, a change takes place: "then." The devil quickly
jumps in to remove the seed. Thus when God's Word is spoken, either
the listener gets it, or Satan takes it. If we don't latch on to the words, we
lose them – completely. That's scary.

II. Some listeners are *picky*

Jesus' interpretation of verse 6 is in verse 13: *"But the ones on the rock are those who, when they hear, receive the word with joy; and these have no root, who believe for a while and in time of temptation fall away."*

This picture suggests softer soil than the first ground, but soil that has a sheet of rock beneath. Don't envision seed falling in the middle of pebbles or around rocks. Rather it's a large rock or a sheet of rock beneath several inches of soil. Matthew states it this way: "Others fell on the rocky places, where they did not have much soil; and immediately they sprang up, because they had no depth of soil" (Matthew 13:5, NASB).

Perhaps "no depth of soil" made the rock beneath a thermal bank which kept the soil warmer and encouraged more rapid germination so that "immediately they sprang up" (Matthew 13:5).

But the arrival of the sun caused a problem. The rock prevented the roots from finding moisture. The sun normally stirs up photosynthesis and gets the chemicals buzzing, which causes a need for water. A message is sent to the roots to go deeper and find water, but here the roots only hit rock. Thus the designated instrument of growth, the sun, becomes the instrument that fries the plant.

What do the rock and the sun represent in this parable? Luke 8:13 indicates that the sun represents a "time of temptation." "Temptation" is the word "trouble," or "difficulty," or even, "persecution." Sun gives a picture of affliction or persecution that arises "because of the word." God's Word, which initially brought such excitement, now brings difficulty, trouble and persecution, and the plant withers. They "fall away."

It's the hard times, the perplexing days, where the sun is actually shining. The difficulties and trials are generating spiritual photosynthesis. James commands, "count it all joy . . . knowing that the testing of your faith *produces* endurance" (James 1:2-3 NASB). The word "produces" introduces us to the power of trials in our lives. They possess an energy like the sun, that gets our chemicals buzzing and causes spiritual photosynthesis.

Have you seen trials at work in your life pushing you to prayer, to Christian friends, to God's Word for answers? That's good. We hear testimonies of people who say, "it's been a rough experience, but what a blessing to meet God." That's the sun at work.

But not all listeners react well to their trials. The fact that this picky listener fell away doesn't tell the whole story. The Greek word for *fell away* in Matthew 13:21 and Mark 4:17 is *scandalidzo*. You can see the word "scandal" in there, and that's what happened. He was scandalized by what the sun did to him! It gave him an attitude. He became indignant.

It would be like Job saying, "the audacity of God to command me to 'count it all joy' when I have just experienced the death of all ten of my children!" "Who does God think I am?" Job's wife was scandalized by the incident and recommended that he, "curse God and die" (see Job 1:19-2:9).

It's as if something weird entered the life of this soil and he reacted violently. Something in his heart refused to tolerate the challenge introduced by the trial. He was fixed on his own agenda, his definition of good. When something entered that didn't meet his goodness specifications, he shut down his auditory apparatus.

He "listened," but had *requirements* as to what the message could expect of him. The rock represented his expectations. The message was valuable as long as it featured free gifts. When difficulty assaulted him he quit listening. The key was the arrival of the sun. That which God designed to help a plant grow, didn't benefit this soil.

This person was not a *passive* or *hardened* listener like the first soil, but rather a *picky* or *finicky* one. He surfed the available messages and got excited over free gifts or entertainment. He had a rating system in his heart that scored messages in terms of difficulty, danger, threat to personal comfort, expense, embarrassment, or just plain work. He made sure to ask himself, "How much will it cost if I obey this word from the Lord?" He had drawn a tolerance line: "too much danger and I'm out of here;" "too embarrassing, too humbling, count me out."

Does this sound like American Christianity? "Give me that old time religion, as long as it is not hard, as long as I can do what I want to do, and as long as it makes me comfortable."

Once a person has chosen the easy way, he dumps the words that don't fit his expectations. "Take up your cross and follow me," Jesus commanded. "What do you mean cross?" he asks. "I will jump into my BMW and follow you." The listener is excited by the promises of heaven, and joy and peace, and answered prayer. He's insulted by the suggestion of trials, difficulty, or pain.

We may be teaching our children to listen this way. Not only is there a natural bent to selective listening, but today's media encourage it. We surf for what we like, and teach our children to do the same thing. There may be nothing wrong with that on a personal level, but when it comes to the Word of God, selective listening guarantees that His seed will never produce fruit in us.

Have you noticed how hard it is to listen? To your children? To your parents? To a friend who is trying to tell you something you may not want to hear? One of the descriptions of the last days is that people will not be able to listen to sound doctrine because they will want to have their ears "tickled:" "For the time will come when people will not put up with sound doctrine. Instead, to suit their own desires, they will gather around them a great number of teachers to say what their itching ears want to hear" (2 Timothy 4:3 NIV).

Paul suggests that people will be surfing for ear-scratching teachers because they have become picky listeners. They will refuse sound doctrine because it takes more work than they want to invest, and involves more difficulty than they want to tolerate.

III. Some listeners are *too busy*

Jesus' interpretation of verse 7 is in verse 14: "*Now the ones that fell among thorns are those who, when they have heard, go out and are choked with cares, riches, and pleasures of life, and bring no fruit to maturity.*"

These seeds germinate, spring up, but then have to compete with weeds and thorns, which are thirsty plants. Observe that they "go out and are choked" by "cares, riches and pleasures of life." They encounter God's Word as they *go out*. They are making money or on the way to the beach as the seed falls onto their soil.

They have priorities and ambitions and accomplishments. Yes, they're willing to give a couple of minutes to the reading of God's Word. They're willing to stop at church for a morning service on their way to an afternoon football game. But their minds are crowded. God's message doesn't get the attention it needs. Processing the message takes more time than they have to give. Other things call.

They are multi-taskers. They are proficient at texting while they drive and keeping track of the score of the football game as they listen to a preacher. In fact, they perhaps never really listen to their friends. Have you met those kinds of people? They're looking at you; they're sitting across the table from you, but you're not sure they actually hear what you are saying?

Have you ever listened this way? Maybe you've worried about what will happen to your job as you read your Bible? Or thought about the direction of the stock market and its impact on your finances? That's weedy listening, and trying to do both only improves your chance of missing God's message.

Since we normally can think much faster than anyone can speak, our minds race ahead and stop to consider other things. But God gave us the ability to think fast for a reason. To really listen, we need to harness our mind's ability to review and summarize for ourselves what a speaker is saying.

The point is that we are not going to really hear what someone is saying until we stop and concentrate on their words. It was Dr. M. Scott Peck, the author of *The Road Less Traveled,* and *The People of the Lie,* along with other books, who said, "you cannot truly listen to anyone and do anything else at the same time."[12]

But it's hard to slow down and concentrate. It's like collecting all the abilities of your brain to follow a person who seems to be walking on crutches – or jogging behind a turtle.

But slowing down is worth it. I heard the story of a student who took a class on listening, and then said:

> We learned some techniques for listening to boring mate-
> rial and boring people. I said to myself as I left class, "who
> could be more boring than my wife?" I decided to use the
> techniques to really listen to her, and the strangest thing
> happened. She actually was interesting.

Once it was obvious that he was listening, the student's wife began relating things that she had never told him before. "All of a sudden," he marveled, "we were like newlyweds." He claimed that a class in listening saved his marriage!

Men are often poor listeners. Wives complain that husbands don't *really* listen to them. The truth is that we are busy. We have much to do and we are behind. There are many things crowding our minds. I would encourage men to surprise their wives by actually listening to them.

Push everything else that is on your plate aside, clear your agenda, and say to her, "OK, you are getting my full attention." Actually get in to what she is saying. Ask her questions about what she means and what she really intends. Don't think about how you are going to respond or how you will fix anything. Spend time with nothing else to do but listen to her. It will be a valuable experience. Do the same with the Word of God. Approach it with nothing else on your schedule.

And I would encourage wives to surprise their husbands by listening fully to them. Push your plate aside, clear your agenda of what you were going to say, and say to him, "OK, you are getting my full attention."

When you stop everything to look someone in the eye, and seek to find out what they are really saying, *you honor the speaker.* Your behavior says, "you are the most important person to me at this moment. There is nothing more valuable than understanding what's on your heart." Ignore your phone. Don't let your eyes glaze over. Don't daydream. Concentrate.

Henry David Thoreau said, "the greatest compliment that was ever paid me was when one asked me what I thought, and listened to my answer."[13] Dr. Joyce Brothers said, "Listening, not imitation, may be the sincerest form of flattery."[14] David Augsburger said, "being heard is so close to being loved that for the average person, they are almost indistinguishable."[15]

Busy listeners find that the precious seed of God's Word gets *choked*. The seed may be doing its job; it's the competition vying for the same piece of dirt and water. Other plants that are stronger, take over, and win the dirt battle. Good listening involves pulling weeds, and thorns that distract.

IV. Some listeners *really listen*

Dr. Watson Pindell, the former president of the Prince George's Community College, used to describe the college educational process as one where "the notes of the professor are transferred to the notebooks of the student without going through the mind of either." The first three soils have pictured for us three ways such a fruitless transfer can occur.

But listening doesn't have to be brainless. Jesus explains what makes for good listening in verse 15: *"But the seed in the good soil, these are the ones who have heard the word in an honest and good heart, and hold it fast, and bear fruit with perseverance"* (NASB).

What makes good ground good? Why does good soil listen more effectively than the others? Jesus points out three responses of the good soil, which highlight *three responsibilities every listener has* – to capture the Word, to protect what one captures, and to obey the Word with persistence.

A. The listener has to *capture* the Word. It's like fishing. Fish don't jump into the boat. The Word appears for a split second as a public speaker creates it, and then disappears. The listener has that split second to catch, understand, and file it in a safe place. Or one can read the Word and have a slightly longer time to catch, understand, and file it.

The first three soils weren't ready, didn't capture the listening event accurately, and the potential blessing of the Word disappeared.

"Wait a minute," I can hear someone say. "You are telling me that an unbeliever, who is 'dead in trespasses and sins' has to capture God's Word?" Yes, that's exactly why Jesus commanded, "he who has ears to hear, let him hear."

I will answer the question, "can dead people really listen?" in the next chapter. But first let me answer these earlier questions: (1) Who makes one's heart "honest and good"? Is it a gift that God gives to certain people or does every human have this responsibility and ability? (2) What does it mean to have a "honest and good" heart? How do we define those words? (3) From where do these qualities come? What's involved in getting an honest and good heart?

1. The listener has the full responsibility to make his heart honest and good. Verse 15 states that the listener comes with "an honest and good heart." Three verses later Jesus warns, "so take care how you listen; for whoever has, to him more shall be given; and whoever does not have, even what he thinks he has shall be taken away from him" (Luke 8:18 NASB).

"So take care how you listen," because it's not the sower, it's not the seed, it's not the circumstances, it's the listener who has the full responsibility of making sure he has an honest and good heart. It doesn't matter if the preacher is boring; it doesn't matter if his message appears disorganized, or how hot the room may be, each listener has the responsibility before God of preparing the soil of his heart to capture God's Word.

Christ's very purpose for giving this parable was to get His listeners to listen: "When He had said these things He cried, 'He who has ears to hear, let him hear!'" (Luke 8:8). "Let him hear" is emphatic: "by all means *listen!*"[16] Thus we shouldn't be sitting around expecting that God will someday give us the ability to listen. He has placed that responsibility squarely in our laps. His blessing is promised to those who put in the effort to concentrate and actually "hear."

2. It's the *heart* that makes listening effective. Each of these soils describes the *heart of the listener.* Jesus started with three bad examples: (a) a hardened heart in soil one, (b) a picky heart determined to find something free and easy in soil two, and (c) a busy heart that tried to catch the Word on the fly in soil three.

But the heart of the good soil is described with beautiful words in the Greek language. "Honest" means "beautiful," and "noble" and "honorable."[17] Absent from this heart are the characteristics we saw in the first three soils.

The word "good" means "useful," "suited for its purpose," and thus, "fertile soil."[18] It describes a person who is just, kind, and ready for the event of listening to God's Word because he is free from the sin which interferes with the Word.

James says that we should prepare to listen to the Word by "putting aside all filthiness and all that remains of wickedness" so that we can "in humility receive the word implanted" (James 1:21 NASB). Peter similarly instructs, "putting aside all malice and all deceit and hypocrisy and envy and all slander, like newborn babies, long for the pure milk of the word, so that by it you may grow in respect to salvation" (1 Peter 2:1-2 NASB).

Sin clouds the listening event by distracting our minds and distorting our ears. The Word is only heard correctly "in an honest and good heart."

Think of why you go to church. There are hundreds of motives for entering the front door: to show off a new outfit, to get together with friends, to see if a certain couple is still together, to evaluate the pastor's sermon, or the choir, or the music. Perhaps simply to get it over with so we can get to the beach Sunday afternoon. The question is, "have you ever approached the listening event with an honest and good heart *to hear God speak to you?*" "Have you ever sung a congregational hymn *to God?*" "Have you ever asked God to *meet you as you listen to His word?*" It's your heart.

3. Even an unbeliever can prepare to receive God's words. Soil one starts with an unbeliever, who will never believe until his hardened heart is softened to receive God's Word. So I would assume that each of these soil pictures begins with an unbeliever. Soil two doesn't receive God's Word honestly, receiving only what it wants. Soil three doesn't take the time to honestly listen. He doesn't understand the requirements of listening and won't interrupt whatever else he is doing.

Are there unbelievers with listening ears that are better than the first three soils? I think so. Zacchaeus, for example, was a wealthy Israelite, but he stopped what he was doing to pursue Christ. He literally climbed a tree in his zeal to connect with Christ! How often do we see that kind of interest in listening to Christ's words? (Luke 19:1-10).

Another example is Cornelius, who Luke described as: "a devout man and one who feared God with all his household, who gave alms generously to the people, and prayed to God always" (Acts 10:2). That may sound like Cornelius was a believer, but the angel who appeared to him instructed him to call for Peter because he "will tell you words by which you and all your household will be saved" (Acts 11:14). Thus when Peter arrived Cornelius and his household were ready to listen, and the Word produced fruit in their lives.

Can an unbeliever have an honest and good heart? Not in his own strength or ability, of course. But does the Holy Spirit, who convicts the world of sin, righteousness and judgment (John 16:8-11) respond to a sinner with strength and ability for him to change his heart attitude, even going so far as to send an angel? Zacchaeus and Cornelius are examples of a *yes* answer.

Something happens in the heart of the good-ground listener *before* the seed ever enters his mind. The seed *finds* good soil; it doesn't *make* it. The soil is ready when the message arrives because things happened beforehand. It took work to understand the message (soil one didn't attempt), a humility to accept all parts of the message (soil two rejected), and an interruption of his pursuits to give the message his full attention (soil three would not entertain).

We see examples of good listening on display constantly. Simply watch a young man and woman after they fall in love. All of a sudden they want to get off by themselves to talk. Their ability to listen changes, because their heart attitudes change. It's not that they have read a book on "how to listen" or hired a listening coach; it's simply that they have fallen in love. Instantly, without any instruction, they develop skill in listening! It's a heart thing.

B. The listener has to *remember* the Word. Verse 15 says that the good soil "holds it fast," which suggests that the listener keeps and protects the words. The phrase means "to hold back, to detain . . . from going away."[19] As displayed by the other three soils, the Word is going to *get away* unless the hearer does something. It's either going to be *stolen* (by Satan) or *fried* (by the sun) or *choked* (by weeds), unless some kind of proactive effort is made. When we hear the Word, it doesn't just sit there, motionless. It's moving. It's on its way out unless we restrain it. This listener grabs and grips it because he understands its value.

Seed does not instantly sprout. It takes time, sometimes a week, sometimes two weeks before it germinates. I planted ghost pepper seeds one spring which advised that they may not germinate for 35 days. In a similar way, God's Word may have a time delay in its productivity. It may take two or three weeks for a life changing message to bear fruit. The question is whether it's still in our hearts that much later. The Word of God energizes change when listeners prevent it from leaving.

We use excuses to diminish our responsibility: "I'll come back to it later," "I can replay the video any time I want to," "This isn't the ideal moment to focus on the message." "Hold it fast" suggests that we will never again have the same, perfect opportunity to capture this precious Word.

That's why there is such an emphasis in the Bible on keeping and guarding God's words: "Your word I have treasured in my heart, that I may not sin against You" (Psalm 119:11 NASB); "This book of the law shall not depart from your mouth, but you shall meditate on it day and night . . ." (Joshua 1:8 NASB).

Every listener has a responsibility to prevent the Word of God from slipping away. We must gain possession of it and make it ours because *God doesn't keep it for us.*

That's why it's helpful to take notes as you listen to or study God's Word. It's helpful to organize what you hear, to memorize main ideas or verses, all for this reason: God's Word easily takes flight and disappears from the desktop screen in our brain. It's pushed out by the cares, riches and pleasures that crowd into our lives. It's fried when we decide that it's a little too hard to handle. It's stolen when we don't see its incredible preciousness.

C. The listener has to *do* the Word. I get this out of the phrase, "bear fruit with perseverance" in verse 15. Fruitfulness involves "perseverance," or "endurance". That means we don't necessarily bear fruit the first time we set out to obey.

It's like training for any sport. When you start practicing for the high jump you may miss more times than you get over the bar. But you keep practicing. The first time you miss you don't say, "I'm simply not cut out for this; I think I will quit." No, you practice the technique repeatedly.

James says, "Count it all joy when you fall into various trials" (James 1:2). There is a learning curve of turning to Christ and thanking Him when you face events that look threatening.

One of our big trials was when our 15-year-old son ran away. He stole our van in the process even though he didn't have a driver's license, and took two 13-year-old girls with him, driving off into the night. For three days we heard nothing. We had difficulty the first day counting the event as "joy." In fact we went through having anger at him, anger at God, frustration, hopelessness, coupled with sympathy for him and the girls, and fear as to what would be the outcome. After a day or more we were better able to stop and thank God for the situation, knowing that He intended to use it for our good (James 1:3).

It was 78 hours later that we received a phone call from LAPD. They had arrested our son and the girls in Hollywood after they had successfully driven there from Washington DC. That brought great relief because they were safe, but along with it came another series of trials. "Will there be a court case?" "How will we get the three teens back?" "Where is the van?" "What should we do?"

Each trial presented us with the question, "will you listen to and obey God's Word by (a) considering it all joy (James 1:2-3), and (b) determining to go through the situation God's way (James 1:4), and (c) asking God for wisdom (James 1:5)?" The event called for endurance and a determination to do trials God's way.

"God's way" covers many of life's experiences, like doing worries God's way (1 Peter 5:7) or suffering God's way (1 Peter 3:14, 4:13), or facing temptation God's way (James 1:13-16). To "bear fruit" suggests a change in the way we handle life's experiences. The picture is transfiguration, a supernatural change on the inside, as we renew our minds and reject the world's advice (Romans 12:2). And it all comes by reading and listening to God's amazing Word, the only document in the world that can completely revolutionize our lives (2 Timothy 3:16-17)!

By means of this parable Jesus tells us that there are at least four different ways to listen, but only one that is worthwhile. You will find that at times you probably listen like soils one, two or three. The question Jesus asks is, "how often have you listened like soil four?"

Good-ground listening is *active listening*, where you make a conscious effort not only to hear what someone is saying, but to personalize it, by evaluating what God wants you to do and how He wants you to do it. It takes your full attention, your determination to prevent the Word from leaving you, and endurance to obey and obey again when you mess up.

So I would encourage you to get a notebook, write things down, and review what you have written. Ask God for enablement to obey Solomon's advice: "My son, give attention to my words; Incline your ear to my sayings. Do not let them depart from your sight; Keep them in the midst of your heart. For they are life to those who find them And health to all their body" (Proverbs 4:20-22 NASB).

V. Careful listeners receive what other listeners lose

Jesus applied this parable to His audience by saying: "*Therefore take heed how you hear. For whoever has, to him more will be given; and whoever does not have, even what he seems to have will be taken from him*" (Luke 8:18).

"How" is the key word in the command – "take heed *how* you hear. . ." There are at least four different responses a person can choose, three of which are fruitless. All four types of soil actually heard God's Word. They were there; they got the message, probably from the greatest Speaker that ever walked the earth, but only one benefited.

"Take heed," Christ warns, because "whoever has, to him more will be given." Whoever has what? Faith? Salvation? No, "whoever has the right kind of listening," whoever listens like soil number four. It's the right kind of listening that brings blessing from God.

Jesus' point is that God gives or withholds additional gifts from us depending on whether *we really listen to His words*. Whoever listens the right way, "to him more shall be given." Whoever doesn't listen the right way, "even what he thinks he has will be taken away."

The gospel of Mark confirms this emphasis on listening when he records Jesus as saying, "Take heed what you hear. With the same measure you use, it will be measured to you; and to you who hear, more will be given" (Mark 4:24). The promise of more is given to those who hear the right way.

What about the other three soils? Jesus doesn't present the less-than-good listeners in a neutral way. "Whoever does not have," *loses even what he thinks he has*. How will that happen? *Life's agents will take it away*. Satan *steals* it from the first ground, the sun *fries* the plant in the second soil, and the weeds *choke* what's growing in the third soil. In the end God's life-changing Word disappears from people *who think they have it*.

What happened to soil two where the person "fell away" or soil three which brought no fruit "to maturity?" What did each lose? The point is, *whatever happened wasn't good.* Verse 18 makes it clear that Jesus was satisfied only with ground number four.

People may ask: "was ground number two saved? It says that the person *believed for a while.*" Yes, but it's the "time of temptation" that tells the tale (Luke 8:13), and they fell away. Did they really have salvation? Did they lose it? We don't know for sure.

The same is true with ground three. From the way Jesus described it, it looks like something might have grown in the weedy ground. But it didn't last. And verse 18 assures us that ground three lost what it thought it had. Whatever happened, Christ's point was that it was "NOT GOOD!" And He urges us: "DON'T LISTEN THIS WAY!" *Be a good-ground listener!*

The purpose of this chapter has been to show that Jesus explained fully and clearly what it means to listen the right way. He made it so simple that anyone can understand. The truth is that every one of us has listened the way pictured by the first three soils – with hardened, picky, or busy hearts. *The question is: how often have we listened like the last soil, with a good and honest heart, holding it tightly and bearing fruit in patience?* That's the kind of listener to whom "more shall be given." That person will bear fruit, eternal fruit, delicious fruit!

Chapter 7

Can unbelievers respond to God's Word?

S ome Bible teachers argue that since unbelievers are dead in their sin they are incapable of listening. In fact, the process of salvation could be compared to God walking through a spiritual morgue and choosing which corpses He will raise to life.

These teachers claim that unbelievers can do nothing. Thus they have to receive life from God before they can even listen, believe and obey. As a result, faith and obedience are seen as something subsequent to regeneration. God has to regenerate a person before he or she can believe.

For example, Pastor John Piper, who has blessed many of us for years with his teaching, states that "faith is the evidence of new birth, not the cause of it."[20] This means that sinners are not saved by faith, because no unsaved person has faith until *after God gives him the gift*. God first chooses who will receive regeneration and gives those people life and faith. The exhibition of their faith demonstrates their new birth.

That's a significant statement because it suggests that the first six chapters of this book have been misguided. I've assumed too much, namely that dead people can do something, like listen with a good heart, believe, and call on Christ for salvation. According to Pastor Piper, the reality is that unbelievers can't do anything more than a rock can do. They can't hear anything, believe anything, or obey anything, until God chooses to give them that ability.

How does that conclusion fit in with Romans 10:13 which assures us that "whoever calls on the name of the Lord shall be saved?" And what did the apostle mean when he described unbelievers as "dead in trespasses and sins" (Ephesians 2:1)? How are we to understand the meaning of the word, "dead?" Is the real issue regarding faith that unbelievers *can not* believe? Or is it that they *will not* believe? The difference is enormous.

I. Deadness is not the issue in the parable of the sower

In the last chapter we looked at Jesus' instruction on listening. He taught His audience how to listen using the picture of seeds falling on different types of soil. Is there any way we can fit Pastor Piper's conclusion into this parable and view at least the first soil as dead and incapable of listening?

A. Jesus made no indication that the first three soils were defective because they were "dead." The fact that ground one was deaf to the message, that ground two filtered out the hard parts of the message, and that ground three was too busy to listen well, didn't suggest that they were *dead* in the sense of *incapable of listening*. Nothing Jesus said implied the listeners *couldn't hear.*

In fact, if they couldn't hear, the parable would be unnecessary. Why warn dead people to be careful how they hear when they can't hear anyway? The instruction would be senseless. You would think that somewhere in this parable of listening, Jesus would have mentioned that unbelievers are dead, and the dead can't listen. But there is no such information.

Instead Jesus viewed the state of each listener as a heart issue rather than an incapability issue. He assumed that everyone had ears and could hear if they would put their minds and hearts to it. The problem was not their *inability* to hear but their *unwillingness* to listen. That's why "as He said these things, He would call out, 'He who has ears to hear, let him hear'" (Luke 8:8 NASB). Even though many in His audience were probably unbelievers, they had ears to hear and "faith comes by hearing."

In fact, the parable becomes an enigma if the soils represent spiritual corpses. Take, for example, the first soil, the hardened ground. Jesus said, "then the devil comes and takes away the word out of their hearts, lest they should believe and be saved" (Luke 8:12). The word "lest" suggests that if the devil didn't remove the Word from their hearts *they might believe and be saved.*

But if the listeners are incapable of believing, why would that be a danger? If they're not going to believe and be saved until God chooses to give them life, what's the devil worried about? The truth according to ground number one is that unbelievers *can* listen and believe. That's why Satan hyperventilates, to prevent the seed from germinating, which he knows has the awesome power to create faith. The fact that he can't wait to steal it suggests that the issue is not the *inability* but the *unwillingness* of the listener which affords him permission.

B. Jesus placed the emphasis on "how you listen." He ended with, "therefore take heed how you hear. For whoever has, to him more will be given; and whoever does not have, even what he seems to have will be taken from him" (Luke 8:18).

How suggests that there are a variety of ways to listen. *How* suggests that there is individual responsibility. Why would Jesus talk about *how* anyone listens if their destiny had already been chosen, if they couldn't listen anyway? The parable almost insists upon human responsibility. Lack of responsibility would make the parable purposeless.

The very presence of this parable suggests that every person can listen in the right way. And those who are listening poorly can change and start listening in the right way if they take care how they listen.

If the audience was "dead" in the sense of "incapable of listening at all," wouldn't it be more accurate for Jesus to encourage them to pray and ask God for the gift of hearing?

So the fact that Jesus gave this parable of warning indicates that the nation of Israel had a responsibility to get her Messiah's message straight. From the evidence in the parable, at least three quarters of the nation wasn't paying attention to what He was saying.

C. Israel was judged for her refusal to listen. "Wait a minute," someone will say. "Have you read verse 10? "To you it has been given to know the mysteries of the kingdom of God, but to the rest it is given in parables, that 'Seeing they may not see, And hearing they may not understand.'" "There it is. The disciples were given the ability to listen and the others were given deception so that even as they saw or heard they didn't really see or hear anything. You need to read the context, Schuppe."

In answer to that, notice that verse 10 (as well as Mark 4:11-12 and Matthew 13:11-15) is a quotation from Isaiah 6. That's the chapter where Isaiah volunteers for missionary service, and God sends him to pronounce judgment upon the nation of Israel. After Isaiah hears the Lord ask, "Whom shall I send, And who will go for Us?" he then answers,

"Here am I, Send me." In the next two verses, God explains his job description:

> Go, and say to this people: "Keep on hearing, but do not understand; keep on seeing, but do not perceive. Make the heart of this people dull, and their ears heavy, and blind their eyes; lest they see with their eyes, and hear with their ears, and understand with their hearts, and turn and be healed" (Isaiah 6:9-10 ESV).

Isaiah was being sent to chosen people with a message of judgment. Isaiah 5 detailed God's lamentful case against His people. He had planted a lush vineyard, given it everything it needed, but it only produced wild grapes. So God chose to bring judgment on the vineyard by taking away its hedge and letting it be burned and trampled down (Isaiah 5:5-6).

In Chapter 6, Isaiah became the prophet who announced the coming judgment. Instead of announcing that God had chosen to give listening ears to select people (and he was speaking to God's chosen people), he was informing them that God had taken away their ability to hear.

Thus in Luke 8:10 Jesus was quoting a judgment passage from Isaiah to explain to His disciples why He was speaking in parables. The disciples raised the question apparently because His method of teaching with parables was unusual. The interchange is captured in Matthew:

> And the disciples came and said to Him, "Why do You speak to them in parables?" He answered and said to them, "Because it has been given to you to know the mysteries of the kingdom of heaven, but to them it has not been given . . . Therefore I speak to them in parables, because seeing they do not see, and hearing they do not hear, nor do they understand. And in them the prophecy of Isaiah is fulfilled, which says: 'Hearing you will hear and shall not

understand, And seeing you will see and not perceive; For the hearts of this people have grown dull. Their ears are hard of hearing, And their eyes they have closed, Lest they should see with their eyes and hear with their ears, Lest they should understand with their hearts and turn, So that I should heal them . . ."" (Matthew 13:10-11a, 13-15).

The parables were part of God's judgment on Israel because she had refused to listen and had rejected her Messiah (Matthew 11:20). She listened like the first three soils. The phrase, "to them it has not been given" refers to His listeners with closed ears who will only see the parables as puzzles. At the same time it was an introduction of new, hidden truth (Matthew 13:34-35) to those with listening ears to hear, like the disciples. Thus we cannot conclude from verse 10 that God chooses which people will listen. The command to listen fits everyone who possesses ears.

D. Jesus made no indication that the last soil was good because it was "elect." According to some, the good ground should have been good because God chose it to be good. But since Jesus was speaking to those who were already chosen, election wasn't the issue. Even members of the chosen nation, the elect, needed to be careful how they listened.

The parable makes clear that the good ground refers to the disciples ("blessed are your ears," and "to you has been given . . ." - Matt. 13:11; Mark 4:11-12; Luke 8:10), and the first three soils refer to Israel ("but to them"). Could the first three soils have listened like the good ground? Absolutely. That was the purpose of the warning.

The parable assumed that everyone possessed "ears to hear." No one present was "dead" in the sense of incapable, and waiting for God to enable them.

E. Jesus placed the major responsibility on the listener. What then made the difference in the listeners if God wasn't choosing some to listen? It was the heart. Each soil in the parable pictured a heart, the attitude of one's mind toward God's Word. Whether one *wanted to listen* was the larger issue, because Jesus assumed everyone could listen.

So the command, "he who has ears to hear" was not about the ears as much as it was about the "to hear." "To hear" is the crucial element in our life with God. God has spoken. His complete message is available –to those who will pay attention.

How well you listen will be revealed by what happens afterwards. The seed will be either stolen, fried, choked, or fruitful. According to Jesus, the difference will be based entirely on how well you listen.

II. Dead people can listen to God's words

Can a person who is walking according to the course of this world, according to the prince of the power of the air (Ephesians 2:1-2), actually "listen" to God? Does such a person have the power, the ability? The parable of the sower suggests that the answer is *yes*. And there are other indications throughout Scripture that the answer is yes.

Paul says, "'The word is near you, in your mouth and in your heart' (that is, the word of faith which we preach):" (Romans 10:8). Its nearness makes it sound like it is possible to confess with the mouth and call upon the name of the Lord. Is calling something special that God has to enact after choosing an individual? or can a normal unsaved person listen to the nearby truth, believe it and obey?

A. Israel could have listened and obeyed. Paul assumed as much in Romans 10:16-21. Israel's listening problem wasn't that she was dead (she was), or that she was incapable of hearing (she wasn't), but that she was unwilling to listen, believe and obey. He asks, "But I say, have they not heard? Yes indeed: 'Their sound has gone out to all the earth, And their words to the ends of the world'" (Romans 10:18).

Paul surmises that one possible explanation for Israel's failure to respond to the gospel is that perhaps she never heard the gospel. She somehow missed the message. To answer that notion Paul refers to Psalm 19 which states that the good news had gone out into all the earth. Israel should have heard because she was *the chosen messenger to carry that message* (Isaiah 43:9-12; 44:8-9)! If the words went out to the ends of the world, why didn't the carriers get blessed the same way they blessed others? They announced them, even taught them (Romans 2:17-23), but didn't personally pay attention to or obey the words that were in their mouths.

Paul then brings up the possibility that Israel simply didn't understand the gospel:

> But I say, did Israel not know? First Moses says: "I will provoke you to jealousy by those who are not a nation, I will move you to anger by a foolish nation." But Isaiah is very bold and says: "I was found by those who did not seek Me; I was made manifest to those who did not ask for Me" (Romans 10:19-20).

The problem was how Israel could be ignorant when other nations, like Nineveh in Jonah 3, which Israel viewed as beneath her superior intelligence, understood the message and repented. Given her exceptional discernment, how could she miss what they understood? Ignorance was definitely not the problem.

This passage would be a perfect place to identify Israel's unbelief as "because she was dead and couldn't hear or believe." Or "she couldn't believe because she wasn't chosen." Either of those conditions would have identified the true limit of Israel's responsibility, or even explained her lack of response.

But Scripture places the responsibility directly on Israel. True she was dead in trespasses and sins, but she had ears, she had the convicting work of the Holy Spirit (John 16:7-11), and she could have called on the name of the Lord and been saved. Why did she not? Here's the answer: "But they have not all obeyed the gospel. For Isaiah says, 'LORD, who has believed our report?' So then faith comes by hearing, and hearing by the word of God" (Romans 10:16-17).

She refused to listen, believe and obey. She was the elect of God. Messiah came specifically to her. What was her problem? It was her will. Paul concludes, "But to Israel he says: 'All day long I have stretched out My hands To a disobedient and contrary people'" (Romans 10:21).

Why would Paul talk as if this great responsibility belonged to the nation of Israel when in reality it was God's responsibility, and He hadn't chosen her? If God selectively distributed the ability to listen, couldn't Paul have expressed that truth a little more clearly?

Instead, the point in this passage is that God didn't selectively withhold the ability to listen from some of His chosen people. Instead, He supplied everything any Israelite needed to capture His words, if only they would use what He supplied. That's the point of Jesus' oft-repeated command, "he who has ears to hear, let him hear."

B. Jesus affirmed that the dead could hear God's words. Here's the context:

> Most assuredly, I say to you, he who hears My word and
> believes in Him who sent Me has everlasting life, and shall
> not come into judgment, but has passed from death into
> life. Most assuredly, I say to you, the hour is coming, and
> now is, when the dead will hear the voice of the Son of
> God; and those who hear will live (John 5:24-25).

When Jesus said, "an hour is coming and now is," He wasn't talking about a future resurrection, but present time. It "now is." Dead people will hear the voice of the Son of God. Yes all the dead will hear at the final resurrection (5:28-29), but at the present time only "those who hear will live."

The "most assuredly" statement of verse 25 follows the "most assuredly" statement of verse 24 which promises eternal life to "he who hears My word and believes Him who sent Me." And this can happen to people Christ called, "dead."

C. Jesus emphasized "whoever." He promised, "For God so loved the world that He gave His only begotten Son, that whoever believes in Him should not perish but have everlasting life" (John 3:16). Again He promised:

> Whoever drinks of this water will thirst again, but whoever
> drinks of the water that I shall give him will never thirst.
> But the water that I shall give him will become in him a
> fountain of water springing up into everlasting life (John
> 4:13-14).

What are we to make of "whoever"? "Whoever is chosen"? "Whoever God gives faith to"? Does "whoever" really mean, "whoever"? If it does then the issue is not their inability-to-hear state, but their refusal-to-listen state.

Jesus said as much concerning the nation of Israel:

> O Jerusalem, Jerusalem, the one who kills the prophets and
> stones those who are sent to her! How often I wanted to
> gather your children together, as a hen gathers her chicks
> under her wings, but you were not willing! (Matthew 23:37).

Observe the immense contrast between Jesus' desire (I wanted to gather) and the response of the nation (not willing). It wasn't that the nation couldn't come to Christ, but that they wouldn't. Remember that Jesus was speaking to the elect of God. Chosen, but dead; Israel was invited to the banquet but unwilling to attend (Matthew 22:3, 5, 8). Anyone could have come had they listened and believed. There were no inhibiting factors as far as God was concerned.

III. A corpse is not a good picture of "dead in trespasses and sins"

We may think, "a dead person is a dead person is a dead person," right? Yes, unless the word, "dead" is a metaphor. What does a metaphor have to do with the definition of a word? It can change it significantly.

For example, "a car killed him." We would expect to see that a man died because of being run over by a car. "Her hat killed me." Now what? Same word, but a metaphor. I'm using the word "killed" to explain my reaction to her hat. I didn't die, she didn't die, and the hat didn't die. I'm making a comparison to help explain my reaction to her hat. What was my reaction? I was horrified. Perhaps I laughed.

Using a word metaphorically can change the definition greatly. "His affair killed our relationship." "Our marriage is dead." "When my boss laughed at me, motivation for my job died." Are we to see corpses? Of course not.

A. Metaphors need to be interpreted carefully. A metaphor commonly takes one slice of a literal picture and compares it to something else in a new way. Jesus said, "tell Herod, that fox . . ." What was it about Herod that made him a fox? "God is my rock." What is it about God that makes it possible for us to picture Him as our "rock?" "I am the bread of life." What is it about Jesus that makes Him "bread?"

It would be wrong to see Herod as a literal fox, God as a literal rock or Jesus as literal bread. A metaphor asks us to view Herod as cagey as a fox, God as solid and unmovable, and Jesus as the food supply for life. Each comparison chooses one feature of the literal picture. That's all. No more. To make two comparisons, or three or four, or to say that one *is* *the other* is dangerous.

"Dead in trespasses and sins" (Ephesians 2:1) describes our relationship with God before Christ. "Dead" is a metaphor. Does the picture of a corpse present an accurate definition of this metaphor? I don't think so. In fact, these dead people were walking "according to the course of this world, according to the prince of the power of the air." They were active.

What happens when you use a literal picture for a metaphor? In this situation, the literal picture (corpse) adds the concept of being "incapable" to the description. "Dead in trespasses and sins" normally means separated from God and incapable of repairing the separation. But does "incapable of repairing the separation" mean "incapable of doing anything?" That's what the corpse picture would suggest. Is that what Paul intended by choosing this metaphor?

As far as I know, when the word "dead" is used as a metaphor, it doesn't mean incapable of action. For example, Jesus puts the words into the mouth of the prodigal's father, "this my son was dead and is alive again . . ." (Luke 15:24, 32). Did He mean that his son beforehand was incapable of responding positively to the father? Or that he was unwilling? Does "dead in trespasses and sins" mean incapable of responding to God's grace," or unwilling to respond to God's grace? A literal corpse is incapable. Metaphorically dead is capable but unwilling.

The fact is that unbelievers are "dead in trespasses and sins." Their relationship with God has been broken. They are separated, and there is no hope of them repairing the damage. They are totally depraved and everything they do results in "filthy rags" (Isaiah 64:6).

But does that mean that we should picture their state as that of a corpse? No. No more than when business partners say, "our relationship is dead," are we to see corpses. The intended picture for "dead in trespasses and sins" is not that of a corpse. It refers to their current hopeless separation from God and their inability to fix the problem. But it doesn't mean that they can't listen to God's solution, believe it and respond by calling out to Jesus, the One who can fix the problem.

B. The Bible usage of dead helps us define the metaphor. Does Paul see a picture of a corpse when he uses "dead" metaphorically in other places? For example, observe his use of metaphors in Romans 7. I have added emphasis to help us see them:

> What shall we say then? Is the law sin? Certainly not! On the contrary, I would not have known sin except through the law. For I would not have known covetousness unless the law had said, "You shall not covet." But sin, taking opportunity by the commandment, produced in me all

manner of evil desire. For apart from the law sin was *dead.*
I was *alive* once without the law, but when the commandment came, *sin revived* and *I died.* And the commandment, which was to bring *life*, I found to bring *death*. For
sin, taking occasion by the commandment, deceived me,
and by it *killed me.* Therefore the law is holy, and the commandment holy and just and good. Has then what is good
become death to me? Certainly not! But sin, that it might
appear sin, *was producing death in me* through what is
good, so that sin through the commandment might become exceedingly sinful (Romans 7:7-13).

In verse 8 we have the fact that sin was dead apart from the law –
dead in a metaphorical sense. What does that mean? In verse 9 sin revived. What does that mean? We also see that Paul was alive in verse 9,
but then subsequently died. And verses 10, 11 and 13 emphasize that the
effect of the commandment was Paul's death. Sin killed him in verse 9
and the commandment killed him in verse 11.

Obviously the corpse picture doesn't fit here. What was once dead
springs into life, and what was once alive dies. How does Paul intend that
we understand this word? His deadness wasn't permanent, neither did it
make him incapable; neither did it disconnect him from social discourse.

In verse 8 the commandment "produced in me all manner of evil
desire." Paul summarizes that experience in verse 9 as, "I died." He was
using the metaphor of death to describe his out-of-control state of sinful
desire.

Also in verse 8, sin was dead "apart from the law." What did that
mean? It meant that sin was dormant. It didn't have power in Paul's life;
it didn't affect him. But when the commands of the law came, things
changed. For Paul, "dead" meant having *out-of-control desire*. And for the
law, "dead" meant *dormant*.

Do you see how a metaphor changes the definition of a word? That's why we need to be careful in reading, "dead in trespasses and sins." A corpse is not an accurate picture of what it means to be unsaved because it adds the idea of being *incapable of responding* to the situation or invitation.

IV. God is no respecter of persons

"If everyone is a spiritual corpse, then obviously God has to choose which corpse will get life. And it's obvious that God has not chosen everyone." Is that an accurate picture of God? to see Him walking through the cemetery, choosing certain of His creations to eternal blessing and passing over others, leaving them for eternal torment?

It's true that many are going to end in eternal torment, but Scripture claims that they do this of their own will. God wants no one to perish (Ezekiel 33:11), and has at great expense provided salvation for all through the death of Christ. But the gift has to be received (John 3:18). And the way people choose eternal torment is by refusing the gift.

Scripture claims that God is "no respecter of persons" (Acts 10:34 KJV). What does this mean? Does it imply that He treats all alike? He does not give to one what He withholds from another? That's obviously untrue. Some have advantages of birth that others never see. Think about the opportunities of Americans. Even those at the poverty line are wealthier than most everyone else on Earth. God grants certain people to be born in privileged circumstances. He doesn't treat everyone alike in respect to their birth, or parents, or opportunities.

So what does it mean that God is no respecter of persons? In what kind of contexts is this assurance given?

It's used in God's instructions to Israel's judges. They were to judge righteously between fellow Israelites because God was impartial (Deuteronomy 1:16-17). They were not to give special treatment to Jewish people over aliens or to important people over unimportant (2 Chronicles 19:6-7).

It's used of God's instructions to Israelites to be careful how they treat insignificant people like orphans and widows and aliens. They were to execute justice and fairness to all (Deuteronomy 10:16-19).

It's used of God's treatment of non-Jewish people. He shows no partiality, welcoming from any nation "the man who fears Him and does what is right" (Acts 10:34-35).

It's used of God's impartial response to every person in light of his or her response to the truth (Romans 2:8-11).

It's used of God's judgment of everyone's work. There is no partiality (1 Peter 1:17). Peter uses this truth to encourage us to make life choices carefully (actually *in fear*).

It's used as an example and command to Christians to be impartial to others as their Lord has been to them: "My brethren, do not hold the faith of our Lord Jesus Christ, the Lord of glory, with partiality" (James 2:1). Since Christ died for all, we ought to be gracious and merciful to all.

In fact, Paul states as much: "For God has committed them all to disobedience, that He might have mercy on all" (Romans 11:32). Everyone acknowledges that God has committed all to disobedience (Romans 3:23). The second part is likewise true: that God did this in order to have mercy on everyone!

Does this mean that everyone will go to heaven? No, Jesus Himself said, "Enter by the narrow gate; for wide is the gate and broad is the way that leads to destruction, and there are many who go in by it" (Matthew 7:13). The warning doesn't say that God has chosen many to enter the broad way. The command is for Jesus' listeners to choose the narrow gate, because the default gate leads to destruction.

God will have mercy on everyone who listens, believes His Word and obeys. As Paul says again, "But the Scripture imprisoned everything under sin, so that the promise by faith in Jesus Christ might be given to those who believe" (Galatians 3:22 ESV).

It's difficult to conclude from these verses that the impartial God picks and chooses to bless certain select people when He has stated that His promises are given to "those who believe."

V. The God who commands us to be impartial is Himself impartial

The commands we read in Deuteronomy 1:16, 10:16, 2 Chronicles 19:6 and Job 34:17 require impartiality in our treatment of people under us because of God's character. We represent Him and He wants to be seen as absolutely fair and impartial.

Is it possible to envision a God picking and choosing certain ones when God declares Himself as impartial? Would we come to that conclusion in light of the statement, "not willing that any should perish but that all should come to repentance" (2 Peter 3:9b)? Does He actually desire every person to be saved?

Here's the way John Calvin answered that question:

> but it may be asked, If God wishes none to perish, why is it that so many do perish? To this my answer is that no mention is here made of the hidden purpose of God, according to which the reprobates are doomed to their own ruin, but only of his will as made known to us in the gospel.

> For God there stretches forth his hand without a difference
> to all, but lays hold only of those, to lead them to himself,
> whom he has chosen before the foundation of the world.[21]

Calvin suggests a hidden purpose of God that differs from God's revealed purpose. Although Peter states that God desires none to perish, Calvin claims that this declaration is modified by God's secret will, "according to which the reprobate are doomed to their own ruin." It sounds like Calvin is trying to suggest that God publicly affirms one thing while privately practicing another. Doesn't that thought turn God into a hypocrite or perhaps a liar? Surely Calvin couldn't have meant to do that in light of the truth is that God is impartial.

But the conclusion that God says one thing and yet holds another thought in His heart can interfere with clear affirmations of God's Word. For example, John Calvin comments on John 3:16 by saying:

> Let us remember, on the other hand, that while life is
> promised universally to all who believe in Christ, still faith
> is not common to all. For Christ is made known and held
> out to the view of all, but the elect alone are they whose
> eyes God opens, that they may seek him by faith.[22]

According to Calvin, the "whoever" in John 3:16 is not actually announcing that the opportunity to believe is available to all. It is only possible for those whose eyes God has chosen to open. Thus, "whoever" means, in reality, "only those God chooses as He walks through the cemetery."

Does that sound like God is impartial? How could that be the God Peter identified with ". . . in every nation the man who fears Him and does what is right is welcome to Him" (Acts 10:35 NASB)?

There are followers of John Calvin who admit that we as humans recoil from the unfairness of this teaching. For example, Wayne Grudem says,

> the love that God gives us for our fellow human beings and the love that he commands us to have toward our neighbor cause us to recoil against this doctrine, and it is right that we feel such dread in contemplating it. It is something that we would not want to believe, and would not believe, unless Scripture clearly taught it.[23]

Grudem admits that there is something inhumane and dreadful about this doctrine. It goes against the grain of common human kindness to one another. How would you like to choose which of your children will go to heaven? Which parent would not earnestly desire every one of his or her children to go to heaven?

Yet at the same time Grudem assures us that it is clearly taught in Scripture. Why would anyone assume that Scripture teaches us that God operates differently than what He commands of us?

Doesn't God command us to love our neighbor because that's the way He responds to His neighbors, and even His enemies (Matthew 5:44-45)? Didn't Christ die for His enemies (Romans 5:8)? Doesn't Jesus claim that we will be sons of the Most High when we love our enemies without expecting anything in return, because "He Himself is kind to ungrateful and evil men" (Luke 6:35 NASB)? How can "kind to ungrateful and evil men" fit the Calvinistic picture of God selecting a few cemetery plots and overlooking many others? Should we really imitate that example of "kindness?"

Jesus places the responsibility of listening on every human being: "take care how you listen" (Luke 8:18) because "faith comes by hearing" (Romans 10:17). Faith is not a gift that God awards to some and withholds from others. He makes it available to everyone who will listen. That's why John 3:16 can say "whoever."

VI. The "corpse picture" changes the gospel

Let me point out four adjustments that have to be made in the gospel message when unbelievers are seen as literal spiritual corpses:

(a) It eliminates almost every command to an unbeliever, because corpses have no abilities. The invitations to "listen," to "believe," to "come," to "call on His name," to "receive," will fall on unresponsive ears, because every command is impossible to obey until God chooses to regenerate a person.

That fact makes Christ's repetition of the command to believe strange. Why lecture a dead horse? Why command a corpse? Why emphasize again and again the importance of listening to those who can't hear? It doesn't seem reasonable to waste so much print on those who are incapable of responding.

In addition, is there any need for such repeated commands when God by irresistible grace is going to give life to those He chooses? Won't He give faith to the elect whether they listen or not?

(b) It also eliminates God's repeated appeals to the human will. The issue in salvation is a person's will. We mentioned earlier Jesus' cry to the nation of Israel, "O Jerusalem, Jerusalem . . . How often I wanted to gather your children together, as a hen gathers her chicks under her wings, but you were not willing!" (Matthew 23:37). It wasn't that Israel *couldn't* repent, it was that she was *unwilling*. But the corpse picture replaces the human will with God's choice. "Are you chosen?" is made more important than "have you chosen to listen and obey God's Word?"

The tragedy is that the simple gospel message is revised. The Biblical mandates to "believe," "come to Christ," and "receive Christ" are downplayed. For example, one preacher advises unbelievers to "seek" to find out "whether you have any capacity for faith," and to "place yourself where the means of grace are most commonly concentrated."[24] In giving advice to unbelievers this preacher makes no reference to the many commands to "believe," "come," or "receive."[25]

(c) It makes the invitation to unbelievers misleading. For example, why did the Apostle Paul instruct the Philippian jailer to "believe?" Here's the text: "And he brought them out and said, 'Sirs, what must I do to be saved?' So they said, 'Believe on the Lord Jesus Christ, and you will be saved, you and your household' " (Acts 16:30-31).

Why didn't Paul command him to pray for the gift of salvation, or "seek to discover whether you have any capacity for faith?" Why didn't Paul say, "it depends on whether you are of the elect?" Was Paul's command misdirected? Could the man actually believe? Wasn't he dead in his trespasses and sins? If he actually was a spiritual "corpse" all he could hope for would be that God had chosen him. But Paul seemed confident that he could believe and be saved.

(d) It impugns the character of God because it presents Him as partial. Those with the corpse picture maintain that they hold a "high view" of God. But at the same time they talk about a God who has favorites. And those He hasn't chosen would be mistreated (eternity in Hell) in comparison with the others. It misrepresents the love of God. How could He in "love" choose to overlook a large quantity of His creations? If God loved that way, why can't humans love that way?

If three young brothers were drowning and I had the ability to save all but choose to save one, I would not be hailed as a great savior. Instead my love would be questioned, even by the one I saved: "why did you choose to save only me when you could have saved my brothers?"

Thus, Wayne Grudem is correct: "the love that God gives us for our fellow human beings and the love that he commands us to have toward our neighbor cause us to recoil against this doctrine, and it is right that we feel such dread in contemplating it."

But his next sentence which states that Scripture clearly teaches such a doctrine is incorrect. Scripture doesn't teach it. Instead Scripture clearly teaches that God so loved the entire world that He sent His Son to die for its salvation (John 3:16-17). It's right for us to recoil against it and feel dread in contemplating it, because it is a false picture of our God's awesome glory.

I've spent twenty-one pages arguing against the corpse picture because *if it is true, then this book is misreading Scripture and misleading you the reader.* If the Bible presents unbelievers as incapable of listening and believing, then "faith comes by hearing," and "be careful how you hear" have to be understood differently, because *faith can't come by hearing.* And if God selects certain to believe then the unbeliever has no responsibility. He awaits God's sovereign choice and hopes he is included.

My purpose in these pages is to make clear the Bible's announcement that *dead people can listen!* Unbelievers can hear, believe and call on the name of the Lord! The truth of the matter is that God is gracious and fair, just and loving and "desires all people to be saved and to come to the knowledge of the truth" (1 Timothy 2:4). Praise His name! and love Him! by listening to His Word!

Chapter 8

Motionless definitions of the word *believe*

We spent Chapters 4 through 6 discussing the beginning step in faith: *listening*. In the last chapter we tried to affirm that those who are dead in trespasses and sins can listen to God's Word. In the next two chapters, I would like to explain how the Bible defines the second step in faith, *believe*. Then in Chapter 10, I want to talk about what it means to *obey*.

Believe it or not, the word *believe* is confusing. People define it in strange ways; as a leap into the dark (suggesting that we are trusting what we don't know) or as a feeling (suggesting that we are trusting what affects us emotionally), or as something unusual like a dream or vision of someone in white that "obviously" comes from God. Some people are convinced they have believed because they suddenly feel peace, or have a new awareness of life.

When we add theology to the definitional discussion, the atmosphere becomes even hazier. Some teach that believing is only possible for those who are already regenerated. That means that one is not regenerated by faith but in spite of one's lack of faith. Only after regeneration are people responsible to believe in order to be saved. Does that sound confusing?

Others believe that faith is a kind of receptivity that involves no response on the part of the human will. It's an actionless thing where a person is kind of pulled along by the Holy Spirit. I use the word "motionless" in the title of this chapter to cover definitions of faith that are effortless or decision-less. Such definitions would not agree with the title of this book because for them, faith does not involve a human *reach*.

I maintain that the definition of *believe* in Scripture is identical to the definition of *believe* in the standard dictionaries. It's an active process of ascertaining the truthfulness of a statement or a person making a claim, accepting and placing confidence in a truthful claim so as to live on the basis of the claim and/or join the person making the claim.

The normal definition means "to accept as true or as conveying the truth" (I *believe it; don't believe him; believes what he is told*).[26] Such a definition involves thinking (which is the second definition in Oxford), and placing confidence or trust in a person or on what they advise or promise (the third definition in Oxford).

This definition is active because it places a responsibility on individuals to sort through competing truth-claims in order to commit themselves to the right one.

Such active definitions are common in Scripture. We've talked about them. But an important question is, "Does the normal, active definition of faith fit *what the Bible says to unbelievers?*" Does faith require someone to think and evaluate competing claims to arrive at a decision, and then to make a decision? Is faith a *conscious choice* and a *personal responsibility?* Or does the Bible require a special definition of faith, one that is not in the dictionary?

Before I explain how the Bible defines *believe* in an active way, which I will do in Chapter 9, let me introduce a couple of ways Bible teachers suggest a special definition for faith, one where the recipient is motionless or has little responsibility.

I. Some teach a *passive* definition of faith

I'm sure you remember the three verbal "voices" in English from your days in the seventh grade. In the *active voice* the subject accomplishes the verb: "I hit the ball" (subject "I," verb "hit," object "ball") or "the young teen sang beautifully" (subject "teen," verb "sang"). In the *middle voice* the subject acts on itself: "I drank the water myself" or "the teen sang the song herself." In the *passive voice* the subject is acted upon by someone or something else: "He was hit by the ball," or "she was overwhelmed by the song."

Observe that in the passive voice the subject has little responsibility. Instead, the activity comes from somewhere else. How do people define faith in a passive way? Let me mention three ways it is done.

A. God gives faith to certain individuals. The notion that faith is a gift originates from the conclusion that sinners are dead like corpses and thus can do nothing to listen or exercise faith. Because of that, nothing happens spiritually in anyone's life until God gives regeneration and faith to certain people, "a gift which God lays in the lap of the soul."[27]

For example, G. C. Berkouwer teaches that man can only be "completely passive in the process of conversion," and there can be no "cause within men for their different reactions to the gospel."[28] He's saying that the reason some believe and others don't is due to God's choice.

Berkouwer rejects any "correlation which makes the election of God dependent on our act of faith" and "every interpretation of the election in Christ in which faith would become the condition of election."[29] Thus faith has absolutely nothing to do with conversion, and the first seven chapters of this book are misguided or plainly wrong.

John MacArthur adds, "Faith is our *response,* not the *cause* of salvation."[30] That is correct; the *cause of salvation* is not our faith but the Grace of God. Faith is simply our response to God's gracious invitation. However, in the next sentence MacArthur claims, "Even faith is 'not of ourselves'; it is included in 'the gift of God'" (Ephesians 2:8-9).

Wait a minute. What does that mean? How can *our response* be God's gift? Isn't that a contradiction? Does MacArthur want us to believe that faith is *both our response* to God's Word and a *gracious gift* from God? You would think it to be one or the other.

Let me quote from one more brother in Christ who teaches passive faith. R. C. Sproul claims that since unbelievers lack the ability to believe, "regeneration occurs when the Holy Spirit comes to a person who is spiritually dead and makes him spiritually alive!"[31]

This means that regeneration occurs *without faith,* and that human ability and responsibility to believe only begin *after regeneration.* Sproul claims that "the ultimate reason why some people respond in faith to the gospel and others do not is that some (and not others) are regenerated by the Holy Spirit."[32]

But didn't Paul command the Philippian jailer to believe *in order to be saved?* According to Sproul that's the wrong order. In fact, the notion that people believe and then are regenerated "seems to be on a collision course with everything the NT teaches about regeneration."[33]

In answer to the question, "why doesn't God give the gift of faith to everyone?" Sproul gives one word, *election.* He explains the essence of election as God determining to give the gift of enablement to certain people.[34]

These men teach that salvation does not come "by grace through faith" but "by grace through God's choice." Norman Geisler describes the strangeness of this position:

> Ironically, while one of the central principles of the Reformation was justification by faith alone (*sola fide*), some who strongly claim to be heirs of the Reformation (i.e., the Reformed) do not believe there is even one condition necessary for a human being to receive salvation.[35]

These men teach a concept of faith that is *passive*. Their Bibles do not command unbelievers to believe on the name of the Lord Jesus Christ for salvation. Rather those commands are addressed to individuals God has already regenerated.

B. The Bible presents faith as active. In light of the assurances of Warfield, Berkouwer, MacArthur and Sproul, why would anyone conclude that faith is active, and that every unbeliever has a personal responsibility to listen and believe? The short answer is that the Bible clearly presents faith as a personal responsibility.

For example, the statement, "without faith it is impossible to please Him" (Hebrews 11:6) doesn't make sense when the faith to please Him is a gift from Him. That would have to mean that God decides who gets the faith to please Him. But the context emphasizes the opposite.

Rather than viewing faith as a gift, the entire 11th chapter of Hebrews views faith as an active response that encourages the reader to trust God and obey Him, as Abel and Enoch and Noah and Abraham and Moses and others did. Indeed, the chapter would have little encouragement to suffering believers if the highlighted people accomplished what they did because God chose to supply them with faith. Instead, it would "encourage" them with, "hope that God chooses you for faith because there is little else you can do."

Scripture repeatedly emphasizes the human responsibility to listen and choose the right response. Faith is a response to God. For example:

> As they have chosen their own ways, And their soul delights in their abominations, So I will choose their punishments And will bring on them what they dread. Because I called, but no one answered; I spoke, but they did not listen. And they did evil in My sight And chose that in which I did not delight. (Isaiah 66:3b-4 NASB).

God's judgment in the form of "punishments" and "what they dread" is based on "they have chosen their own ways." They had the opportunity of choosing a different way because God "called" and "spoke." Why did God *call?* Did He actually expect a response from people who were dead in their trespasses and sins? Could the people have listened and responded if they had wanted to? Could they have wanted to?

The point is that Israel's lack of faith was not an issue of *could not.* It was Israel's *would not.* Passive faith doesn't fit this passage. No one is giving a person the faith to believe; no one is making a person believe. Instead, the One calling and warning is waiting for a person's active response.

II. Some teach a *non-active* definition of faith

There are other Bible teachers who disagree with the passive faith idea but teach a faith that is more or less effortless. For example, Professor Zane Hodges says, "faith is *not* an '*actus*' in either the Roman Catholic or Arminian sense. It is 'pure receptivity' to the offer of the Gospel. Faith is a *persuasion* of the heart, not an *'act'* of the human will."[36]

The word *actus* is a Latin word that means "an act or thing done." Hodges wants us to believe that faith is not the result of someone choosing to accept God's Word as true, but rather *pure receptivity* to the offer of the gospel. That distinction is difficult to follow. How does one receive something without choosing to receive it? Does pure receptivity involve evaluating competing claims? Doesn't listening involve evaluating and choosing, which would place it into the category of *actus*?

To clarify that it's not an act of the human will but pure receptivity, Hodges refers to Martin Luther's great statement: "Faith holds out the hand and the sack and just lets the good be done to it. For God is the giver . . . we are the receivers who receive the gift through faith that does nothing." Hodges then states, "this is my view of faith, too."[37]

Hodges agrees with Luther that faith "holds out the hand and the sack" but doesn't seem to accept that holding out the hand is an act of the human will. What does it take to hold out the hand? Doesn't it involve a choice and the output of some kind of energy? How can one hold out a sack without effort?

Thus it looks like Hodges defines faith in a way that is both active and passive. He pictures faith as holding out the hand and sack toward God the giver (involving both will and effort) while at the same time he identifies that act as "pure receptivity" to God's offer (passive). He seems to want to define faith in an active way but doesn't want to call it active.

Holding out the hand and sack in response to God's promise is a beautiful picture of faith. That's the *reach of an empty hand* as the title of this book suggests. God sends out ambassadors announcing that He has reconciled the world unto Himself through the death of His Son, and commanding listeners to be reconciled (2 Corinthians 5:19-20). In effect

He is saying, "hold out your sack and I will fill it with My forgiveness and goodness." Those who hold out the hand and sack, do they "receive the gift through faith that does nothing?" Or is their response "an *act* of the human will?"

The difference is significant. One looks like a passive faith ("receive the gift through faith that does nothing") and the other requires some sort of human *actus*. Which of these pictures did Jesus present when He said, "let him hear" or "come to Me" or "you would have asked of Him for living water?" He was looking for an act of the human will.

Thus, Professor Hodges dismisses the action involved in faith while at the same time uses action verbs associated with believe, like *hold out*. He argues against any effort or *actus* while agreeing with Luther's picture of a faith which involves effort.

III. Some ignore the verbs associated with belief

Another way to make faith passive is to overlook the verbs like *call* (Romans 10:13) and *come* (John 6:35) which are often combined with *believe*. These verbs tell us that believing involves a response to God's invitation. But some Bible students tell us that these verbs are to be understood passively.

Pastor Charles Bing, for example, argues that the verbs are simply synonyms for the word *believe*. He mentions the words "look," "hear," "enter," "feed," "come," and "receive" in the gospel of John and summarizes them all with the statement, "these pictures of faith all denote receptivity, agreement, or trust. All are essentially simple activities and essentially passive. None communicates the idea of merit, work, effort, or achievement."[38]

It's true that none of these verbs communicates merit or achievement, but what about the word "effort?" To "come," to "enter," and "feed" are "essentially passive?" Here's how Bing explains it:

> to eat and drink is to appropriate or receive something
> upon which life depends. There is no work or merit asso-
> ciated with these activities. Rather, the benefit is from what
> is appropriated, which corresponds to the object of faith,
> which is Christ.[39]

He adds, "to *come* is to trustingly approach Christ for help. It entails no human merit or effort."[40]

But how can someone eat, drink and receive with no effort? Don't those verbs involve a decision and action to turn to Christ? Who eats and drinks passively? The fact that Pastor Bing can put these action verbs together with the word *passive* is confusing.

Bing even seems to acknowledge that faith is more than passive when he states, "Christ's revelation demands a response."[41] That is correct. The problem is how he can hold the demand for a response and the word *passive* at the same time. The gospel of John pictures unbelievers listening (John 5:24-25), searching God's Word for truth (John 5:39-40), and responding by coming to or rejecting Him (John 5:40). These descriptions involve *actus*, personal effort.

The bottom line, as Pastor Bing says, is that "Christ's revelation demands a response." And that response must come from the heart and will of the individual. George MacDonald, a nineteenth century preacher, novelist, and storyteller puts it this way:

> Nor will God force any door to enter in. He may send a
> tempest about the house; the wind of His admonishment
> may burst doors and windows, yea, shake the house to its
> foundations; but not then, not so, will He enter. The door

> must be opened by the willing hand, ere the foot of Love
> will cross the threshold. He watches to see the door move
> from within.[42]

A beautiful picture of active faith. The door must be opened "by the willing hand" "from within." The passive idea doesn't fit Scripture.

How then do we define believe *actively?* What is meant by "the willing hand" and "from within?"

Chapter 9

An active definition of the word *believe*

"Loan me $100 and I will pay you back tomorrow." "This is the best life insurance plan you can purchase." "I love you; will you marry me?" These are all invitations to faith.

All of them call for action on the part of the listener. All of them hear a message which is the first step of faith. The second step involves evaluating the truthfulness of the claims. Who is it that promised to pay back $100 tomorrow? Does the guy know life insurance or is he simply a salesman for an insurance company? And who is it that wants to marry me? Does this person really love me? Each question analyzes the person making the claim as well as the claim itself. "Believing" involves discovering who is true and what is true in order to accept as genuine their word of promise or declaration of truth.

Bible writers connect faith with confidence. An example is Hebrews 11. Here are the first few verses:

> Now faith is the assurance of things hoped for, the conviction of things not seen. For by it the men of old gained approval. By faith we understand that the worlds were prepared by the word of God, so that what is seen was not

made out of things which are visible. (Hebrews 11:1-3
NASB)

It's simply an "assurance" of things that God has announced and a
"conviction" of unseen things which are only available in His words.
Faith is believing what God has said.

The King James and New King James translations substitute *substance*
for "assurance" and *evidence* for "conviction." The NKJ reads "Now faith
is the substance of things hoped for, the evidence of things not seen."

The danger of using "substance" and "evidence" is that they tend to
make faith sound like something material, or that on which "things
hoped for" are based. Sort of like, "faith itself is the foundation on which
your hope is based, and it's the evidence of things you can't see."

The truth is that Christ is the foundation of things we hope for; His
Word is the evidence of things not seen. Faith is not a substance that
assures me that what I hope for is real. Rather faith is a confidence in
what Jesus said. The guarantee of things unseen does not come from our
faith but from Christ.

When we maintain the "substance" definition of faith, we may get
the notion that God wants us to have confidence in our faith.

I. Some encourage us to have faith in faith

Plenty of people believe that faith itself is the foundation of things
hoped for and is its own certification or proof. It's even taught as gospel
truth by the "Word of Faith," or "Positive Confession" group.

Kenneth Copeland, for example, a well-known American televange-
list and charismatic preacher, views faith as material energy. "Faith is a
power force," he claims. "It is a tangible force. It is a conductive force."[43]

"Faith is a spiritual force… It is substance. Faith has the ability to effect *(sic)* natural substance."[44] As "the force of gravity…makes the law of gravity work . . . this force of faith…makes the laws of the spirit world function."[45]

He even thinks that faith is God's source of power:

> everything that you're able to see or touch, anything that you can feel, anything that's perceptive to the five physical senses, was originally the faith of God, and was born in the substance of God's faith.[46]

What this means, according to Copeland, is that, "faith was the raw material substance that the Spirit of God used to form the universe."[47]

He believes that our faith is released by our words because words are spiritual containers and we have the ability to actually create things by our words. We can create spiritual containers with energy. When we say, "it's a great day," we are creating a great day. When we say, "it's a miserable day" we are creating that.

He goes so far as to claim that "Jesus existed only as an image in the heart of God until such time as the prophets of the Old Testament could positively confess Jesus into existence through their constant prophecies."[48]

Wait a minute; is he claiming that Jesus is not the eternal God but came into existence because of human prophetic words? It sounds that way.

His assertions are mind-boggling. To think that we can "confess reality into existence" is ridiculous. It ultimately removes God from His throne in order to install faith by suggesting that humans with enough faith can *make God obey them*. That was Satan's original idea (Isaiah 14:13-

14)! But Copeland affirms that "when we use the spiritual laws that God has set up, God must obey what we request."[49]

The foundation of Copeland's false doctrine comes from his view of Hebrews 11:1 in the King James translation. To him the word *substance* means a fundamental element that makes up the universe like an atom. That element is activated by spoken words. Even God activated the force of faith when He said, "let there be light." He created light by His "positive confession" releasing the force of faith. In a similar way he believes that Hebrews 11:1 promises that we can speak things into existence by our "faith-filled words," or our "positive confession."

Are you familiar with this doctrine? It is being sold on TV by people like Kenneth Hagin, Kenneth Copeland, Robert Tilton, Paul Yonggi Cho, Benny Hinn, Marilyn Hickey, Frederick Price, John Avanzini, Charles Capps, Jerry Savelle, Morris Cerullo as well as the late Paul and Jan Crouch. This group has built a money-making monster out of their definition of Hebrews 11:1.

But doesn't this verse say that faith is a *substance?* No it doesn't. It's a confidence in God's Word. If faith were a substance, *then all the examples in Chapter 11 of Hebrews had the wrong kind of faith.* Noah, Abraham, and Moses weren't making positive confessions that God had to fulfill. Noah didn't come up with the idea that he needed an ark any more than Abraham positively confessed sacrificing his son Isaac on an altar. Instead, they were simply obeying God because of their absolute confidence in His words.

Think about how these "Word of Faith" teachers would try to explain Hebrews 11:35-38 which details people who were "tortured" with "mockings and scourgings," and with "chains and imprisonment." They were "stoned, they were sawn in two, were tempted, were slain with the sword." What did they positively confess? What did they envision creating by their words? Not a thing. The notion that faith is a material source of power in the universe is ridiculous.

II. Faith focuses on Someone *outside* of us

The value of faith is not in *itself* but in its *object*. Pastor R. C. H. Lenski says,

> Faith, confidence, and conviction are similar terms. Faith rests on someone or something outside of itself, and *not* on itself. Somebody or something, outside of me inspires faith or trust in me: otherwise, I have no faith. It is this outside ground that shows whether faith is true, i.e., justified, or false, i.e., unjustified. Truth alone justifies me for believing or trusting. No lie ever does that. A lie succeeds in producing faith only when it masks itself as truth.
>
> Religious, Biblical, Christian faith is not different from faith in secular life in this respect, nor is true faith different from false faith in this respect. Satan produced faith in Eve by his lies which he dressed up as truth. Always, always, something or someone impresses us as being genuine, true, right, reliable, in a word, as being trustworthy, and so produces in us confidence, conviction; these are the essence of faith.[50]

The rest of Hebrews 11 demonstrates how that truth works out in life. Each person mentioned displayed his or her confidence in God's Word by obeying His directions. Faith is a confidence that is strong enough to obey.

"By faith Abel *offered*" (4); "by faith Noah *prepared an ark*" (7); "by faith Abraham *obeyed*" (8); "by faith he *dwelt . . . as in a foreign country*" (9). The response shows the level of their confidence. They believed God's

Word enough to go out on a limb in their obedience. To them, God's Word stood as the accurate description of reality in spite of everything visible that contradicted it.

Abel offered a sacrifice different than Cain's. Noah did what no one else in the world had an interest in doing, spending eighty or a hundred years of his life building a boat on dry ground in a land that had never seen rain.

No one did these kinds of things without a strong confidence in God's Word because obedience took virtually everything they had. Building an ark for eighty years would not be something akin to a leap into the dark. One would need a lot of light before making that kind of radical commitment. The light came from God's Word and His trustworthy character.

III. Faith is a response to truth

As Lenski said above, "*truth alone* justifies me for believing or trusting." Everyone is on a search for truth. The word *believe* is associated with someone who has found the truth (I *believe it; don't believe him; believes what he is told*).[51] That's the end result of a search which involves thinking, evaluating and choosing.

It's important to recognize that we commonly use the word *believe* in two significantly different ways. I'm going to call these the "A" and "B" definitions. The "A" definition is like "two plus two is four," and the "B" definition is similar to the cry "fire." "A" sounds like a response to a math statement: "to accept something or someone as true." It's acknowledging the truthfulness of the sum of two plus two.

But the "B" definition adds a *response component*. When someone shouts "fire," acknowledging the truthfulness of the statement involves *action*. The Bible uses the word believe in both of these ways.

A. In definition "A" *believe* **means** *confidence in a person or report as true.* "A conviction of the truth of anything,"[52] or to "believe (in) something, be convinced of something."[53] Sometimes it is expressed by *believe that . . .* followed by the content of what is believed.

We commonly use this definition to make faith statements: "I believe in creation" or "I believe in evolution," or "I believe in global warming," or "I believe in the Trinity," or "she believes in alternative medicine." We express confidence in evidence presented by someone else. That confidence suggests that we have analyzed the credibility of the statement and/or the person who made it and we accept it as genuine.

"Confidence" is the way Paul intended the word *believe* to be understood in Romans 10:14. After someone hears and understands the good news that Jesus Christ died for our sins and offers forgiveness and salvation to all who call upon Him, the next question is, does that person *believe that this news is true?* Paul's point is that no one will actually call upon the name of the Lord for salvation until they accept the message as true.

We see this definition used when people talk about the gospel: "oh I believe that Jesus was the greatest;" "I believe in God;" even "I believe that Christ died for my sins." Whether or not these people are saved depends on whether they are using the word in the right way, with a verb, like *call* or *come* or *receive*. It's possible to have confidence in one of Christ's statements without actually coming to Him for salvation. Paul adds the word *call* in Romans 10:13 to make clear that accepting the gospel as true does not save a person until she or he responds to the Lord by calling on His name.

Can you remember when you heard the awesome news that Jesus saves, but didn't respond for a while? You had to think about it and evaluate it before you actually believed it?

I can remember questioning the validity of the gospel message because it sounded unrealistic to promise heaven and forgiveness of sins to anyone who simply *called*. And I wondered if the promise of salvation would include me, since I wasn't sure I was "religious enough" at the age of seven. I had heard the gospel many times by that age, but had not accepted it as truth.

B. In definition "B" *believe* **means** *responding to a person or report*. This definition adds action to the "A" definition above. It's "a conviction, full of joyful trust, that Jesus is the Messiah – the divinely appointed author of eternal salvation in the kingdom of God, conjoined with obedience to Christ."[54] It combines *confidence* with *obedience to Christ*.

Many of the truth statements in Scripture contain implications that we could compare to hearing the cry of "fire" in a crowded building. As soon as someone states the fact or calls out "fire," there is an expected response. In fact the announcement forcefully *insists* on a response. In a similar way, the fact that Jesus is the only way to the Father calls for a certain response (John 14:6).

Suppose someone responded to the cry of "fire" with, "oh I believe there's a fire in this building"? Is that faith? Or how about saying, "the person who made that cry is very trustworthy;" "I happen to know that person and she has never made a false statement in her life;" "in fact she has a PhD in chemistry; if anyone can spot a fire, she can!" None of these statements exhibit faith no matter how good they may sound, *until the person making them responds by getting out of the building*. In fact, what the person says is not as important as what the person does!

The cry of "fire" insists on a rapid move toward the exit. In a similar way, when John the Baptist and Jesus announced that the Kingdom of Heaven had arrived in Israel, they insisted on a response of repentance (Matthew 3:2; 4:17). Instead listeners responded by admitting that Jesus was amazing, like John the Baptist, or Elijah, or Jeremiah, or one of the prophets, as they refused to repent (Matthew 16:14 and 11:20).

Peter instructs, "casting all your care upon Him, for He cares for you" (1 Peter 5:7). Definition "A" can be fulfilled by a personal assurance that God cares for you. But definition "B" goes a step further by directing us to cast all our cares on Him. In effect it says, *don't tell yourself that you believe God cares for you if you haven't cast your cares on Him!*

The difference is significant. It's similar to Jesus saying, *don't tell yourself that you believe that I am the bread of life if you haven't come to Me* (John 6:35). *Don't tell yourself that you believe that I am the door to eternal life if you have not entered by Me* (John 10:9). Jesus wasn't talking about believing a certain content about Him (even though that is the starting point), but believing *in Him,* a "coming-to-Him" commitment.

The "B" definition is what Paul commanded in Acts 16:31: "Believe on the Lord Jesus Christ, and you will be saved, you and your household." Paul is not asking them to simply accept facts about Jesus as true but to also receive Christ as Savior by calling upon His name for salvation.

That's the sense of John 3:16 and 3:18, as well as 1:7; 4:42, 48; 5:38, 44, 46, 47; 6:29, 30, 36, 64; 8:24, 30, 45, 46; 9:38; 10:38; 11:15 and many other verses.

John makes definition "B" clear when he contrasts coming to Christ for salvation with the reaction of the nation of Israel: "He came to His own, and those who were His own *did not receive Him.* But *as many as received Him,* to them He gave the right to become children of God, *even to those who believe in His name"* (John 1:11-12 NASB italics added). Those to whom Jesus gave the right to become children of God were those who actively *received Him* by believing in His name. That's definition "B."

IV. Substituting the "A" for the "B" definition causes confusion

You probably have asked sometime in your spiritual relationship with Christ, "am I really saved?" "Did I pray the right prayer?" "Was I repentant enough?" "Did I need to cry more and really mourn?" "Did I need to humble myself more by publicly kneeling in front of the church and confessing my sins?" "Maybe my attempt to do anything was wrong, and I should have waited for God to assure me that He has saved me?" The questions arise partly because of the difference between definitions "A" and "B."

A. The "A" definition of *believe* may not lead to salvation. We cannot say to unbelievers, "accept the fact that Jesus died for your sins and you will be saved." Why not? Because the verbs associated with *believe* push us beyond definition "A" to an active response. To *believe* means to *receive Him* (John 1:12).

I had a friend who assured me that he had received Christ. We spent a half hour in my car every Tuesday evening driving to help work on our church. He came from a Catholic background and assumed that he received Christ at every Mass he celebrated. One night I asked him, "Stan, have you ever personally invited Jesus to be your Savior and forgive you of your sins?" He thought for a while and then said, "yes."

I asked him if he could remember when. He again thought for a while and then said, "yes" and gave me a date.

I congratulated him on trusting in Christ. That's all I can remember of our interaction. Six months later he signed up to become a member of a local Bible church. A year later he was the chairman of Men's ministry at the church and invited me to speak at a Saturday morning breakfast. He introduced me that morning as "the man who led me to Christ."

I asked him afterwards, "Stan, when did I lead you to Christ?" His answer was, "do you remember when you asked me when I personally invited Jesus into my life?" I said, "yes." He continued, "well I lied." "Worse than that, I knew that you knew that I lied!" "And I set out to find out what you were talking about and found Christ."

That experience was a lesson to me about the difference between definitions "A" and "B." Stan was convinced he had believed in Christ according to definition "A." My question simply probed as to whether he understood *believe* from definition "B."

B. Definition "B" expects a *response*. Definition "A" implies an inner acknowledgment: "yes I believe that two plus two equals four;" "I believe in global warming;" "I believe that there is a God;" "I even believe that Jesus died for me." Sometimes people tend to view the facts of salvation as affirmations to add to their doctrinal statement: "I now believe in God the Father, maker of heaven and earth; and in His Son, Jesus, who was born of the Virgin Mary, suffered under Pontius Pilate . . ."

But definition "B" expects a response because it provides the *only answer to our problems*. Remember Peter's warning to the Jewish leaders: "This is the 'stone which was rejected by you builders, which has become the chief cornerstone.' Nor is there salvation in any other, for there is no other name under heaven given among men by which we must be saved" (Acts 4:11-12).

It's not only that Jesus provides the answer to the human condition; it's that He is the *only answer under heaven* to the human condition. It's the unique capability of the gospel that gives the facts their force, and invites, even insists, even demands a response of faith. Like the cry of *fire* in a crowded church, there is only one possible response.

We see this kind of insistence all through Scripture. The Great Shema, which states that "God is one" insists on complete love for Him, because *there are no other gods;* there is nothing else to worship (Deuteronomy 6:4-5). "God, who has reconciled us to Himself through Jesus Christ" insists that we be reconciled to God (2 Corinthians 5:18-20). The fact that God has given to every believer incredible mercies insists that we present our bodies to Him as a living sacrifice (Romans 12:1). The fact that we have a Great High Priest over the house of God insists that we (a) draw near with a sincere heart, (b) hold fast the confession of our hope, and (c) consider how to stimulate one another to love and good deeds (Hebrews 10:21-24). The facts insist on a response by those who believe them.

We are admonished to treat God's words with great care because they involve the *salvation of our souls* (James 1:21). They are not simply a list of "facts to agree with to admit you to our Christian club," but they are *the only facts that will save our souls!* The Bible is filled with these divine facts that insist on specific human responses because in reality *there are no other answers.*

Thus, in its full sense (definition "B") faith describes a *response to God's directions.* Sometimes the full sense is wrapped up in one word like *come* (Matthew 11:28; Revelation 22:17). Sometimes it's expressed by the word *faith,* (Romans 3:22; Ephesians 2:8-9). Sometimes the words, *submit* (Romans 10:3), or *obey* (Hebrews 5:9), or *follow* (John 8:12), or *heed* (Romans

10:16), or *hearing with faith* (Galatians 3:2), or *repentance* (Luke 24:47) are used as synonyms for the "B" definition of *believe*.

V. Faith is *relational*

"I love you; will you marry me?" is perhaps the ultimate human expression of faith. It's a statement and question that calls for the commitment of one's all. In that regard it serves as a prime picture of definition "B" – an active response that requires one's best abilities of listening and evaluating in order to make the wisest choice of believing and obeying in order to ultimately walk through life together.

God desires a love relationship with His creations. He could force us to love Him, or manipulate us, or pay us, but instead He seeks a relationship based on faith and trust similar to marriage. That means the relationship is voice-activated; it's based on words. Individuals need to talk to each other and come to trust one another's words.

How does a human being develop an intimate relationship with the eternal God? Jesus explains it this way:

> All things have been delivered to Me by My Father, and no one knows the Son except the Father. Nor does anyone know the Father except the Son, and the one to whom the Son wills to reveal Him. Come to Me, all you who labor and are heavy laden, and I will give you rest. Take My yoke upon you and learn from Me, for I am gentle and lowly in heart, and you will find rest for your souls. For My yoke is easy and My burden is light (Matthew 11:27-30).

It starts with the striking statement that no one "knows the Father!" And the only way to know Him is through knowing the Son. Jesus explains how with three commands, "Come," "Take," and "Learn" that serve as invitations. Human response to each one is a response of *faith*.

This means that one needs to *listen* to each command, then believe that, (a) He will give rest; (b) His yoke is good; (c) His educational system is the best, and (d) obedience will result in a heart transplant that enables one to daily discover rest. These directions diagram how to come to know the most wonderful person in the universe through His Son Jesus! Let me develop each one:

A. The first response of faith is to trust Christ's invitation for salvation (v. 28). "Come, and I, I myself," an emphatic promise, "will give you rest." The promise is a gift to be completely supplied by Christ. The "wise" and "prudent" of verse 25 are making similar offers but leaving their listeners "heavy laden," because they don't actually know the Father.

Salvation, the beginning of a relationship with the Father, is given to those who *come* to Christ. You come to Him by talking to Him, admitting where you are and asking Him to give you His rest.

B. The second response of faith is to trust Christ's invitation to discipleship (v. 29). The fellowship Jesus wants us to enjoy with Him is in a *yoke*. A yoke doesn't sound very nice. It's a load, an effort, a struggle. It's difficult, not exciting; it's boring and repetitive; it's a grind. Who wants to take a *yoke*? That's sweat; that's exhaustion. That's where we were before we came to Christ. Didn't Christ promise to free us from the labor and weariness of a yoke? Why is that a part of the invitation?

A yoke suggests assignments we don't enjoy. They probably will start with our circumstances. Jesus may say, "I want you to go through this new difficulty My way." "I want you to forgive your brother; and let's start by writing him a letter right now." "I know that what he did was very embarrassing; I know it makes you emotional just to think about it, but let's start the letter of forgiveness right now."

A yoke gives you a job that may be hard, like forgiving someone as Christ forgave you (Ephesians 4:31-32). But your obedience of faith will open your eyes to the excitement and joy of God at work to repair the damaged parts of your life. He actually intends to turn that broken relationship into a new friendship (Romans 12:17-21).

The bottom line is that *God doesn't force anyone to do this, and many Christians opt out of it.* Discipleship in a yoke is not an American ideal. We think there are better ways of attacking the problem. "I'll buy a study Bible and read all the notes;" "I'll increase my giving to the church," are usually seen as improvements over taking a yoke and forgiving an enemy.

C. The third response of faith is to trust Christ's invitation to education (v. 29). "Learn from Me" pictures a classroom which involves work, study, assignments, tests, papers. The Teacher is gracious, but He seriously wants us to get up to speed with the curriculum (Hebrews 12:5-11).

Case in point. While writing this chapter suddenly my wife of fifty years was discovered to be with stage 4 bone cancer. She had no symptoms other than pain in her right shoulder. We went to an orthopedic doctor who quickly determined that the shoulder and ball of the socket were both fractured. After ordering a CAT scan he showed us the pictures. She was lit up like a Christmas tree with cancer in both shoulders, ribs, vertebrae, hips knees and feet.

We walked away from his office and for the first time Martha asked, "what are you going to do after I die?" I don't think I'd ever seriously considered that question. I was positive I would go first and needed to make preparations for her to live after me. All of a sudden the price tags in life changed. Death was now in the equation and a lot of other things lost their value. Death was in the equation before, but it was less important because it was more distant.

As I write this Martha is on hospice and we are rejoicing in the Lord for each day He gives us. We find great joy in having our children, grandchildren and great-grandchildren around us. Old friends are coming around to talk about the former days. Driving her to the Oncology center is a chance to live in the anticipation of the unknown together. Sometimes I feel like I'm holding my breath, waiting to see where the next foot will drop.

But what's so bad about stage 4 cancer if it brings all twenty-nine of our family members together and provides great times of fellowship with friends? A friend of ours who was dying with cancer stood up in church one Sunday and testified, "this is a win-win situation!" "If Jesus heals me I will keep holding my grandchildren in my lap. If He doesn't I will be kissing His feet!"

She had learned something in the yoke. She had answered some of the questions we ask about the heart of God, such as: "how can He love us and allow stage 4 cancer?" "why doesn't He heal like He did before?" "can we dare to believe that stage 4 cancer comes from a gentle and lowly heart?"

We can know a great deal about God without knowing God Himself. Like the Pharisees of old we can absorb a lot of theology, a lot of arguments, and yet never get to know the Father through the Person of Christ. They were classic examples of abundant knowledge, Bible students of great distinction, who didn't know the One of whom the Bible was speaking (John 5:39-40). May they not become our mentors.

D. The goal of obeying Christ's invitations is a *heart transplant*. The university of Jesus teaches about a *heart* that is in contrast to our default heart, described as "gentle and lowly."

Getting to know any person is a process of getting to know his or her heart. What they love, what they hate, and what makes them laugh and cry are all a part of their *heart*. It may sound strange, but the ruler of the universe has a heart described as "gentle and lowly!" Have you ever pictured God that way?

What's the value of learning His heart? Why bother? It changes us! The Psalmist says, "Though the LORD is on high, Yet He regards the lowly; But the proud He knows from afar" (Psalm 138:6).

The point is that *we will never come to know the Father until our hearts are changed,* because God actually "resists the proud, but gives grace to the humble" (James 4:6). The proud will never know God, no matter how hard they try or how brilliant they are.

The root issue is our *hearts*. A humble heart is only *learned* in the yoke with Jesus. Humility is not a normal part of our DNA. But Jesus teaches it in our daily life experiences.

So where have we been in this chapter? We've said that the word *believe* must be understood as something active, and, as *our* responsibility to analyze, choose, and respond to truth statements. Believe means to accept something or someone as true. That's the "A" definition which the Bible uses often. But that definition is insufficient to describe the relationship God wants us to have with Him. Thus Bible writers emphasize the word *believe* with the "B" definition that includes an active response of obedience and commitment.

And the "B" definition leads to personal interaction with God Himself, an intimate relationship where you actually share your life with Him. The end result in that "you will find rest for your souls. For My yoke is easy and My burden is light" (Matthew 11:29c-30). Don't miss it!

Chapter 10

What does it mean to "obey?"

Faith is obedience to an invitation

The word *obey* is a dangerous word to use in a definition of faith. It immediately sounds like human accomplishment, like keeping the commandments, or public confession, or signing up for a discipleship program.

Every discussion of faith has difficulty deciding where to draw the line on works. It's clear that our salvation is "not of works lest anyone should boast" (Ephesians 2:9). But once you conclude that humans have some kind of responsibility in faith, the question becomes, "how can human-inaugurated activity to choose and to will be *not of works?*"

Back in Chapter 1 my first experience with faith was going forward and receiving what was in the closed hand of a preacher. He identified my activity as *faith,* and said to the other people still seated, "as you sat there in your pew, you may have said to me, 'I believe you that you have something valuable in your hand,' but you didn't believe me because you didn't move. This lad believed me. You may think you believed, but you didn't."

What should we call that simple act of going forward and receiving what the preacher had in his hand? Was it good works? It was *work* in the sense of effort. But no, it wasn't *good works* of any kind. Yet it was such an integral part of faith that I didn't actually believe until I moved to get up and go forward.

Some would argue, "your going forward was the *fruit of faith.*" "Because you believed the preacher (faith) you went forward (fruit)." In that way, my work would be separated from my faith and I could say that I received the dollar *not of works* but simply by *believing.*

But somehow that explanation doesn't seem answer the questions. Did I receive the dollar because I went forward to get it? Was that going forward an act of faith? Or was it works? Somehow the walking forward had to be an integral part of the faith, or I would have remained as dollar-less as the rest of the people.

In this chapter I would like to expand on *the expected response of faith.* What does it mean to *obey?* What kind of move does God prescribe for those who are dead in trespasses and sins? I find that the Bible defines faith in a way that includes action, includes effort, even work, but is not earnings. The key is that *faith is a response to an invitation.*

I. Obedience begins with our *hopelessness*

Oddly enough a response begins with what one *can't do.* It's because a person understands the devastation of his sinfulness that he turns to God for grace.

There are times in life when the definition of a word is critical. Understanding the response of obedience depends on understanding the significance of the word GRACE. "By grace you have been saved through faith" Paul said (Ephesians 2:8). Grace and faith work together. We mentioned grace briefly in Chapter 3, but let's think about how spectacular the word is.

The Greek word for grace is *charis,* which means "beauty and charm" and "that which gives pleasure," and "lovingkindness and goodwill," and "the appreciation that comes from having received grace." All of this is connected with a gift. Thayer says, "moreover, the word *charis* contains the idea of kindness which bestows upon one what he has not deserved."[55] It's an undeserved gift. Salvation is a gift no one deserves. That's a key in understanding obedience.

Perhaps one of the best descriptions of grace can be seen in the parable of the Prodigal Son. You remember the story in Luke 15 about the father who had two sons. One felt that it was an appropriate moment to claim his share of the inheritance. His father obliged, and he packed up and left the family to go find life in a distant country. He thought his dream had arrived, to live life the way he wanted. No more farm chores; this was going to be party time! But alas it wasn't long before he blew through all the money, and his grand plan crashed.

Of course, at that point, a severe famine hit the land, and verse 16 says, "no one gave him anything." He wound up, as a Jewish lad, working in a pig pen and drooling over their food. Pig pens can be educational; the lad's life was changed, and he returned to his father. Upon arrival he received what he had never expected, far beyond what he could have ever dreamed: *grace.*

I view this parable as a description of God's grace to unworthy sinners because of the setting. Jesus was receiving complaints from the Pharisees and scribes for eating with tax collectors and sinners (Luke 15:1-2). His response to them was a three part parable that explained why

He did this (15:6-7, 10, 28, 31-32). At the same time it also invited them to join Him.

The parable introduces us to grace displayed by the responses of three individuals: a shepherd, a woman and the Father (15:5-6, 9, 22-24). They not only treated their lost object with a joy like they had just found the pearl of great price, but their excitement compelled them to call others, like friends and neighbors (15:6, 9) or the older son (15:28) to the celebration.

The father's grace is especially highlighted in his response to the returning prodigal: (a) he *ran* to him, an undignified, even embarrassing response for an old man, in reality an act of humility; (b) he *kissed* him, which was usually a pledge of reconciliation and peace (Genesis. 33:4); (c) he *ordered* the best robe be supplied for him (which indicated *status*) and a ring be placed on his hand (which indicated *authority*), and shoes be put on his feet (to indicate he was a *freeman* not a slave), and the "fattened calf" be slaughtered and prepared for a feast (a meal reserved for *special* guests); (d) he commanded the gathered people to "eat and be merry" (23), to feel the excitement, to make the place rock! Because his excitement had to be shared by everyone, (e) he then invited the elder son to join in the celebration (28).

Why such strange behavior from the father? Why a response that looked every bit like he had won the lottery? Because repentance was the greatest thing that could have ever happened to his son. The father compared his return to a *resurrection* because his long dead son was now alive (Luke 15:32).

The father's strange behavior was also intended to make a statement to the prodigal as well as to everyone else. He engraved on the heart of his son the words *forgiven, accepted, received into the family, book closed on past actions, let's celebrate!*

That's our Savior's picture of grace, a picture of His Father in action, a picture of the angelic eruption in heaven over a repentant sinner coming home (Luke 15:7, 10)!

Question: "where did all this begin?" When the prodigal came to the realization that he had lost everything. He was dying of hunger, he had sinned against heaven and against his Father (15:18), his family connections were gone, and he was "no longer worthy to be called your son" (15:19, 21). He knew he had forever thrown away incredible opportunities.

He saw his true, hopeless condition. He had fallen below the level of life his father's servants enjoyed. There was no way he could earn what he had lost. His leverage with his father was gone and nobody else cared about him. He understood, perhaps for the first time the horror of his sin and wondered if there was any hope.

For grace to be grace, *every person who ever comes home to God must come this way,* with no credit in his or her heavenly bank account, with no hope of paying for help. God's grace cannot be connected with what a person *has* or *can do.* Once someone thinks he has a molecule of earnings, or thinks he can do something, there can be no grace. By definition, grace cannot be earned or paid for. It must be an absolutely free, complete gift. The hand of faith must be empty when it reaches.

Once a person sees himself as a hopeless sinner imprisoned and dominated by sin, without any way to get God's attention, then the gospel becomes great news. *Christ died for your sin, and offers complete forgiveness!*

The major question with grace is, "is the person bankrupt enough to receive a gift?" Does the sinner approach God with nothing to contribute? A grace-gift stands in direct opposition to any supposed accomplishment on our part. Grace and payment are mutually exclusive. This means that we can *never* pay for God's gifts, either before we receive them or after. God must remain *eternally uncompensated* for His grace.

That's where the prodigal was. There was nothing he could do; he was at zero. Have you ever seen yourself as helpless, un-religious, and going to Hell, with no hope of heaven? That's where Grace begins.

II. Obedience is *receiving,* not *committing*

There is the danger that when one speaks of obedience some will get the idea that initial faith involves some kind of *commitment.* The thought is that faith is not genuine until one submits to Christ as Lord. Thus receiving Christ as Savior involves committing oneself to Him for life.

For example, Pastor John MacArthur says, "the gospel Jesus proclaimed was a call to discipleship, a call to follow Him in submissive obedience."[56] He makes a contrast between "easy believism" and true grace which is "costly." He is convinced that the lazy, uninterested state of many so-called Christians results from being taught a weak definition of faith. According to him genuine faith includes a commitment to discipleship.

A co-pastor, Marc Mueller, explains, "the saviourhood of Christ is actually contingent on obedience to His Lordship."[57]

And "obedience to His Lordship" involves reading conditions into the salvation message that Jesus gave to His *disciples.* For example, "If anyone comes to Me and does not hate his father and mother, wife and children, brothers and sisters, yes, and his own life also, he cannot be My disciple" (Luke 14:26), or "If anyone desires to come after Me, let him deny himself, and take up his cross, and follow Me" (Matthew 16:24).

MacArthur believes that in order to come to Christ, the unbeliever needs to resolve the personal submission issue by taking up his cross to follow Him. For him faith is not only receiving a gift, but making a commitment.

Pastor James Boice agrees with this concept and explains, "discipleship is not a supposed second step in Christianity, as if one first becomes a believer in Jesus and then, if he chooses, a disciple. From the beginning, discipleship is involved in what it means to be a Christian."[58]

This teaching looks Scriptural because it highlights the seriousness of turning to Christ. Receiving Christ is not the same as choosing between two brands of toothpaste. It's more than "try a little Jesus in your life," or "put your hand in the hand of the man who stilled the waters."

And the emphasis on the Lordship of Christ sets the gospel in its proper context: He is Lord and we are not. We don't deal with *The Lord* on our terms; only on His. And His terms are dogmatic: "no one comes to the Father except through Me" (John 14:6). Yes, coming to Christ involves submission.

But the question as I see it is, *can we define faith as a commitment to discipleship?* Is faith an act of commitment or the reception of a gift? Does Matthew 11:28 picture the gospel when it commands, *come to Me* and receive rest, or does Matthew 11:29 picture the gospel with *take My yoke upon you?* I think that there is a difference.

Suppose you prepared a delicious meal to give to a homeless person, took it downtown and called out to someone sitting on a heating grate, "come over here and I will give you a good meal." Would it be the same thing to call out, "come over here and I will give you a good meal if you will obey me for the rest of your life?" Or, "I will give you this meal if you become my disciple?" Does the insertion of "if" add another condition to the promised gift?

Scripture tells us that faith has a condition: "Whoever calls on the name of the LORD shall be saved" (Romans 10:13), or "If you knew the gift of God, and who it is who says to you, 'give Me a drink,' you would have asked Him, and He would have given you living water" (John 4:10). "Calls on the name of the LORD" and "you would have asked Him" are conditions. They require a response. But do they involve a further commitment?

It seems to me that one of the problems with the *discipleship* definition of faith is that it can't accomplish what it's trying to do. It's trying to make people serious about trusting Christ, realizing that there is more to salvation than simply grabbing a gift and running away.

But can sinners offer Him *commitment?* How does the homeless man know whether he will obey tomorrow? He may promise with the best of hopes, but what if he doesn't obey tomorrow? Does he lose the food he ate today? Perhaps the discipleship definition of faith would argue that the lack of obedience tomorrow was evidence that he never genuinely received the meal today.

But think of Jesus' disciples. Did they offer Him commitment when they started following Christ? True, they became disciples, but did they follow Him in "submissive obedience?"

Take Peter for example. As a leader among the disciples he was the first to acknowledge that Jesus was the Messiah when he confessed, "You are the Christ, the Son of the living God" (Matthew 16:16). But he was also the one who rebuked his Master six verses later when he announced: "God forbid it, Lord! This shall never happen to You" (Matthew 16:22 NASB). "God forbid" doesn't sound like submissive obedience.

Was Peter saved at that time? Certainly! Did he realize that discipleship was involved when he came to Christ? Certainly! He *was a disciple.* But even *as a disciple* he had difficulties with submission to the will of

Christ. In fact all the disciples had difficulties. Their submission problems arose over the demands of discipleship.

Imagine Jesus saying to Peter, "now Simon before I forgive your sins you need to submit to my Lordship so that you will not deny Me at My trial before the Jewish leadership." How would Peter know what he would do at that future moment? Somehow he hadn't successfully solved the submission issue at salvation. He was still working on it *as a disciple*.

Jesus asked Peter the *disciple* to submit when He said, "If anyone desires to come after Me, let him deny himself, and take up his cross, and follow Me" (Matthew 16:24).

But Pastor Boice assures us that "discipleship is not a supposed second step in Christianity, as if one first becomes a believer in Jesus and then, if he chooses, a disciple." Wasn't the invitation to Peter a second step? Wasn't Christ asking him to choose to deny himself, take up his cross, and follow? If Boice is correct, then Matthew 16:24 was unnecessary because Peter had already taken up his cross when he was first saved.

The fact that Jesus gave this invitation to His disciples shows us that discipleship is an issue for *believers*. They are the people who have trouble with the new level of commitment that God asks for when He leads them into difficulties.

It was Peter the believer, the disciple, who balked when he heard for the first time that Christ the Messiah was willingly headed for a *cross*. His doctrinal statement up to that time didn't allow the combination of the words *Messiah* and *cross*. He knew for sure that Messiah had come to rule and reign. The cross idea was a shock and one he refused to accept, at least initially.

Peter balked again when facing the question at Jesus' trial, "do you want to die with Him?" Three times he had the opportunity to say *yes*.

But he didn't want to be associated with that part of Messiah's purpose, and denied knowing Him.

I can relate to Peter's fears. There are times in the past when I have denied association with Christ, even though I am a committed disciple of His. Did that mean I wasn't saved? Did that mean I wasn't saved *the right way?* If I had settled the submission issue at salvation would I have not had these problems? The answers are "no," "no," "no," to each of those questions because discipleship is not a salvation issue but a Christian life issue.

The distinction is between salvation and sanctification. Salvation is becoming a child of God by faith (John 1:12; Matthew 11:28)); sanctification is growing up as a child of God by faith (Ephesians 4:13-15; Matthew 11:29-30). The "cost of discipleship" is not settled at salvation but is met and settled at various growth spurts in the Christian life.

The biggest problem with the discipleship explanation of salvation is the change it makes to the definition of faith. Back in Chapter 8 I referred to Martin Luther's great statement: "Faith holds out the hand and the sack and just lets the good be done to it. For God is the giver . . . we are the receivers who receive the gift through faith that does nothing."[59]

I maintain that when we add commitment to that picture we distort the definition of faith. Instead of holding out the hand and the sack to receive God's gift it asks us to make a deal with Him.

It's to believers that Paul said, "I beseech you therefore, brethren, by the mercies of God, that you present your bodies a living sacrifice, holy, acceptable to God, which is your reasonable service" (Romans 12:1).

Paul beseeches "brethren" who have received "the mercies of God." This is not part of the salvation message. It's a part of growing up in Christ. We grow up as we worship our Lord by presenting our bodies a living sacrifice to serve Him. *Virtually every command to believers in the New*

Testament is a discipleship issue. Disciples have submission issues. And it is wrong to assume that believers who balk at submitting to Christ, as Peter did, are demonstrating that they are yet unbelievers.

Discipleship, or "Making Jesus Lord of my life" is not what is meant by *obedience* because salvation is a gift. Commitment to discipleship may look like obedience but it is something (a) no unbeliever can do, (b) no believer can do initially, because (c) it's the kind of obedience that the twelve apostles only developed as they grew in Christ.

This discussion is important in helping us define faith. Faith is the reach of an empty hand in response to the promise that God will fill it. There is not even commitment in the empty hand. If we don't get the definition correct at this point, we won't understand faith when it comes to discipleship. As we will see in Chapter 12, discipleship is likewise an act of faith and the reception of a gift.

III. Obedience is coming to Christ not a confession

The prodigal was practicing his confession on the trip home. He was going to say, "I am no longer worthy to be called your son" (Luke 15:19), but he apparently never got a chance to finish it. Some, however, teach that salvation depends on *confession,* actually *confessing Christ publicly.*

After all Romans 10:9 says, "if you confess with your mouth." An unbeliever obeys that invitation by a *verbal announcement in a group.*

As a young twenty-something-year-old, I was allowed into a prayer room where a pastor was leading a man and wife to the Lord. The pastor asked all four of us to stand and repeat a certain doctrinal statement. After we had done that he asked the couple if they believed what they had just declared. When they said "yes" he pronounced that they were saved. They had *declared* their faith. They had *confessed with their mouths* Jesus as Lord, which Romans 10:9 instructs.

However, something about that experience didn't ring true to me, even though I couldn't put my finger on why I was dissatisfied. I never used that method when I directed people to Christ. I would always encourage an unbeliever to pray directly to Jesus, ask Him for forgiveness, receive Him, and commit himself or herself to Him.

Only years later did I realize the danger of that method of leading people to Christ: it's based on weaker definition of *believe,* definition "A." The pastor asked them to state their *confidence* in a doctrinal statement: "do you have confidence in the truthfulness of what you have just declared?"

The couple in the prayer room may have truly received Jesus Christ as Savior. I hope so, and if so, Praise the Lord. But *they could have also misunderstood the directions.* It's possible to *accept and acknowledge something as true* without personally receiving Christ as Savior or calling on His name. The response of "I believe," even when made as a public statement, may not be a genuine response of faith.

Think of why this idea is risky. Jesus pointed out the weakness of a verbal confession with this parable:

> But what do you think? A man had two sons, and he came to the first and said, "Son, go, work today in my vineyard." He answered and said, "I will not," but afterward he regretted it and went. Then he came to the second and said likewise. And he answered and said, "I go, sir," but he did not go. Which of the two did the will of his father? They said to Him, "The first." Jesus said to them, "Assuredly, I say to you that tax collectors and harlots enter the kingdom of

God before you. For John came to you in the way of righteousness, and you did not believe him; but tax collectors
and harlots believed him; and when you saw it, you did not
afterward relent and believe him" (Matthew 21:28-32
NASB).

Observe the importance of the words *went* and *go*. The first son *went*
after saying "I will not." The second son did not *go* even after saying "I
go." If the first son had only "repented" and said, "I'm sorry that I refused to go; I now say that I will go," and yet still *did not go*, would he have
been any different than the second son? No, his "confession" would have
been as worthless as his brother's.

When the command is to *go* the only obedience is to go. It doesn't
matter what you say before, after, or while you go, as long as you go.[60]
The first son confessed "I will not," but did the will of his father. He
exemplified the response of the tax collectors and harlots who entered
the kingdom of God. The second son made a good confession when he
said "I go, sir," but didn't actually do the will of his father.

As Pastor Lloyd-Jones says, "Faith is always an obedience. I am not
talking about works that are going to follow all this."[61] Thus confession
is good and could be a step in the right direction, but without actually
receiving Christ, confession does not save.

IV. Obedience responds to a *specific invitation*

It's like Jesus asking, "who wants a drink? Raise your hand" (John
4:10). Faith raises its hand. "Who wants rest from your overbearing load?
Come to me and I will give it to you" (Matthew 11:28). Faith comes to
Jesus.

God does not look for us to participate in the salvation process, as if we could make some useful contribution. That's impossible. But God wants us to respond to His invitation by saying, "yes" and reaching out our empty hand. That's the command. "Come to Me" does not mean "save yourself," or even "help Me save you" because salvation is one hundred percent the work of Christ.

But "come to Me" is *an invitation that expects a response*. Jesus pictured this invitation process in His parable about a wedding feast:

> The kingdom of heaven may be compared to a king who gave a wedding feast for his son. And he sent out his slaves to call those who had been invited to the wedding feast, and they were unwilling to come. Again he sent out other slaves saying, "Tell those who have been invited, 'Behold, I have prepared my dinner; my oxen and my fattened livestock are all butchered and everything is ready; come to the wedding feast.'" But they paid no attention and went their way, one to his own farm, another to his business, and the rest seized his slaves and mistreated them and killed them. But the king was enraged, and he sent his armies and destroyed those murderers and set their city on fire. Then he said to his slaves, "The wedding is ready, but those who were invited were not worthy. Go therefore to the main highways, and as many as you find there, invite to the wedding feast" (Matthew 22:2-9 NASB).

Observe the amazing statements and the point of this parable:

A. This wedding feast was not only for the king's son, but, THE King's Son, THE Crown Prince, THE Heir of the universe! The Pharisees understood that, and in fact, had already plotted His death in the previous parable (Matthew 21:33-46).

B. A select group of people had been invited. They had received a "save the date" invitation. It probably was more like, "wedding coming," since they didn't actually know the date. But they received ample warning.

C. Servants were sent out to "call the called." The word, "invited" is the word, "called." The response was a surprising, "they were unwilling to come." No explanation, simply, a unified "NO."

D. The king, not willing to take "no" for an answer, sent another group of servants to the same invited people with a new message of urgency: "everything is ready." Jewish weddings were normally celebrated for seven days. But this one was beyond spectacular. The magnitude was indicated by the plurals, "oxen," and "fattened livestock." There was plenty of meat because the expectation was for hundreds of guests. Nothing needed to be done. "Just come" was the call. "All you need to do is show up." The wedding was on. Everything was in motion. The bride was there; the food was ready; the only need was for the guests to assemble.

E. There were two responses to this second invitation: one group ignored the message and turned away, one to his farm and another to his business. The invitation was an irritating interruption. They had much more important things to do than the wedding of their crown prince. The other group was far more antagonistic. They took the king's persistent invitation as an insult, and laid hold of the messengers, treating them shamefully, and even killing them. Incredible! All that, for inviting them to the greatest of all celebrations?

F. The king concluded that, "those who were invited were not worthy." What made them unworthy? They had received ample warning. The wedding was the event of the century, actually *the event* in the history of the universe. No one in his right mind would turn down this ticket. How did they make themselves unworthy? They were *unwilling to come*. They refused the gracious invitation delivered in the command to *come*.

The parable introduces us to the presence of two wills. There's the will of the King for all invited to come to His wedding celebration. And there is the contrary will of His subjects. The fact that a certain group (Jewish people) was invited showed the attitude of the king. He viewed them as an important part of his kingdom. Their reactions showed what they thought of Him, that His desires and plans were insignificant.

Observe that this invitation doesn't allow for any of the three responses we have mentioned above. It wasn't expecting that the called ones would do "good works," or "submit to the king as lord," or "confess that the king is their lord." The only acceptable response was to come. Those who didn't come were not predestined to reject the invitation. Instead, it was the response they chose after the king had done all in His power short of coercion to make it easy for them to obey.

This parable is a beautiful picture of the obedience of faith. Those who were called heard the invitation three times. But they didn't believe it important enough to obey. They may have even sent in an RSVP promising to come. But when the moment came, commanding a specific action on a specific day, they rejected the invitation. Their choice brought the judgment of the king that they were *not worthy*. In a similar way people today make themselves unworthy by their refusal to come to Christ (John 3:18).

Christ's invitation continually goes out in many different forms represented by many different commands, such as "come to Me," "receive Him," "ask of Him," "believe on Him." Each command is an invitation to the wedding of the ages.

Who made the choice as to what individuals enjoyed the wedding? Was it Christ who chose to save some and overlook others? Or was the responsibility in the hands of the sinner to hear, believe and come? This parable places it completely in the hands of those who were "called." All they were expected to do was obey an invitation.

VI. Salvation is completely the work of God

What did the guests contribute to the wedding? What did they do to earn their way in? What did they do to please the king or to help him prepare for the celebration? Everything was ready by the time they were to come. They could do nothing except obey the gracious invitation. The wedding feast was one hundred percent the work of God. The sovereign King envisioned a wedding feast full of guests. He wrote out the guest list but there were some guests who of themselves chose to skip the feast.

That's the picture of the brazen serpent. What could the snake-bitten Israelites do to provide for their salvation in Numbers 21:5-9? Nothing, except look in order to live. The snake bite remedy was 100 percent the work of God using a human-made brass serpent as the anti-venom.

That's the picture of the Passover lamb in Exodus 12. What could the bound Israelites do to free themselves from Egypt? Nothing except obey the directions to slay the sacrificial lamb. The tenth plague was 100 percent the work of God.

That's the picture of salvation for the world. What can dead humans do to free themselves from the deadly effects of sin? Nothing except turn to the cross of Christ where it has all been provided.

The bottom line is that faith has to involve an exact response to God's invitation to be faith. The effort has to match the command. And that response is not in the Biblical category of works^{earnings}, even though it may involve personal effort.

People today think they are going to Heaven because they do something religious or believe something biblical. They miss the specific stipulation of faith to *call on the name of the Lord* for salvation.

My question to you, dear reader, is, "have you actually obeyed God's invitation to call on the name of the Lord?" You may have decided to turn over a new leaf, to increase your prayer life, to get baptized, to give more money away, to read a book on faith, but have you ever specifically obeyed the gospel command and called on the name of the Lord for salvation? That's the key.

Chapter 11

Faith as completed action

How long does one have to believe, to truly believe?

Okay, the Prodigal Son came home and met massive amounts of grace and surprising amounts of love. His dad stamped on his heart, *forgiven*, with the gifts of robe, ring, shoes and the plantation-wide celebration. Question: "What happened after the party was over? The Father was probably too excited to check his commitment level to find out whether his son was actually promising to obey for the rest of his life.

What happened in Luke 15:33? There's actually no such verse, but what I mean by that question is "what was life like the next day?" How should the prodigal now live with his robe and ring and shoes, all which suggest that he possessed a new status and authority? Was it *same-ole, same-ole* as in the past? Was the prodigal going to go back to his old ways or would there be a change? Luke doesn't tell us because Jesus was more interested in getting the elder son, the Pharisees, to join the celebration.

So what is supposed to happen *after* one calls on the name of the Lord and is saved? We're now talking not only in terms of *initial* response, but *subsequent* response. Does faith automatically continue? Is it the same kind of faith? Can someone lose faith? Does one have to continue believing for awhile in order to really believe? Or is believing a momentary event?

These are the kinds of questions I would like to discuss in the next five chapters. Up to this point we have focused primarily on the definition of faith as it involves unbelievers. But now the question becomes, "how does a person who has placed genuine faith in Christ Jesus live?" Or, how does one who has been justified, live from faith to faith? (Romans 1:17).

Let's start in this chapter by answering the question, "does faith ever get *finished?*" Is it possible for you to say "I believed" in a finished way, or do you need to continue trusting and obeying to actually believe?

I want to answer this question in two ways: (a) by showing that faith is a single act of response to God's invitation ("faith as completed action") that doesn't have to prove its genuineness by never wavering; and (b) by showing that a single act of faith for salvation does not guarantee another act of faith.

Let me illustrate these two concepts by going back to the homeless man for whom you prepared a steak dinner (Chapter 3). He heard your promise of food from across a four-lane highway; he believed it and came over to your gracious supply of a sumptuous meal. He enjoyed the meal because of a single act of faith. When the meal was done his genuine act of faith was completed. That's issue number one.

Now suppose as he is cleaning up the meal, you promise him another steak dinner the next day. Will he accept? Who knows? Do you see that the next day he has to believe again and come get it again? The fact that he believed you once suggests that he probably will believe you the second time. But it doesn't guarantee that he will show up the next day. It wouldn't be an issue of "continuing to believe you" as much as "trusting your word again."

This chapter is addressed to people who are asking, "How much faith is enough faith?" "Have I believed enough?" "My faith wavers and I'm not sure I have believed long enough or hard enough to really get saved." "Am I guilty of easy believism?" Let me explain how the completeness and temporary-ness of faith are developed in Scripture:

I. Faith is one act at one moment in time

One of the interesting things in the Gospels is the number of places where Jesus scolds His disciples because they *don't believe*. In Matthew 8:26, for example, Jesus calls them men "of little faith" (also in 6:30, 14:31, 16:8 and 17:20 [unbelief]). Why describe His disciples this way? Weren't they following Him because they believed in Him? How could they have *little* faith? What is the difference between little and big faith? The Syro-phoenician woman was described as having "great faith" (Mark 7:26). What did she have that the disciples didn't have?

It looks even worse when Jesus questions His disciples with, "do you still have *no faith*?" (Mark 4:40 NASB). How could men who had left their businesses for Him possess *no faith*? Who else was sacrificing for Christ the way His disciples were? Had they now quit believing? Were they not yet genuine believers who needed more time to learn to truly believe?

These questions are good because they help us see the temporary-ness of faith. The disciples had undoubtedly listened to, believed in, and come to Christ. So what had happened to their faith? It was genuine; it was still there; it simply hadn't grown by trusting Christ in a new or different area.

If faith is the beginning of a relationship (and it is), it's also the beginning of something that varies up and down, in and out. It's similar to love. Love is fickle. For some reason we can be strongly in love with someone one day and question the relationship the next day. Why? How can such fickleness be part of *real love*? How can the disciples' fickleness be part of *real faith*? Did they have real faith? Absolutely!

The truth is that, like love, *faith is a one-time act that needs to be repeated.* One act of faith doesn't necessarily continue as an attitude of faithfulness. To grow in faith one needs to *believe God again*.

A. Paul speaks about faith that has been completed. He says to the Ephesians: "In Him you also trusted, after you heard the word of truth, the gospel of your salvation; in whom also, having believed, you were sealed with the Holy Spirit of promise" (Ephesians 1:13). Paul speaks as if his readers are *saved!* He's not saying, "you know if you keep doing this for the next five years there is eternal hope for you." No, it's all *finished!* They "trusted" after they heard the word of truth and afterward they were "sealed with the Holy Spirit of promise." And like the father of the prodigal, God said, *forgiven, accepted, and received into the family, book closed on past actions! Let's celebrate!*

Does that encourage you at all? Some people live for years hoping that they are inside the door, hoping that they have believed enough, maintained hope long enough, or jumped through the right hoop to get saved. Paul talks about faith in the past tense as if it is finished and that they already have been sealed with the Holy Spirit! He's not saying that they are getting sealed or hoping that they will get sealed somehow. It is an *accomplished fact in their lives!*

We see this finished state of faith repeatedly in Scripture. Paul said in another place, "But God be thanked that though you were slaves of sin, yet you obeyed from the heart that form of doctrine to which you were delivered. And having been set free from sin, you became slaves of righteousness" (Romans 6:17-18). His readers were former "slaves of sin." They had been in bondage, but they believed and "obeyed the message "from the heart" and were "set free from sin"!

He talked similarly to the Galatians: "This only I want to learn from you: Did you receive the Spirit by the works of the law, or by the hearing of faith?" (Galatians 3:2). He writes to readers who have received the Holy Spirit. The word "receive" speaks of a definite point in their spiritual history. After they believed they received the Holy Spirit. It was finished.

That's why he commanded his Corinthian readers to "Flee sexual immorality" (1 Corinthians 6:18), because their bodies were "the temple of the Holy Spirit who is in you" (1 Corinthians 6:19). The Corinthian church had many problems. But Paul was confident that the Holy Spirit was *in them*. They believed God's Word at a point in time and received the Holy Spirit.

B. Jesus spoke of faith as one act at one time. Jesus made this amazing promise: "Most assuredly, I say to you, he who hears My word and believes in Him who sent Me has everlasting life, and shall not come into judgment, but has passed from death into life" (John 5:24).

Jesus declared that the person who has heard His Word and believed "in Him who sent Me" *has everlasting life*. Does that mean the person will receive eternal life after he or she dies, or after continuing to believe for a period of time? No, eternal life begins the moment a person believes in "Him who sent Me."

To make the point more emphatic, Jesus added, "and shall not come into judgment, but has passed from death into life." What an incredible addition! One act of faith and a person's future completely changes. He will not come into judgment. He has *already* passed out of death into life.

Just by listening to Christ's words and believing on the Father who sent Him! That's why the gospel is so dynamic; it changes people's futures.

Have you passed from death to life? Can you remember when you received Christ by believing on the One who sent Him? According to Jesus, not only were you given eternal life, but you were removed from the "judgment" line up and you passed out of death into life! That's quite a striking list of benefits for simply listening to and responding to God by receiving His gift.

And that's only the beginning! Lewis S. Chafer, former president of Dallas Theological Seminary, claims that thirty-three things take place in a person's life the moment he or she trusts in Christ![62] You were made a child of God, you were given the Holy Spirit, and you were transferred from the kingdom of darkness to the kingdom of light in addition to at least thirty other amazing gifts! That should cause us to praise His name for the rest of our lives, no matter what happens to us.

Observe that Jesus is talking about one act of faith in John 5:24. It all takes place in a moment of time. You hear, you believe on *Him who sent Me* and you pass from death to life. No statement of continuing in faith until the end of life, or even for a certain period of time. There's no suggestion here that *as long as you believe you enjoy eternal life*. The implication of Jesus' promise is that all these benefits come upon us as soon as we believe, as soon as we call.

C. Some claim that faith needs to *continue* to be genuine faith. Some people argue that the verb *believe* is in the present tense in John 5:24, a tense in Greek that suggests repetition, or *continual action*. These people use that fact to claim that this verse should be re-translated to emphasize that *as long as a person continues to believe she/he will continue to have* *eternal life*. In other words, once that person stops believing they stop enjoying eternal life. Faith is something that needs to be maintained.

According to them John 3:16 should read: "For God so loved the world that He gave His only begotten Son, that whoever [continues to believe in Him] should not perish but [continue to have] everlasting life." And they point out that the Greek verb for *believe* appears in the present tense fifteen times in the gospel of John (3:15, 16, 18, 36; 5:24; 6:35, 40, 47, 7:38; 11:25, 26; 12:44, 46 and 14:12).

So what do we do with the present tense of the word *believe?* It's true that the present tense often implies repetition or continual action, but it doesn't always require that. Think of the thief on the cross: "Lord, remember me when You come into Your kingdom" (Luke 23:42). The quick response the thief heard was, "Assuredly, I say to you, today you will be with Me in Paradise." The promise wasn't, "you'll be with Me if you continue in faith for the remaining 30 minutes of your life."

The jailer in the town of Philippi was ready to end his life. Paul commanded him, "believe on the Lord Jesus Christ, and you will be saved, you and your household" (Acts 16:31). The man believed that night, his household also believed, and they were all baptized. The effect of their salvation appeared immediately: "when he had brought them into his house, he set food before them; and he rejoiced, having believed in God with all his household" (Acts 16:34). Salvation was by *one act of faith* – he listened, he believed, and he obeyed. He knew that night that he was saved!

Even John 5:24 doesn't support the view of continual faith. Although the verse has five present tense verbs in it (there are actually 7 verbs or verbals in the verse) one verb clearly argues against the need of faith continuing for salvation to continue. Trace the verbs here: "Most assuredly, I say (present tense) to you, he who hears (present participle) My word and believes (present participle) in Him who sent (aorist tense, point action) Me has (present tense) everlasting life, and shall not come (present tense) into judgment, but has passed (perfect tense) from death into life".".

Notice that the last verb is in the *perfect tense*. The perfect tense implies that *the action has been completed, permanently.* It assures us that the transfer from death to life is finished!

Thus we must read the verse this way,

> He who continually hears My Word and continually believes in Him who sent Me, continually has everlasting life, and continually does not come into judgment, but *already has passed in a final sense from death into life!*

How can someone only maintain eternal life as he continually hears and believes, when he has already finally passed out of death into life? The theory of faith continuing in order to be real faith doesn't fit the verse and doesn't make sense.

Jesus doesn't speak about conditional eternal life that depends on the faithfulness of our faith. *He is talking about one act of faith with permanent, eternal, wonderful results — because of God's grace.* Like the thief on the cross, like the Prodigal Son or the Philippian jailer, one act of faith forever changed their futures. By grace they were placed into God's family (John 1:12), by grace they were rescued from the kingdom of darkness and transferred into the kingdom of His dear Son (Colossians 1:13).

D. "Continual faith" changes the definition of faith. What is faith if it has to be something that continues? The Bible's definition we came up with in Chapter 2 said, "faith is listening to God's Word, and believing it enough to obey." Could we legitimately change it to, "hearing God's

Word and believing it enough to obey continually for the rest of your life, or for a certain probationary period of time?" That would imply that Romans 10:13 ought to be understood as, "Whosoever shall continue to call upon the name of the Lord shall be saved." As long as you call you stay saved. Once you quit calling, you lose it, or prove that you never had it. Is that what Paul meant?

How often would you have to believe or call on the Lord's name to remain saved? Once a day? Once a week? And how many times would you have to neglect believing to lose its benefit?

Wasn't the nation of Israel saved out of Egypt by one act of faith, sacrificing the Passover lamb and applying the blood to the lintel and doorposts? Didn't God's grace bring incredible, forever results that resulted in never returning to bondage and slavery in Egypt?

All this was in spite of the fact that Israel *didn't continue believing*. They murmured, they complained, they rebelled, they tested God ten times (Numbers 14:22-23). As a result God's conclusion of them was, "they always go astray in their heart, And they have not known My ways" (Hebrews 3:10). In spite of everything that happened afterwards, Israel was saved from Egyptian bondage never to return again.

The truth is that faith is listening to, believing and obeying God *at a moment in time*. That faith is blessed by God in supernatural ways. It doesn't require that act to continue for awhile to demonstrate that it is genuine.

But isn't it true that God *wants us to continue in faith?* Absolutely! Do parents want their children to grow and make the right decisions? Absolutely! But if they don't it doesn't change the initial gift of life.

It's important to understand the finished nature of faith. Faith is not real faith because it continues throughout life; it is real when we obey.

Jesus said, "come to Me" (Matthew 11:28). Faith is completed when we come to Him.

E. A common way of expressing the Christian life is, "continuing to believe." God's desire is for all His children to continually believe and obey Him. But *is that the way we should define the word "believe?"* Does faith have to continue for a period of time in order to be genuine faith? Some people apparently think so. Here is a fairly representative quote by a good Bible teacher, Pastor Stephen Cole. It's based on John 3:36, which says, "He who believes in the Son has eternal life; but he who does not obey the Son will not see life, but the wrath of God abides on him" (NASB):

> You might expect that John would say that whoever believes in Christ has eternal life, but the one who doesn't *believe* is under God's judgment. But instead, he uses a different word, saying, 'he who does not *obey* the Son will not see life.' He does this for two reasons. First, not to believe in Jesus is to disobey God, who calls on all to repent and believe. Second, genuine saving faith is obedient faith, whereas false faith claims to believe, but denies that claim by disobedience (Matt. 7:21; Luke 6:46; Titus 1:16; James 2:18-24; 1 John 2:3). Of course, none of us can obey God perfectly, but the overall direction of our lives should be that of obedience to Christ.[63]

The statement, "genuine saving faith is obedient faith," is true. Faith obeys, as we defined the word *obey* in the previous two chapters. But the assumption of Pastor Cole seems to be that in order to be genuine, faith needs to *continue obeying*. Did you catch the qualification, "the overall direction of our lives should be that of obedience to Christ?" We know we can't obey God perfectly, but for "genuine saving faith" there must be *overall obedience*. Salvation faith involves obeying God, not perfectly, but in such a way that the overall direction of our lives is obedience to Christ.

Two things make that a fuzzy statement: (1) How many commands does one have to obey to possess (or demonstrate) saving faith? Is it God's desire that we obey Him "perfectly," while at the same time accepting less than perfect attempts? How much less-than-perfect obedience can be tolerated in genuine saving faith and still have "overall obedience?" (2) How long of a period are we talking about? For the rest of one's life? What is included in "the overall direction of our lives?" If one strays for a month or a year, does that prove that the original faith was false?

I'm positive that Pastor Cole doesn't believe in salvation by works or by perfect obedience, but do you see the issue? The way it is stated sounds like if one doesn't continue believing, his faith is not genuine. But if faith is not one act at a moment in time, then who determines "overall obedience?" How does Ephesians 1:13 fit in where it says, "having believed you were sealed with the Holy Spirit of promise"? At what point in time can a person say that? How can Paul present the picture of salvation as accomplished if instead it means it's accomplished only if they continue in faith?

And what happens if a new believer doesn't see the overall direction of her life to be obedience? Let's say that she had bad habits as an unbeliever that still drag her down. Can she ever experience the happy assurance of Ephesians 1:13? What is actually necessary for "genuine saving faith?"

Have these questions ever bothered you? I mean, if your faith depends on continuing faithfully in obedience, would you have trouble with assurance of salvation? Would you question your salvation every time you disobeyed? I would. And I have.

The truth is that at a point in time faith is complete in the sense that the benefits are ours, permanently. There is a point in time when we can sit down and eat the fattened calf meal like the Prodigal. Of course, there is the expectation of "overall obedience" as Pastor Cole says, but that's an issue of Christian growth, not initial faith. The example provided by the nation of Israel can help us understand this process.

II. Israel provides a picture of faith growth

Paul states that things which were written in the Old Testament were written for our learning (Romans 15:4); and that things which happened to the nation of Israel were designed to be examples for us (1 Corinthians 10:6, 11). What example do they provide?

A. Israel was rescued from Egyptian bondage by faith. The nation believed and obeyed. It started back in Exodus 4:31, when Moses and Aaron returned to Egypt from the desert and announced God's promise. The people "believed and worshiped."

When it came time for the tenth plague, Moses gave instructions on how to prepare the Passover lamb. The people believed and obeyed. As a result the Death angel passed over the houses where the blood of a lamb was visible on the door posts. That didn't include Pharaoh's house and the angel stopped in at midnight. It must have been awful.

That visit opened the door for Israel to exit Egypt. They were petrified at the Red Sea when they saw Pharaoh's army pursuing them, but, "by faith they passed through the Red Sea as by dry land . . ." (Hebrews

11:29). Pharaoh's army didn't find dry land for long. Their chariots sunk into the mud and the entire army was swallowed by the water (Exodus 14:23-28).

By Exodus 15 Israel was completely free from Egyptian bondage. They were safely on the other side of the Red Sea, singing and dancing their praises to the Lord for His incredible victory. No more chains! No more Egyptian taskmasters. No more Pharaonic persecution. They were free! They were a new people, rescued by the Grace of God. What an amazing experience, to realize that because of simple trust in God, they had become a new nation. With no military effort on their part, they had witnessed the fall of the greatest military power in the world!

A parallel thing happens today when a person comes to Christ. After spending time attempting to please God on their own, the individual receives the gift by simply holding out the empty hand of faith and calling on His name. The light enters, the bondage of sin is broken, and they are free.

Question: was Israel's faith dependent on continuing in obedience? No, she was out, never to return. Her faith that brought salvation from Egypt was complete.

B. Salvation from Egypt brought new expectations of faith. But there was a serious problem. Look where Israel found herself now that she was out from Egyptian domination. Yes she was free, *but on the wrong side of the Red Sea!* The food supplies, the grocery stores, the water tanks, the infrastructure for normal life, were all on the other side. She was free, but in an endless, sandy desert, with nothing! Simply providing water in a desert for a million people was impossible. And food? Shelter? Clothes? Nights are cold in a desert. Yes she was free, but only for a couple of days. She would soon die in the desert unless God intervened.

Did Israel think at all about her future needs? It doesn't look like it. She was singing, dancing, on cloud nine over her new life, when suddenly she ran out of water (Exodus 15:22). Why did God allow her to run out of water?

It was an invitation to a new step of faith. She was now in God's training program. The lack of water brought her to a fork in her now redeemed journey, "would she trust God again, as she had done back in Egypt and at the Red Sea?" "Could He now supply water?"

They were standing on a different stage now, with different scenery. The kids and the animals were a part of the picture because of dehydration. New realities were setting in as everyone began to realize the horror of the possibility that *they might not make it through this awful place!*

Finally they came to water (v. 23). Can't you see them all running to it, crowding around for a drink? And the water was *bitter!* – undrinkable! What would you think at that moment, with your wife and kids and animals crying around you? Would you have said, "hey, wait. The God who recently freed us from bondage to the greatest nation in the world, is leading us. Let's trust Him and ask Him to meet our need?" Or would you have said (with most of the Israelites), "we're dead!?" "There's no hope!" Being in the desert with no water was a challenge of their faith. Would they *trust God, or trust appearances?*

C. Salvation from Egypt provided new opportunities for growth. The purpose for the lack of water was so that Israel would trust God again and grow in their understanding of His love for them. Faith grows *by exercise.* Since she had sacrificed the Passover lamb by faith (Exodus 12:28) and walked through the Red Sea by faith (Hebrews 11:29), one would expect that she would automatically repeat her faith response by trusting her God to supply water.

But somehow *Red Sea faith* didn't transfer to *present-need-of-water* faith. She needed to stop, *listen* to God's directions and *believe* them enough to *obey*. Her murmuring was testimony that she didn't. *As a group of believers, Israel didn't believe.*

God didn't immediately supply the water Israel needed because He wanted her to turn to Him. Here's the way He explained it to her:

> And the people complained against Moses, saying, "What shall we drink?" So he cried out to the LORD, and the LORD showed him a tree. When he cast it into the waters, the waters were made sweet. There He made a statute and an ordinance for them. And there He tested them, and said, "If you diligently heed the voice of the LORD your God and do what is right in His sight, give ear to His command- ments and keep all His statutes, I will put none of the dis- eases on you which I have brought on the Egyptians. For I am the LORD who heals you." Then they came to Elim, where there were twelve wells of water and seventy palm trees; so they camped there by the waters (Exodus 15:24- 27).

"There He tested them." A test is an opportunity presented by expe- riences in life to listen "to the voice of the LORD, to do what is right in His sight, to give ear to His commandments and keep His statutes" (v. 26).

The other option is to listen to one's own voice and do what one thinks right, to give ear to what one wants and do it one's way by mur- muring and complaining. In other words, a test brought them to a fork where they had to choose whether they were going to believe and obey God, or trust their own judgment. Had they trusted God by consulting and obeying Him, they would have met "the LORD who heals (15:26)!"

Every believer faces life-forks, usually every day. James describes it this way:

> My brethren, count it all joy when you fall into various tri-
> als, knowing that the testing of your faith produces pa-
> tience. But let patience have its perfect work, that you may
> be perfect and complete, lacking nothing. If any of you
> lacks wisdom, let him ask of God, who gives to all liberally
> and without reproach, and it will be given to him (James
> 1:2-5).

How you respond when your car has a flat tire, or your hot water heater gives out, or someone embarrasses you in public, or your child hurts you, reveals who you trust. Like Israel's bitter water, tests like this appear suddenly and without permission. And Satan is usually the first on the scene to give his recommendations as to how to react ("scream," "throw something," "hit him," "pay her back"). God has already written down His directions: "Consider it all joy" (thank God for the situation, knowing that He intends to use it for your good), "let endurance have its perfect result" (determine to go through it the right way to extract all its benefit), and "ask God for wisdom" (as to how to respond correctly to the challenge).

Each of these responses is a faith response. The tests are intended by God to help us grow in "endurance" (v. 3). That's the identical reason for the apple in the Garden, and the lack of water for Israel in the desert. They're props on the stage of life that force us to make a choice. We can't *not choose*. We have to do something, either believe and obey God's Word, or believe and obey our desires and/or Satan's word.

Thus it didn't take continuous faith to rescue Israel from Egypt. They believed and obeyed at the Passover, they believed and obeyed at the Red Sea and they were out. Even though they refused to believe and obey when they ran out of water, that didn't change their status in regard to Egypt. They were out permanently. Their faith at the Passover was genuine; so was their faith at the Red Sea. Continuing to believe was not what made their initial faith genuine.

III. The disciples provide a picture of faith growth

The twelve had followed Christ because they believed in Him. They all probably had a similar confession as Nathanael, "Rabbi, You are the Son of God; You are the King of Israel" (John 1:49). What then did Jesus mean when He asked them "Why are you afraid, you men of little faith?" (Matthew 8:26). Luke records the question as, "Where is your faith?" (Luke 8:25). Mark says that He asked "Why are you so fearful? How is it that you have no faith?" (Mark 4:40). Their fear of the winds and surging sea was an issue of faith. But they were believers. They were disciples. They had followed Him in faith. The only reason they were in the boat with Him was because they believed that He was their Messiah.

What was their problem? It was similar to Israel's problem in Exodus 15. God had set up a stage on the Sea of Galilee, had called in some wind and waves, to bring them to a fork in the road: "will you trust Me in this new environment?" They knew He was Messiah, but had no concept that Messiah ruled the winds and sea. It's interesting that after Jesus performed the miracle, Mark records, "And they feared exceedingly, and said to one another, 'Who can this be, that even the wind and the sea obey Him!?'" (Mark 4:41). The experience was an eye-opening shock that introduced their Messiah as the One in charge of the winds and seas (*i.e.*, God!), to them a fearful realization.

When Peter walked on the water at the beckon of Jesus, he got nerv-
ous and began to sink. As Jesus stretched out His hand and gripped him,
He said, "You of little faith, why did you doubt?" (Matthew 14:31). Sinking into the sea showed Peter's wavering faith. But back in the boat after
the wind stopped, the disciples "worshiped Him, saying, 'Truly You are
the Son of God'" (Matthew 14:33). Water walking provided new insight
into the glory of Christ. The purpose of the test was to strengthen Peter's
faith and understanding of Messiah.

In a similar way the "various trials" in our lives test our faith. They
force us, if you will, to reveal who we really believe, God, Satan, or ourselves. The apple in the Garden of Eden became a test of Adam and
Eve's faith. Would they trust God's description of the apple (don't eat,
it's damaging for you), or Satan's description (you won't die), and their
observations, (it looked good and non-damaging)? *What they chose showed
who they believed.*

What trials have you encountered this week? Think of how they have
tested your faith. "Where is God when I lose my job?" "Where is God
when my car quits on the Interstate?" "Where is God when my child is
arrested for shoplifting?" Each of these is a "test," a fork that brings a
choice into your life. You can't skip it. You have to choose whether you
will trust God's Word, or murmur, complain and do your own thing.

Trials come our way *because* we have trusted Him for Salvation. They
provide opportunities to grow in Christ and meet Him in new ways.

IV. Christians grow in faith at different speeds

What did Christ do when Peter failed the test? He said to him, "You
of little faith, why did you doubt?" (Matthew 14:31). What did Christ do

when Peter denied Him three times, even cursing (Matthew 26:73-75)? Did He kick him off His disciple band? Did He tell him that his original faith wasn't genuine? No! He responded the way any loving parent responds to their young child learning to walk. Like Israel and Peter, sometimes it takes us a while to exercise faith on a new and strange stage of life.

I can remember the day when I trusted and obeyed James 1:2 for probably the first time. I had been a believer for perhaps twenty years, but that verse had never clearly gotten my attention. One Sunday afternoon I got my 1965 Mercury Comet stuck in a stone quarry. After driving around exploring a new section of Maryland, I had steered down into an old quarry. At one point the car slid on gravel, the back wheel shot out over a rather large ditch and stopped dangerously tilted toward the ditch with the axle sitting on the ground. I was stuck. I got out, surveyed the situation and said to myself, "you are an idiot."

I had an appointment to lead a group of young people at six that evening, it was now about three and I was forty five miles away, in the middle of nowhere, with no one around and little hope of getting out. I was standing beside the leaning car, condemning my decision, when James 1:2 popped into mind: "consider it all joy, my brethren, when you encounter various trials."

My immediate reaction was, "that surely doesn't fit this situation; I didn't fall into a trial, I jumped. It was my fault; it wasn't something God brought into my life." Then I thought, "well the verse says, 'various trials,' the command is to thank God for the situation because (v. 3) He wants to strengthen my faith. So I should stop, consider it all joy, and thank God for it."

After some further argument and discussion, I bowed my head, and thanked God that I was facing a trial, even though self-caused, thanked

Him that He knew how to get me out, and asked for wisdom as to what to do (v. 5), reminding Him that I had an appointment.

It was an interesting experience. I started walking and praying, asking God for wisdom as to where to turn. I got out of the quarry and could turn either right or left. I turned left and after awhile came upon a house, with no one home. But behind the house I found a man hanging tobacco in the attic of a barn.

I explained my situation to him. He responded, "help me hang this tobacco and when I get done I'll see what I can do for you." After hanging tobacco awhile (a new experience) he showed me his tractor, with a plow on the front! After scraping out a road for me he pulled my car out and I was at the youth meeting by six!

What happened? *I met God in a new way.* I realized His interest in the minor details of my life, even those caused by my own stupidity. What I saw in the situation said to me, "this is hopeless; you'll never get out of here until the quarry workers come back to work tomorrow." My insides said to me, "grumble, complain, condemn yourself, throw rocks at the stupid car" (there were plenty). But the Word said, "count it all joy," and "ask God for wisdom."

That four-verse package (James 1:2-5) has become one of my favorite passages. It became the feature of our lives when our eldest son borrowed our van without a driver's license and drove away with two 13-year-old girls, as I mentioned in Chapter 6, and then when we had no job and six children under the age of 16, and then when our youngest son passed away at the age of 22, as well as many other times.

The questions that come in each trial are, "are you going to believe God by thanking Him for the situation, trusting that it comes from the hand of Someone who loves you and intends to bless you? Are you going to seek His wisdom? Or are you going to decide on the basis of what you can see, and grumble, complain and solve the problem the best way you can?"

Let me summarize what I've said in this chapter: faith is *point action,* at a *moment of time.* The effects of faith are *permanent* because what Christ does in response to our faith is eternal. In addition, the one initial act of faith introduces new opportunities to believe, and therefore expects faith to grow.

Thus faith is *temporary* in the sense that one act of faith doesn't guarantee another act of faith or continuous faith. The listening-believing–obeying process has to be repeated. Trusting God's Word for salvation doesn't guarantee that a person will immediately trust God by "counting it all joy" when he gets stuck in a gravel pit.

And the fact that twenty years elapses between trusting Christ for salvation and trusting him in a gravel pit doesn't call into question the genuineness of that initial salvation experience.

Chapter 12

The unity of faith – faith is faith

The faith by which Christians grow is the same kind of faith by which they were saved

People invent different kinds of faith. There might be head faith, heart faith, and the faith that leads to salvation contrasted with faith that produces good works in a Christian. Some talk about "easy believism" and want to make sure that faith is a total commitment. Is there a different kind of faith that one needs after the initial faith for salvation? Maybe the way to ask it would be, "what is the difference between faith *before* salvation and faith *after?*" The answer impacts how we define faith.

Early on in my Christian experience someone introduced me to Colossians 2:6 which says, "as you therefore have received Christ Jesus the Lord, so walk in Him." The "as/so" connection compares receiving Christ Jesus with walking in Him and declares that they are or should be the same process. As believers we walk in Christ in the same way that we have received Him, *by faith.* Salvation and the Christian life are to be based on similar responses to God's Word.

Is that true? Was Abraham's faith for salvation in Genesis 15 the same type of response as the faith of sacrificing his son in Genesis 22? Bible writers seem to view faith in a consistent way whether the person is an unbeliever or believer. For Abraham, faith for salvation was the same hearing and believing process (Genesis 15:6) as it was to leave Ur (Hebrews 11:8) as it was to stay in Canaan (Hebrews 11:9) as it was to sacrifice Isaac his son (Hebrews 11:17).

Where is the evidence that faith after salvation is of the same fabric as the faith that leads to salvation? How do we know that the faith the righteous are to live by (Romans 1:17) is the same faith by which they became righteous?

I. Some teach a Christian-life faith that doesn't seem to match Salvation faith

Problems arise when trying to sort out how a Christian lives by faith. Some answers seem confusing. Let me quote from two examples, that of Professor Zane Hodges and Pastor John MacArthur. Both of these men are excellent Bible teachers and greatly used of the Lord. I explore the difficulties in their explanations simply to show the fuzziness in defining Christian-life faith.

Professor Zane Hodges makes a strong contrast between the faith of salvation and what happens afterwards. He states,

> the Christian experience, therefore, begins with faith. By faith we appropriate God's gift of life with all of its matchless potentials. That much is absolutely free. But from there on there must be diligence. There has to be a willingness to work, and to work hard. To be sure, God will generously

give His help as we do so. But we must *want* that help, we
must *reach out* for it, we must *be willing* to apply all perseverance to the process of Christian growth. There is no other
way to fruitfulness.[64] (emphasis his).

Hodges tells us that the faith which begins the Christian experience
is a "gift" but "from there on there must be diligence." "But from there
on" implies a significant difference. Christian growth depends on hard
work (helped by the Holy Spirit) that a Christian must "want" and "reach
out" for and apply with "all perseverance."

The question is, if *the just shall live by faith* shouldn't life after salvation
be *not of works* in the same way that salvation faith is *not of works*? They
both depend on a faith response because "without faith it is impossible
to please Him" (Hebrews 11:6).

Pastor John MacArthur also contrasts the faith of salvation with the
responsibilities in the Christian life. He explains,

It cannot be overemphasized that works play no role in
gaining salvation. But good works have everything to do
with *living out* salvation. No good works can *earn* salvation,
but many good works *result* from genuine salvation. Good
works are not necessary to *become* a disciple, but good works
are the necessary *marks* of all true disciples. God has, after
all, ordained that we should walk in them.[65] (emphasis his).

Notice that he clearly emphasizes that salvation is "not of works."
What is not clear is how one lives this new, work-filled Christian life *by
faith*.

II. Faith doesn't stop after salvation

The testimony of Scripture seems to be that life after salvation needs to be lived in the same way that we came to Christ. For example:

> I have been crucified with Christ; it is no longer I who live, but Christ lives in me; and the life which I now live in the flesh I live by faith in the Son of God, who loved me and gave Himself for me (Galatians 2:20).

> Therefore, having been justified by faith, we have peace with God through our Lord Jesus Christ, through whom also we have access by faith into this grace in which we stand, and rejoice in hope of the glory of God (Romans 5:1-2).

> For we walk by faith, not by sight (2 Corinthians 5:7).

> For we through the Spirit eagerly wait for the hope of righteousness by faith. For in Christ Jesus neither circumcision nor uncircumcision avails anything, but faith working through love (Galatians 5:5-6).

> Yet indeed I also count all things loss for the excellence of the knowledge of Christ Jesus my Lord, for whom I have suffered the loss of all things, and count them as rubbish, that I may gain Christ and be found in Him, not having my own righteousness, which is from the law, but that which is through faith in Christ, the righteousness which is from God by faith; that I may know Him and the power of His resurrection, and the fellowship of His sufferings, being conformed to His death (Philippians 3:8-10).

These passages speak of faith in the Christian life as if it is the same genre as the faith that brought salvation. When we imply a significant difference between the beginning and the maintaining of the Christian life (one is without works and the other is hard work) we suggest either (a) that there are two different kinds of faith, or (b) that the Christian life is lived by our efforts.

III. The faith process in the Christian life is identical to the faith process for salvation

The truth is that *there is only one definition of faith.* Faith is faith. Abraham's faith in Genesis 15 involved the same process as his faith in Genesis 22. So just as salvation is "not of works lest any man should boast" so the Christian life must be lived "not of works lest any man should boast."

Observe how Paul emphasizes this point, that salvation faith is to be continued as Christian life faith. He asked five insightful questions of the Galatians:

> Did you receive the Spirit by the works of the law, or by the hearing of faith? Are you so foolish? Having begun in the Spirit, are you now being made perfect by the flesh? Have you suffered so many things in vain -- if indeed it was in vain? Therefore He who supplies the Spirit to you and works miracles among you, does He do it by the works of the law, or by the hearing of faith? (Galatians 3:2b-5)

Paul allows two possible ways of receiving the Holy Spirit and two ways of receiving His miracles as a Christian. One is "by the works of the Law," the other is "by the hearing of faith." "Law" represents personal earnings, and what humans can accomplish by their own performance. "The hearing of faith" describes the process of listening, believing and receiving God's gifts.

I'm sure that neither of the Bible teachers above would argue that a Christian is "perfected by the flesh." But Paul doesn't offer any other alternative to "the hearing of faith." It's either faith or flesh. The implication of his third question is that once we have begun by the Spirit we are perfected *by the same Spirit,* by the same *hearing-of-faith* process. The Galatian's error was to suppose that salvation was by faith, but that growth in Christ is by works of the law. Paul's point was that they needed to live life *in the same way they came to Christ:* by grace through faith.

We face the danger of repeating the Galatian error when we draw a contrast between salvation faith and Christian life works. Of course we wouldn't command new believers to get circumcised as the Galatian false teachers were doing, but we make living in Christ more of a human production, more like "get busy and live for Christ by obeying the Ten Commandments and tithing and doing good works."

How does a believer live by faith that is "not of works?" For one thing it starts at the same place the gospel started, with listening to God's Word (Romans 10:17), then believing it to be true, followed by obeying. This means that Christian-life living begins with our ears.

Martin Luther spoke of the Christian life by saying, "there is nothing else required of us, but that we, setting apart all our works, should give ourselves only to the hearing of the Gospel."[66]

That statement points out that both unbelievers and believers have a similar challenge: both need to *listen to God's Word* since that's where faith begins.

In light of Paul's five questions and answers, think of the fuzziness of either Professor Hodges' or Pastor MacArthur's statements above.

How would you fit, "the hearing of faith" into their explanation of Christian growth? It's important to remember that what they say is *true*. The Christian life is described as running a race (1 Corinthians 9:24-27) which involves total involvement and maximum effort; it's described as wrestling against superhuman powers (Ephesians 6:10-13). It depends on wanting it and reaching out for it. But *how do those concepts fit in with "the hearing of faith?"* What keeps Christian living from becoming "the works of the Law?"

IV. Christian-life faith is salvation-faith *repeated* in new contexts

We started back in Chapter 11 with the fact that faith is one act at a point in time. It gets finished with immediate results (John 5:24). The Bible does not talk about an attitude or mood that needs to be continued in order for faith to be genuine. Once a person believes, God does massive and surprising things, like the story of the Prodigal.

We live the Christian life by repeating that same process, hearing God's Word, believing it to be true, and obeying it. Only now the faith is exercised in a different area or in a new context. Israel by faith placed blood on the doorposts of her houses and experienced the salvation of Passover. But shortly thereafter she came upon water to drink that was bitter, calling for a similar process of listening and obeying. Only now she failed to consult God and grumbled instead. She didn't exercise faith. As a result she missed out on God's blessing.

What this means is that growing in Christ is a similar challenge to the initial experience of coming to Christ for salvation. It's the issue of listening versus doing our own thing. And like Israel, we find that responsibility almost as difficult as we did before we came to Christ.

Martin Luther said,

> "ye must be circumcised and keep the law," cannot be utterly rooted out in our minds, but it sticketh fast in the hearts of all the faithful. There is in the faithful therefore a continual conflict between the hearing of faith and the works of the law.[67]

Life is a tension between listening and doing. For example, if we should come to trial number one like Israel did, where everyone is thirsty and crying out for water, how would we respond when we discovered water that was bitter? How many believers are going to say, "now let's stop and (a) thank God for this situation, and (b) determine to go through it properly, and (c) ask God for wisdom" (James 1:2-5)?

Instead Israel's reaction describes the norm: grumbling and exclaiming that "this Christian life doesn't work! I'm going back to Egypt." It's difficult to stop, listen and ask God for His gift of wisdom, especially if the trial we are in is a tough one.

"Tell me how easy a thing it is to hear the word of faith" when you "come once to an earnest trial," Luther said.[68] It's the "earnest trial" that really checks our willingness to stop and submit to the sufficiency of God's Word.

The point is that faith has to be repeated; there are not two definitions, one for an unbeliever and the other for a believer. The process of hearing, believing and obeying fits the Christian life just as it fits that of an unbeliever because "without faith it is impossible to please Him."

V. Faith is a response to God's invitations and commands

Paul and Silas commanded the Philippian jailer, "Believe on the Lord Jesus Christ, and you will be saved, you and your household" (Acts 16:31). Jesus said, "Come to Me, all you who labor and are heavy laden, and I will give you rest" (Matthew 11:28). The gospel often goes out with a command (Matthew 3:2; 4:17; 7:13; 2 Corinthians 5:20).

But since obedience to a command is something we do, how can that response be *by faith* and *without works?*" In a similar way, how does a believer live by faith when Jesus said, "He who has My commandments and keeps them, it is he who loves Me . . ." (John 14:21)?

Aren't the commandments the foundation for Old Testament living? Aren't believers living under *grace?* Does grace involve commandments? Yes. The truth is that we obey God's commands by faith. Let me explain.

A. Commands are the foundation of every relationship. We grew up with commands. "Brush your teeth; wash your hands; don't talk that way to your mother." Somehow there is the idea that when we get older we will grow out of them. Especially once we trust Christ and our hearts are changed we should be free from all commands except the command to love.

We had students at the Washington Bible College who argued that living under Grace meant "absence of commandments." The commands in the student handbook were an irritant. "Why is there a dress code?" "Why tell us when to be back in the dorm at night?" "We're adults!" "Why do we have lights out at 1 a.m.?" "Why do we have to sign in and out?" "Doesn't the administration know how to run a school under Grace?" For these students, commands were inimical to Grace.

Their notion was that living under God's grace meant less rules or no rules because Grace meant "no law." The thought was that since Grace and Law were opposites, we should just love the Lord and be kind to one another, and not steal, and not talk each other down. It would be like the first century church where everyone loved each other, held all their possessions in common and the church was filled with joy!

But wait, aren't those *commands?* "Love," "be kind," "don't steal," "don't talk down"? Aren't those part of the Ten Commandments? "Love the Lord;" isn't that command number one? "Don't steal." Isn't that number eight? "Don't talk down each other." Isn't that number nine?

The notion that living under Grace means no commands doesn't work. Just BE? Be what? The truth is that we can't live without commands, and the Ten Commandments are the foundation for life.

I think it was Martin Luther who said, "love God with all your heart and do what you want to do." We have to be careful how we process that statement because there is only one way to know if we are loving God with all our hearts. Jesus said it, "If you love Me, keep My commandments." That's why *we can't view living under Grace as living without commandments.* Those who succeed in living by Grace obey Christ's commandments. Why is that so important?

B. Commands define our relationship with God. They introduce us to His qualities and characteristics. For example, God said, "You shall be holy, for I the LORD your God am holy" (Leviticus 19:2). The command for us to be holy is based on the fact that He is holy.

A similar thing happens in marriage. For example, when you said, "I do" you came under a whole new set of commands that you perhaps knew little about beforehand. Did you husbands find commands that sounded somewhat like these?

Thou shalt eat any food creation that she designs.

Thou shalt assume the debts of thy mate.

Thou shalt provide for her needs and wants.

Thou shalt listen to her talk and encourage her in it.

Before I was married, I was getting up at six in the morning to go to the Washington Bible College and spend all day there, not coming home until ten or eleven at night, so I could sleep and get up at 6 a.m. and go back to WBC. I married a beautiful Georgia peach and she expected me to be home at five in the afternoon. My initial, very short, response was, "for what reason? I've got too many things to do." In addition she expected me to carry out the garbage, and quite a few other things. None of that was in the marriage contract. None of that was talked about beforehand. *I was blind-sided by the relationship!*

No I wasn't. You should see the list of commands she learned about! She had to quit her missionary job to marry me, and learn to improvise and live on very little, and be ready for strangers that I might drag home for dinner, and always be prepared for sudden events. One night the babysitter arrived at our house before I got home to tell Martha that we were going out to a dress up occasion. It was a great night, but she was frustrated because she didn't have time to get ready. I figured that she was always ready!

So I have learned in more than fifty years that there are certain commands I should obey, certain lines I should never cross if I want to live and remain healthy. How many commands would you say are intrinsic in your marriage relationship? Forty? Eighty? One hundred and fifty? They help define the relationship; they are great!

These are not commands given so that your mate will accept you; he/she already has, that's why you're married. These are commands given because you're already in this relationship. They are inherent in the title *marriage* as descriptors of the arrangement.

Does this mean that we are *under the Law* in a marriage? Absolutely not! It's a love relationship! But in order to enjoy that love relationship, a couple needs to get serious about one another's commands. *They're not optional; they define the expectations.* They help us understand each other's thoughts and motives. They help us live together *by faith*.

C. Commands define the project. God's commands define what the Christian life looks like and where it is going. It's like God saying to the Israelites back in Exodus 20, "here are the ten things that define where I want our relationship to go."

Relationships are duets not solos. That means that two people need to contribute to make the relationship work. If one party does all the work you don't have a relationship, except maybe that of a *parent*. The desired relationship is for both parties to contribute one hundred percent to the marriage. That makes for a *team*.

What God desires is for us individually to become a team with Him. He has already contributed more than His one hundred percent and wants us to wake up to the blessings He has supplied. Waking up involves listening to His commands, believing them and joining Him by obeying.

Let me give an example: "Therefore, putting away lying, 'Let each one of you speak truth with his neighbor,' for we are members of one another" (Ephesians 4:25). "Speak truth" is a command. God wants us to speak absolute truth.

Someone responds with, "why do I need to speak truth?" "I don't feel like speaking truth; it's never been my specialty, and I rather enjoy adjusting words." "Do I have to be honest?" "Will I lose my salvation if I'm not?"

What if you lie to your mate? Do you become unmarried? Her response to your lie may make you wish you were unmarried! But the point is that you are still married, maybe not as happily as you were before.

Speaking truth or lies does not make or cancel a relationship with God. But speaking truth *defines God*. He only speaks truth and He wants us to represent Him on earth, which is only possible by speaking truth.

In addition, the verse says, "for we are members of one another." We belong to each other as members of the Body of Christ. But we only actually join the team *as we speak truth*. Liars cannot build a team. Whether you or I ever become a useful part of the Body of Christ depends on us becoming honest and laying aside falsehood.

Have you ever done that, gotten rid of everything that is not absolutely honest? Do you stretch or bend words? Do you add a little bit to make the story sound bigger or more impressive? All such action harms your relationship with God and other believers. It's no different than marriage. Marriages are based on absolute, complete, full, frank, honesty. Can you be married without honesty? Sure, but you won't experience the relationship you want.

How do you put away falsehood? You do it *by faith*. You *listen* to what He has said, that we are members one of another and the Body of Christ only grows on truth and honesty. You *evaluate* your own performance in light of God's truth, comparing the absolute importance of truth in Christ's body with the deceit in your own heart. You *trust God's Word enough to obey it* by confessing your deceit to God and to those who love you and think you are honest. And you *ask God for another gift* like you did when you were saved. Only this time you ask for *wisdom* (James 1:5) and grace (Hebrews 4:16) and *ability to obey*. And He gives it!

We grow in Christ by believing and obeying His commands. They define our different relationships. We have been brought into a *Family*, and there are family commands ("love your brothers and sisters"). We have been placed into a *Body*, and there are body commands ("the eye cannot say to the hand, 'I have no need of you'"). We are being made into the *Temple* in which God intends to dwell on Earth ("be holy as I am holy"). In addition, we live in a culture with *Government* commands that help us live as lights in the darkness ("submit yourselves to every ordinance of man for the Lord's sake").

Thus, Christian life faith is made of the same fabric as salvation faith. It always begins with listening and obeying God's words whether they are promises, invitations, or commands. And just as married love is filled with commands, so Christian life grace is filled with commands, because "He who has My commandments and keeps them, it is he who loves Me" (John 14:21a).

Chapter 13

How does a believer *live by faith?*

This chapter intends to introduce you to what I often call Schuppe's false doctrine. I'm kidding of course; I have no interest in peddling false doctrine, but I'm talking about my angle or how I view the rubber actually rolling on the road in life. I want to paint my picture of how one lives the Christian life by faith, by hearing, believing and obeying. This is by no means the final word on the subject, but perhaps these thoughts might help.

Remember that Paul presented the Christian life as containing only two possibilities: "works of the law" or "the hearing of faith" (Galatians 3:5, see chapter 12). So how do we live by the hearing of faith?

Early on as a believer I sort of thought that I was to live by obeying the Ten Commandments, going to church, giving a tithe of my income, reading my Bible, praying and telling others about Christ. Then as I would hear a new message or read another book I would add other requirements, like taking up my cross to become a disciple of Christ, loving my enemies and not discriminating against others, and on and on.

That's the Christian life isn't it? What's not to like about it? What was missing was the Person. The "hearing of faith" takes a Person. Otherwise motives go astray. The value of my list depended on why I did it, or for whom I did it. If I did it for status among other believers or extra credit from God it would quickly become "works of the law."

A better picture of the Christian life is of two people walking together. The word "walk" speaks of taking life step by step, with each step involving a discussion and/or decision. A believer needs to talk with God over each issue and event. We see this kind of picture all through Scripture.

For example, we are commanded to "walk in the Spirit" (Galatians 5:16) and "walk in Him" (Colossians 2:6), and "walk just as He walked" (1 John 2:6). Even the Old Testament says things like, "He has shown you, O man, what is good; And what does the LORD require of you But to do justly, To love mercy, And to walk humbly with your God?" (Micah 6:8). Notice "*with* your God."

In order to do this we should "walk according to His commandments" (2 John 1:6) and "walk in the truth" (3 John 1:3), which means we should "walk in love" (Ephesians 5:2) and "walk as children of light" (Ephesians 5:8), and "walk in the light as He is in the light" (1 John 1:7), and "walk in the steps of the faith which our father Abraham had" (Romans 4:12).

All of these directions and many others like them boil down to one thing: *God wants to spend time interacting with each one of us. He wants to be a part of our lives and decisions.* He expressed His intent when He said: "I will dwell in them and walk among them. I will be their God, And they shall be My people" (2 Corinthians 6:16; Ezekiel 37:26-27). How does walking with God by faith work out in practical life? Let me point out four contexts in which we walk with God by faith: (a) our circumstances; (b) God's projects; (c) God's family; and (d) our weaknesses.

I. We walk with God in our circumstances

Like Shadrach, Meshach, and Abed-nego, God shows up when the furnace gets extra hot as we determine to obey Him (Daniel 3). He wants to meet us in every stressful situation.

A. Circumstances provide opportunities to take a step with God. It's similar to marriage where two people dialog as they make decisions about life. Life together forces them to talk about how to approach their finances and schedules and daily tasks and living arrangements and children and friends and social life and . . . The list keeps extending and the couple finds that at times they have to work hard to stay in sync.

Martha and I talked quite a bit before we were married. To my surprise she didn't want to come and live in the two bedroom house that I rented on thirty-five acres of property next to the Little Patuxent River because it was a little "remote." I loved the place, but we moved into an apartment, and then into another apartment. We decided to buy good used furniture instead of cheap new stuff. But she didn't want to buy a used bed. That was the start of our walking-together life.

Connect that picture to your walk with Christ. Have you discussed with Him your finances? Have you asked Him what He wants to supply? And what you should do with the part that you can supply? Does He actually want to meet all your needs? How does He intend to do that? You're not actually walking together until you dialog about your finances. Circumstances bring endless things to dialog about.

Case in point: my wife realized on December 17, 2020, that she had stage 4 cancer. She was fearful and somewhat frustrated, and we talked about "what do we do next?" We prayed that God would not only take us through this but would give her joy in the process. As I write this piece three months later, she is happy, joyful and laughing over the twists and turns that reveal the mercy and goodness of God. What's not to love about that? Stage 4 cancer and delighted with life. That's my woman!

It was the sudden appearance of cancer that brought about our discussion and decision to ask God to give us joy. And He has answered our prayer abundantly. We give Him praise!

B. Circumstances reveal God's character. When things get hard some marriage partners bail out, others clam up, a few get angry. But God uses hard times to introduce us to His incredible characteristics.

Take Job for example: "You have heard of the perseverance of Job and seen the end intended by the Lord – that the Lord is very compassionate and merciful" (James 5:11). The strikingly beautiful words are "very compassionate" and "merciful." Have you ever pictured your God as "very compassionate" and "merciful? Job found those qualities in the middle of incredibly difficult trials.

Remember that he's the one who lost all ten of his children and just about all his wealth in one day. Shortly after he lost his health and suffered miserable pain. Then he tolerated more than twenty chapters of judgmental condemnation from three supposed "friends." Yet in the middle of his intense pain, he met Someone who was full of compassion and mercy! And for the next one hundred forty years of life (Job 42:10-17) his testimony probably said, "I didn't like the journey, but the end result has been awesome!"

Take another example. In 13 chapters of running and dodging King Saul's spear (1 Samuel 19-31), King David met God as his Shepherd. He said, "the Lord is my Shepherd," meaning "the Lord shepherds me." The rest of the psalm details what the title "Shepherd" means. His God gave him green pastures in which to lie and still waters that met his thirst and restored his soul (Psalm 23:2-3).

Even though God steered the walk through "the valley of the shadow of death" and placed him "in the presence of my enemies," David discovered that "You are with me; Your rod and Your staff, they comfort me" (Psalm 23:4). It's almost like God's presence was more vivid in his dark and threatening situations. There He was, preparing a table and anointing David's head with oil so that David declared, "my cup runs over" (Psalm 23:5)! Think of being able to say in your darkest hour, "my cup runs over" because of God's presence in your life!

Is such a relationship possible? If that's a true picture I want in! But maybe David was dreaming a little. Maybe this was only a wishful hope on his part? Actually no; that's the picture God has given us to describe the Christian life. It's walking with Him and experiencing His tender, shepherding care. Every Christian has the privilege of David's discovery as he or she walks with God.

C. Circumstances encourage our participation. One question that comes up when we think about walking with God is, "what can I do?" "He is God and can do anything; why would He need or want me?" "He is infinite; I'm not; He knows the outcome, I don't." It's hard to imagine that God would have anything for us to do other than riding on His back in a knapsack.

Why would God want or need our input? Is there anything we can actually *donate* to His sovereign work? Does the Bible suggest anywhere that God might want a contribution from us as we walk with Him?

How about prayer? Does God want us to discuss our needs and concerns with Him? Jesus said, "And whatever you ask in My name, that I will do, that the Father may be glorified in the Son. If you ask anything in My name, I will do it" (John 14:13-14). We can ask.

But "anything in My name?" Isn't God going to do what He wants to do? But if He intends to ignore our requests, why did He encourage us to ask? The fact that He invites us to get involved says that He views the Christian life as a duet, walking with Him, not as a solo, where we do our own thing as we attempt to please Him. *He wants our requests!* Yes He could do it all alone. But for some reason He wants us to contribute.

Have you ever looked at your God as sort of slowing down His walk so you can catch up, with His ear tuned to your requests, wanting to accompany you into your dark valleys?

Perhaps you question whether God actually engages in that kind of give and take. Think of Amos the prophet. He was a sheepherder who was sent on a short term mission assignment twenty five miles up the path to the city of Bethel in Israel. What kind of relationship did Amos have with God? This conversation appears in his 7th chapter:

> Thus the Lord GOD showed me: Behold, He formed locust swarms at the beginning of the late crop; indeed it was the late crop after the king's mowings. And so it was, when they had finished eating the grass of the land, that I said: "O Lord GOD, forgive, I pray! Oh, that Jacob may stand, For he is small!" So the LORD relented concerning this. "It shall not be," said the LORD. Thus the Lord GOD showed me: Behold, the Lord GOD called for conflict by fire, and it consumed the great deep and devoured the territory. Then I said: "O Lord GOD, cease, I pray! Oh, that Jacob may stand, For he is small!" So the LORD relented concerning this. "This also shall not be," said the Lord GOD (Amos 7:1-6).

Amos had a relationship where (a) God showed him what He planned to do; (b) Amos disagreed with His plans, and (c) God relented and decided not to do it. That sounds like a team at work. Is it possible for humans to have enough wisdom to add anything to God's plans? Amos did.

So I view the Christian life as a walk with God that is similar to marriage, where two people discuss life's circumstances. Marriage has introduced me to the joy of finding a companion totally in love with me and totally faithful. I have been repeatedly amazed at how Martha has handled difficult situations. Finances, counseling angry children, meeting the needs of neighbors, defending me when I was attacked, all these experiences have convinced me that I can trust her completely with money, our children and grandchildren, her walk with the Lord, and with her absolute ironclad determination to back me up in everything. She is my strength and joy. We think alike, we are heading in the same direction, and I find it exhilarating to be with her.

Can you imagine me speaking the same way, with the same emotion, about God? That He loves me totally, that He is totally faithful, that I am amazed at how wisely He handles difficult situations, and finances, and angry people? Isn't that the way it should be? Circumstances should create that kind of testimony in us—by faith.

II. We walk with God in His projects

Some get the idea that walking with God is sort of like wandering together throughout the countryside of life. It's "hanging out with Jesus," or "jogging with Jesus." Isn't that what Enoch did? He "walked with God" and "was not" because he "pleased God" (Hebrews 11:5; Genesis

5:24). Perhaps he took strolls with God, each day getting further and further from home until one day God said, "you know My house is closer than yours; let's go to Mine."

But strolling with God isn't an accurate picture. Noah was getting ready for a worldwide flood as he walked with God. Constructing a five-hundred-foot wooden boat was a project (Hebrews 11:7). In a similar way, moving one's entire family and living as a foreigner in a tent for one hundred years was a project for Abraham (Hebrews 11:8-10). Leading his people out of Egypt was a forty-year project for Moses (Hebrews 11:24-29). For these people it wasn't as much a stroll with God as a project to accomplish. It seems that everyone in Hebrews 11 was working on a project. They

> through faith subdued kingdoms, worked righteousness, obtained promises, stopped the mouths of lions, quenched the violence of fire, escaped the edge of the sword, out of weakness were made strong, became valiant in battle, turned to flight the armies of the aliens (Hebrews 11:33-34).

How can these projects be cataloged as faith? A corresponding question is, "what do their accomplishments teach us about living the Christian life today?" It's clear that the writer to the Hebrews intends that each example in chapter 11 encourage us to live by faith.

Does God have Noah or Abraham-type projects for believers today? Are we supposed to be accomplishing something as practical as an ark as we walk with Him? Absolutely. Think of the twenty-year project when a baby is born. Think of the project of marriage, or organizing and directing a family of children. Jesus said, "He who has My commandments and keeps them, it is he who loves Me" (John 14:21). Some of His commands are instant, like "give thanks," or "don't fear." But others take longer, like projects.

A. Present tense commands serve as projects for believers. The Greek language has a verb tense that often describes on-going action, or repeated action. It's called the *present tense.* It's not identical to the present tense in English because it's not necessarily speaking of what's happening now. It could be action in the future or the past.

We normally view obedience to commands as immediate, but some commands describe a project, like "go to college," which may involve four years. In a similar way obedience to one of God's present tense commands might be a long-term task. Here's an example of projects God has given us. I've capitalized the present tense commands:

> Therefore, laying aside falsehood, SPEAK TRUTH (present imperative) each one of you with his neighbor, for we are members of one another. BE ANGRY (present imperative), and yet DO NOT SIN (present imperative); DO NOT LET THE SUN GO DOWN (present imperative) on your anger, and DO NOT GIVE (present imperative) the devil an opportunity. He who steals NO LONGER (present imperative) ; but rather he MUST LABOR (present imperative), performing with his own hands what is good, so that he will have something to share with one who has need. LET no unwholesome word PROCEED (present imperative) from your mouth, but only such a word as is good for edification according to the need of the moment, so that it will give grace to those who hear. (Ephesians 4:25-29 NASB)

I've skipped the other verbal forms in this section to highlight the eight present tense commands. Don't think of them as commands that need to be obeyed in order to *become saved,* since they are all addressed to believers. Neither are they commands showing us how to *stay saved.* Again, that's not the issue. The assumption is that we are already members of Christ's body (4:25) and stones in God's glorious temple (2:19-22). Rather they guide our growth as believers. They help us accomplish the major command in this section which is to "walk worthy of our calling" (4:1). The commands in 4:25-29 tell us how to be worthy temple/body members in three ways, by (a) putting off the old man and (b) putting on the new man and (c) renewing our minds (4:22-24).

B. The challenge of speaking truthfully. Verse 25 says that there is something to be put off (falsehood of any kind), something to be put on (truthfulness in every area of life), and a new way of thinking that will renew our minds (we are members of one another).

As I mentioned in the last chapter, the command is addressed to those of us who practiced the sport of lying as we grew up, seeking to shade the truth and cover things with almost true words. When Mom asked, "Where are you going?" our response was, "Out." "What are you going to do?" "Nothing." "Who are you going with?" "No one." All the while we knew exactly where we were going, what we were going to do and the three friends we were going to meet. One of my grandchildren has described it as "embellishing the truth." In reality it's old-fashioned lying.

After years of creating almost-truth truth painted over with fuzzy word-definitions intended to cover one's intentions and polish one's image, getting that deceitful urge out of one's system is a *project.* We don't automatically speak absolute truth when Christ enters our hearts as Savior and Lord. It takes living-by-faith work because it depends on believing and obeying God's Word when we open our mouths. As "members of one another," and part of "one body" (4, 12, and 16), our growth in Christ depends on connecting with that body by "speaking the truth in love" (4:15).

Falsehood ruins body life. Suppose your eye lied to your foot and said, "there is no gully there; keep walking." Liars can't contribute to body life because team building depends on trust. Do you see the conundrum? It's difficult to grow up in Christ *without the help of others* in the body; but at the same time it's difficult to share in body life *until we speak truth.* That's why truth is more than a Christian life app. It's essential for our growth and Paul makes it the first command in walking worthy of our calling.

Jesus said, "let your 'Yes' be 'Yes,' and your 'No,' 'No.' For whatever is more than these is from the evil one" (Matthew 5:37). He wants our "yes" to be a genuine "yes" without qualifications or enhancements of any kind. Not a "partial yes" or a "maybe yes," but "real yes" because anything "more than" absolute truth is *of the devil.* Do you ever have trouble speaking exact truth? That's the project.

The fact is that God cannot lie (Titus 1:2). He has nothing to do with anything that is not complete truth. All lies or half-truths come from Satan who is the father of lies (John 8:44). That's why it's impossible to represent Him or advance His interests with lies and half-truths.

C. Three more Christian life challenges. Once you realize the challenge your tongue presents, Paul lists other projects. I have summarized the seven remaining commands of Ephesians 4:25-29 into three projects.

There's a project in verses 26-27. *It's finding and living in the balance between anger and sin.* "BE ANGRY (present imperative), and yet DO NOT SIN (present imperative); DO NOT LET THE SUN GO DOWN (present imperative) on your anger, and DO NOT GIVE (present imperative) the devil an opportunity."

These commands describe the emotional balance between out-of-control sin and anger. Observe that the command is to "be angry." Some Christians attempt to be uber-calm over everything, even the things which make God angry. Should we react as if God is over-worked over nothing? The Psalmist said: "Do I not hate them, O LORD, who hate You?" (Psalm 139:21). Do you hate what God hates? Or do you view it all casually?

Here's the problem: "how does an always-calm Christian express genuine godly anger without sinning?" In contrast: "how does a historically angry Christian express that emotion righteously?" God wants us to develop His kind of balance in emotional situations.

Another project in verse 28 commands us to *conquer the habit of taking what doesn't belong to us:* "He who steals MUST STEAL NO LONGER (present imperative); but rather he MUST LABOR (present imperative), performing with his own hands what is good, so that he will have something to share with one who has need."

Stealing is the lazy way to prosperity that many of us learned early on. As kids we just took stuff, but as teens we learned to re-define the action as "borrowing" or "re-appropriating." As a college educator for many years I couldn't believe how many Christian young people practiced plagiarism as a regular habit. I found that students from certain cultures didn't even view plagiarism as wrong. Using the intellectual property of others is even practiced by pastors today who steal their messages from the web, or other sources. Employees "borrow" materials from their employer, "adjust" the time clock, and devise clever ways of looking busy, which are all forms of theft. Have you ever stolen? You can't serve God as a thief. Such actions profane His name (Leviticus 19:11-13).

This verse gives us two ways to conquer the problem: (a) become a *worker* by asking God for the wisdom and strength to create your own materials and property; and (b) become a *giver* so that you can bless others with what you have developed yourself.

A third project in verse 29 commands: "LET no unwholesome word PROCEED (present tense imperative) from your mouth, but only such a word as is good for edification according to the need of the moment, so that it will give grace to those who hear."

This verse assures us that we can bless others by ministering grace with our speech. Grace is a gift you give to someone who doesn't deserve it. How can you give undeserved gifts with your mouth? By speaking in ways that edify, encourage and strengthen others.

It starts with putting a gatekeeper at the door of your mouth to screen everything going out. Nothing exits that is in the category of "unwholesome." Only words that will edify are allowed out. The gatekeeper asks, "will this word help?" "Does it fit the moment?" "Will it encourage and strengthen?" Anyone can ask God for wisdom to know when to insert the precisely helpful word.

So far this passage gives us four projects that will enable us to walk worthy of our calling by contributing to the growth of God's temple. How many present tense commands are there in the rest of Ephesians? Would you believe *more than thirty-five!?* Not all apply to everyone. Some are for husbands, some for children, some for employers, but every believer will find plenty of instruction for several by-faith projects like Noah. And that's how we walk with Christ, by discussing with Him the commands that He had made His priority.

III. We walk with God in a family

God automatically places every one of His children in a *body*, a group, called the *church*. At salvation we are "baptized into the body of Christ" (1 Corinthians 12:13). That's one reason to get rid of lying and speak truth – "we are members of one another" (Ephesians 4:25). Because of this, walking with God is not just about *God and me*, but about *God and us*. We walk with God as *we link ourselves with other family members*.

Some disagree. They think that it's better to walk with God alone, perhaps in a monastery or perhaps on a golf course. They find the church to be discouraging: too many problems, too many hypocrites. Does the Bible give any clear evidence that walking with God depends on getting involved with a group of believers? Let me give you two indications:

A. The church is the primary place to grow in Christ. We need the input, challenge, and guidance of others to grow. Here's the picture:

> but, speaking the truth in love, may grow up in all things
> into Him who is the head -- Christ -- from whom the whole
> body, joined and knit together by what every joint supplies,
> according to the effective working by which every part
> does its share, causes growth of the body for the edifying
> of itself in love (Ephesians 4:15-16).

The word "causes" is important. Notice what edifies and generates growth in the body. It's when the whole body gets "joined and knit together" as each "joint" or each "part" "does its share." This is a God-defined picture of *how to grow in Christ* – talking truth with other believers in order to contribute to their growth. It's like the oft-repeated adage: "if you want to learn the material well, teach it to someone else;" "if you want to get out of depression, encourage someone else who is depressed;" "if you want to get your barn built help someone else build theirs." The repetition of "someone else" is important.

God uses other believers to help rescue us from our self-centeredness. Initially we tend to view our relationship with God in a private, individualistic way: "I'm walking with God through circumstances and I'm working on His projects for me." That's good. But the fact that we have been placed in a body with many members adds a new feature: *"it's not just about me."* That's the way the apostle Paul talks:

> For as we have many members in one body, but all the members do not have the same function, so we, being many, are one body in Christ, and individually members of one another. Having then gifts differing according to the grace that is given to us, let us use them: if prophecy, let us prophesy in proportion to our faith; or ministry, let us use it in our ministering; he who teaches, in teaching; he who exhorts, in exhortation; he who gives, with liberality; he who leads, with diligence; he who shows mercy, with cheerfulness (Romans 12:4-8).

We can learn from the parallels between our physical bodies and Christ's body. We are "in one body" with "many members." That means that we are "members of one another," we belong to one another. He assumes that we have "gifts" that the body needs, but that they won't bless the body until we "use them." In our physical body all the cells are integrated and function for the benefit of others. Each cell needs other cells to live and help it accomplish its tasks. No cell can strike out on its own and stay alive. It's either a part of the body or it's dead. A beautiful blue eye by itself, sitting on the floor and looking around, is meaningless and soon disappears.

Thus, the directions in this passage encourage us to give our best to contribute our spiritual gift for the benefit of others. The one who leads should do it with "diligence." He should go after it with all his heart. The one who teaches should be the best teacher possible. Why? Because what God is doing on Earth is special. Each part in that project makes a significant contribution. We are not just sitting around waiting for the Rapture. We are growing a body, a temple where God lives, a bride for our Lord! We only get one shot at this. Let's make it our best shot!

The church is an absolutely unique creation. It's developing God's future leaders. When you think about it, virtually the only place on Earth where genuine leaders are trained is in the church. Colleges train leaders that do it for the money, or do it by lording it over others (Mark 10:42). God trains leaders as volunteers who lead by example people that are more like sheep (1 Peter 5:3). Those they lead give very little, if any, appreciation or positive feedback. Yet they keep serving, willingly. Ask Moses what it was like to lead his people in the wilderness. That was leadership. Do colleges teach that kind of selfless service? If they tried, probably few would take the course.

Prophecy, ministry, teaching, exhortation, giving, leading, showing mercy, are all developed more successfully in a church setting than probably anywhere else. The point is that God is doing something on Earth today that is amazing! And He is doing it in *your church*. Are you a part of it?

Some people think that other cells in their body, other members in their church, seem weak, immature and not really worth their best effort. "They are all children or old people." But God says that those insignificant church members are important because He has given greater honor to the individual who seems to lack honor (1 Corinthians 12:24). Investing your best efforts for their benefit is a matter of faith. God says it's worth it even though it doesn't appear that way. Isn't that what the Good Samaritan did (Luke 10:25-37), and Christ Himself? (Ephesians 5:2).

For an example of how it should work, think about the events that took place when the early church began. Without a book of instructions on how to start a church, without any models, here's what happened to this huge group of people who trusted in Christ on the day of Pentecost:

> Then those who gladly received his word were baptized; and that day about three thousand souls were added to them. And they continued steadfastly in the apostles' doctrine and fellowship, in the breaking of bread, and in prayers. Then fear came upon every soul, and many wonders and signs were done through the apostles. Now all who believed were together, and had all things in common, and sold their possessions and goods, and divided them among all, as anyone had need. So continuing daily with one accord in the temple, and breaking bread from house to house, they ate their food with gladness and simplicity of heart, praising God and having favor with all the people. And the Lord added to the church daily those who were being saved (Acts 2:41-47).

It's a picture of three thousand children in a giant family. "All who believed were together." They studied together, ate together, sang together, worshiped God together, helped each other with individual needs. Observe that people were not living "solos" where they went off to their golf course to be alone with God. It was more like a "duet" as each lived his or her life with Christ Himself (Galatians 2:20). Even more than that it was a choir, where each lived and sang in the middle of a worshiping group (Romans 15:8-14)! Does Acts 2:41-47 picture the way you live – in the middle of a group that is eating, singing, studying, worshiping God together?

B. We walk with Christ as we make His priority our priority. Faith says, "Here's where God says the action is; let's get involved." How? It's more than filling out a new member form and signing up in your local church. Paul discusses the way into the project with these words:

> I beseech you therefore, brethren, by the mercies of God, that you present your bodies a living sacrifice, holy, acceptable to God, which is your reasonable service. And do not be conformed to this world, but be transformed by the renewing of your mind, that you may prove what is that good and acceptable and perfect will of God. For I say, through the grace given to me, to everyone who is among you, not to think of himself more highly than he ought to think, but to think soberly, as God has dealt to each one a measure of faith (Romans 12:1-3).

Each of these verses makes an important point. First, *you will never be of "reasonable service" to God until you present your body to Him as a living sacrifice.* Nothing happens until we say "no" to our own ambitions and lay ourselves on His altar. We are walking with One who died on a cross! So don't expect that serving Him will bring you anything different. It all starts when we become a *living sacrifice.*

The second verse says, *you will never know the will of God until you attack the old worldly thinking that runs your operating system.* Living as a sacrifice requires a whole new way of thinking, a paradigm shift. That takes a renewal of your *mind.* The "world" represents our old way of thinking and living, which based everything on what we saw and wanted (like refusing to invest time or energy in anyone that didn't look like they could pay us back). God's perspective lives for the benefit of others, like Christ did. The renewal comes from His Word, as we set our minds on things above (Colossians 3:1-2).

Verse 3 says, *you will never walk with God in serving others until you think soberly about yourself.* The major roadblock is pride. Sin has made us so nearsighted that we can't see beyond ourselves. Thinking "soberly" means "to be in one's right mind" as if pride is being out of one's right mind. Kenneth Wuest calls it a "species of insanity."[69] Contributing to family life depends on getting rescued from self-centeredness.

These three verses tell us that walking with God's family begins when, (a) by faith we present our bodies to Him as a living sacrifice; (b) by faith we get the old way of thinking out of our system, and (c) by faith we view ourselves honestly instead of continuing to live in swelled-head-edness. That's where living-in-the-family starts.

Mildred Wynkoop summarizes the crucial nature of this section:

> Paul's exhortation in Rom. 12:1-2 . . . is not then an added "upper story" to justification, nor a Christian alternative to higher or lower levels of grace, nor a luxury enjoyed by the excessively devoted and almost fanatical fringe enthusiast. It is, rather, the theological point of his whole argument. The whole-body presentation is not the maximum Christian attainment but the minimal Christian commitment. As the Roman letter proceeds, it is seen that all of Christian living, with all its problems and vicissitudes, lies beyond this particular point.[70]

It was John the beloved disciple who said, "Beloved, if God so loved us, we also ought to love one another" (1 John 4:11). You would expect the verse to read, "if God so loved us, we ought to love God." But John understands that our love for God is primarily expressed by loving others. When we assure God of our love for Him, He responds by reading how much we love our brothers and sisters: "If anyone says, 'I love God,' and hates his brother, he is a liar; for he who does not love his brother whom he has seen cannot love God whom he has not seen" (1 John 4:20). It doesn't matter how many times he sings "Oh How I Love Jesus." The truth is in the church and his relationship with those who are less significant.

IV. We walk with God in our weaknesses

As we said back in the first section, "circumstances invite our participation." The problem is that obedience to Christ's commands is sometimes a mission impossible. The commands are beyond our abilities. "Pray without ceasing" may border the impossible, but "love one another as I have loved you" (John 13:34) is clearly out of sight. So in order to walk with Christ we need to wake up to our *inabilities* and understanding what we *can't do*. Then we need to realize what we *can do* about those inabilities.

The big key is that *we can't do it alone*, any more than we can have children alone. There was only one virgin birth. If the Christian life is to ever be lived on Earth by faith the first requirement is for us to realize that walking with God is a duet, not a solo, *and to make the duet happen.* The truth is that *we either get God involved or we don't live the Christian life.* We may live a good life or a moral life but it won't be the Christian life until Christ is living it in us (Galatians 2:20).

What's involved in making your life a duet? It looks like God is willing, so what's the problem? I see three key issues:

A. Step # 1 – realizing that certain of Christ's commands are impossible. We're walking according to God's directions, not ours. Think of Noah getting the ark contract in Genesis 6:14-16. Perhaps Noah's response was, "why an ark?" "Can't I just preach, or conduct prayer meetings, or start churches?" It wasn't only the size or complexity that was daunting, it was the time. Can you imagine working on a project for eighty years? Couldn't God choose a more efficient way for him to employ his time?

For years I would begin the semester of a college class by reading the important points of the syllabus and then adding this command which wasn't in the syllabus: "Each student in this class is to learn the names of all others in the class."

In a class of eight or ten students, the reaction was mild, but when the class contained thirty or forty students there was usually a pause after the announcement and then the conversation went something like this: (a) "Everybody's name?" My answer: "Yes." (b) "First and last name?" My answer: "Yes." (c) "Spelled correctly?" My answer: "Yes."

After I announced my yes answers there was usually class silence as students processed the scope of the project. Then further questions arose like, "May we borrow your class list?" to which I answered "No." Then class brainstorming began: "Let's pass around a sheet of paper so everyone can spell out their name;" "Let's sit in the same location every day so we can connect names with seats."

I think a similar process took place with Noah's contract: "All of three hundred cubits long?" "Yes." "Three separate floors?" "Yes." "All the animals?" "Yes." "Isn't this larger and more complicated than any technology available today?" "Yes."

It's so easy to gloss over Christ's commands with the thought, "He wants us to be as good as we can be." We assuage our consciences with the thought that we are going to be better; in fact we are going to be our best little selves!

But is our "best selves" what Jesus had in mind when He commanded, "Love your enemies?" (Matthew 5:44; Luke 6:27). Our internal translator may read that command as "Hate them less," or "See if you can improve in this field," but was that the intent of the command?

The directions are to "Walk in love, as Christ also has loved us and given Himself for us, an offering and a sacrifice to God for a sweet-smelling aroma" (Ephesians 5:2). How does God expect our human love to replicate Christ's love? Does that mean dying for someone? Isn't the command impossible?

Couple that with the fact that Christ said, "let love be without hypocrisy" (Romans 12:9). Match My example, as the prime picture of *agape* love. He died for a world of people who were His enemies as they shook their little fists in His face and blasphemed His name (Romans 5:8; Ephesians 5:2). That's the only way you and I have been rescued. We were those little fist-shakers, that is, until God's love opened our eyes to the awesome brilliance of His glory. He actually *loved us!* There's the demonstration with all its blood and human body parts at the cross of Christ. And He still loves us today as His children, like we saw with the Prodigal son.

We may not even know how to love without hypocrisy because we've faked it so often. I think most of us have had the experience of faking love. Remember when your mother said, "now I want you to be nice to your Aunt Matilda. She may be a little battleaxe but I want you to act nice!" What was mom doing but asking us to fake it. And we did. Or we didn't. Whichever, it was a lesson in acting.

But Christ genuinely loved His worst enemies by treating them as His best friends (Romans 5:7-8), by dying to pay their debt. Once we understand the scope of this command to love as Christ loved, we respond like my students in class with, "That's impossible." "Does God actually expect me to love *that way?*" "How will that ever happen?" The truth is that, yes, God wants us to display His love through us. And the place to start is with our actual enemies.

When someone goes through life thinking that he has obeyed the command to love by hating his enemy less or perhaps by having a better feeling toward him, that person has never understood the impossibility of the command, the scope of the project, and how much help he needs. Only when someone says, "No, that's beyond impossible, that's off the charts in my book," does he or she see the project in the right light. That's what brings them to Noah's state of mind in Genesis 6:14-16.

The only way to understand what it means to walk with God is to meditate on His commands. Meditate, for example, on 1 Corinthians 13:1-7. When you actually hear what it's saying it puts you in a quandary. You realize that *you may never have correctly obeyed the command to love.* And you realize that you may never be able to, at least not without outside help.

B. Step # 2 – committing one's self to obey an impossible command. In spite of the fact that the command seems out of reach, faith begins when we buy into God's direction. We say, "Yes it's impossible for me to love as Christ loved, but that's the project You have for me and by faith I want to do it with all my heart." After that you can say, "So help me God." Nothing happens until we commit ourselves to take His yoke by obeying His specific command.

Noah probably asked and answered the commitment question every day: "The boat again? I hardly got anything done yesterday. The job is impossible." And Satan probably supplied many excuses to do other things. But when Noah said "yes" and strapped on his tool belt, God gave him whatever he needed to accomplish the day's tasks.

God supplies the grace when we commit to the command. You get started, perhaps by saying, "I sent a note today to my enemy inviting him to lunch at a nice restaurant." "I joined a church." "I started attending a small group Bible study." You have to take Christ's yoke with your own hands and obey (Matthew 11:29). This is not "Let go and let God." You "Take hold of the yoke." And you take it by faith in spite of the fact that you know the job is beyond your abilities.

Think of Abraham. God commanded him to offer his son as a burnt offering (Genesis 22:2). When did God supply the grace he needed to make that offering? Abraham knew it was impossible for him to sacrifice the promised lad he had waited twenty-five years to receive. I'm sure he was telling God as they traveled, "I can't do this; I can't give up my only son. Why would You ask me for this?" Yet he kept walking all the time toward the mountain.

Only after he had traveled for three days and tied Isaac down on the altar, was there an announcement from Heaven that God had provided the sacrifice! Why wasn't the ram delivered to Abraham's tent before he left? Why did God wait for three days? Why put Abraham through such stress? Do you see the answer? Grace was supplied as the command was obeyed *by faith.*

C. Step # 3 – persisting in the request for God's help. It's not only committing ourselves to obey a command that looks impossible but also understanding *what we can do about it.* God encourages to pray boldly:

"Let us therefore come boldly to the throne of grace, that we may obtain mercy and find grace to help in time of need" (Hebrews 4:16). Do you see the word "obtain?" Prayer *obtains mercy and grace.*

Sometimes our requests are granted instantly, sometimes it doesn't look like they will ever be answered. In every situation the directions are, "Ask with boldness and don't quit." Jesus gave a parable to this point:

> Then He spoke a parable to them, that men always ought to pray and not lose heart, saying: "There was in a certain city a judge who did not fear God nor regard man. Now there was a widow in that city; and she came to him, saying, 'Get justice for me from my adversary.' And he would not for a while; but afterward he said within himself, 'Though I do not fear God nor regard man, yet because this widow troubles me I will avenge her, lest by her continual coming she weary me.' Then the Lord said, 'Hear what the unjust judge said. And shall God not avenge His own elect who cry out day and night to Him, though He bears long with them? I tell you that He will avenge them speedily. Nevertheless, when the Son of Man comes, will He really find faith on the earth?'" (Luke 18:1-8).

Observe how this parable fits walking with God:

(a) "always ought." Faith must pray, because it realizes that in some way the task is going to have to be accomplished by God. The fact that the woman was a widow suggests the hopelessness of her task. She had no chance of getting justice from her adversary by herself. The one slim possibility was a judge in the city, but he didn't look promising. "Always ought" prayer is based on the impossibility of the assignment.

(b) he "did not fear God nor regard man." Why would Jesus risk comparing God the Father with someone who didn't fear God or care about humans? Wasn't that dangerous to parallel the One who is love with a man who couldn't give a rip about anyone? There was probably little risk because Jesus had heard His disciples pray and knew they prayed as if God wasn't really interested in their requests. Have you ever thought that God might not really be listening to your requests?

(c) "he would not." What did he care about her adversary? It wasn't his problem. He saw no need to do anything, "for a while." Observe the point Jesus is making: even if God were this way (and He definitely is not according to 18:7-8), there would still be no excuse for lack of results. The unjust judge, who really didn't care, actually answered the woman's request!

(d) "men always ought to pray and not lose heart." This woman would not stop! Jesus' point is, don't quit praying because what you need only comes by prayer. Like the woman, you can't supply it, and no one else can either. You actually have no other place to go! Even though it may not initially look hopeful God has promised to answer our requests. In addition, even though God's "own elect" cry "day and night" and can't seem to get His attention, "He will avenge them speedily!"

(e) the ultimate question of the parable is, "will the Son of Man actually find faith on the earth?" Prayer is a faith issue, and one's faith displays itself by persistently praying even though the situation looks unpromising. The fact that God's elect are "crying out day and night" to Him, that He often "bears long with them" pictures walking with Christ.

God delays His answers to encourage our trust in Him to grow. Of course He will answer! And His answer will be perfectly timed! We sort of think it should be the opposite. When someone receives a quick answer to prayer, we think, "that person really knows how to pray because they get answers." Conversely, people who pray and pray without receiving an answer simply don't know how to pray. Not so according to this parable. Instead, Jesus pronounces blessing on those who persist in prayer even though it looks like the heavens are being ruled by an unjust judge!

(f) Observe what the widow could do and could not do. She could not avenge herself of her enemy, but she could bug the judge! The judge had to do the avenging. Against all appearances she believed that he was her answer! A picture of walking with Christ.

Isn't that the message of Hebrews 11? How many times did Noah take the same position as this widow in the eighty plus years he was building the ark? He probably had hundreds of requests that were answered with "he would not for a while." Abraham actually died in faith without receiving what he requested even though God had promised it (11:13)! How often had he prayed like this widow?

(g) Christ doesn't tell us who her adversary was, but think of who your adversary is. How does your prayer parallel her's? My guess is that your adversary is the same one I have, Satan himself, who has your number in certain of his temptations. You've fallen many times. God must rescue you because you can't defeat him. Will you ever get free? Verses 7-8 are the encouraging promises. The point is that faith persists in making requests of God even though there may be few apparent results. And the opposite of faith is to "lose heart," grow weary and quit (Luke 18:1).

So there's my take on how to live the Christian life. It's similar to marriage in that it is walking with God on a daily basis in at least these four areas: (a) into and through difficult circumstances, (b) tackling projects He has diagrammed in His commands, (c) using His gifts to make His people all that He wants them to become, and (d) repeatedly depending on God to avenge you of your adversary. The truth is that every surprising difficulty in your day is a faith opportunity; every one of God's commands is a faith opportunity; those weak and difficult people in your church are faith opportunities; your prayer life is a faith opportunity. Does God want you to live by faith? Say "yes!"

Chapter 14

What happens if a believer refuses to believe?

Salvation by faith doesn't guarantee living by faith

We ended Chapter 11 with the thought that faith is a completed step in the sense that faith doesn't have to continue believing to believe. Also entwined in that concept is the thought that one act of faith doesn't guarantee another act of faith. This means that trusting God's Word for salvation doesn't guarantee that a person will take the next step and trust God again when facing trials.

Each step of faith is a new experience with God. Step one (salvation) makes step two (counting it joy) possible, even expected, but not automatic. It's almost like one has to go back through the entire process of listening, believing, and obeying each time.

That thought leads to this question: "if salvation-faith is a completed step and needs to be repeated in order to grow, what happens to those who stop after the first step?" Those who don't trust God when they get to Marah (Exodus 15)? Or Kadesh (Numbers 14)? Maybe they're fearful, maybe they've had a bad day, maybe they have rebelled or turned away from the Lord. What happens to them? Are genuinely saved people still saved if they disobey, turn away, and sin? What if they intentionally, deliberately sin?

Probably all of us can point to an example of someone who started well in the Christian life and then ran out of gas, or turned away. The problem with such examples is that we don't know whether they were genuinely born again. We don't have access to their hearts.

Are there any examples in Scripture of believers who refused to believe and obey? How about Jonah? Didn't he rebel after years of faithful ministry as a prophet of God (2 Kings 14:25)? What did his rebellion do to his relationship with God? How about David and Bathsheba (2 Samuel 11)? How about Peter at Jesus' trial (Matthew 26:69-75)? Weren't these genuine believers who turned away from God? What happened to them?

Strangely enough, there are people who, like the Israelites at the door of the Promised Land, decide to chuck it all and go back to Egypt. After having been transferred out of the kingdom of darkness into the kingdom of light, they actually want to go back to darkness. After being rescued from the garbage of sin they want to go back to the garbage (2 Peter 2:21). What happens to them?

I. Life is designed to grow

Jesus spoke to Nicodemus about being born again. That's where it all starts, new life, comparable to the arrival of a newborn baby. We rejoice. But do we stop there? No. Look at that baby at one year old and twenty pounds heavier, and walking! Additional rejoicing! And think of that baby at the age of twenty-five, with his own job, and home and family. A similar thing occurs in the spiritual life.

Let's suppose that you're walking down the street and come upon a young mom pushing a stroller which has the cutest little guy in it. You stop and speak goo-goo to him. He smiles and gurgles back. You ask the mother, "how old is he?" Her reply: "today is his birthday; he's seventeen."

Your next question is probably something like, "what's wrong? A seventeen-year-old ought to be out of a stroller and talking. If he can't do that something is *wrong*.

The same is true in the Christian life. We expect a seventeen-year-old believer to have grown. That's why the writer to the Hebrews was disturbed when he realized that his readers' growth didn't match their age: "For though by this time you ought to be teachers, you have need again for someone to teach you the elementary principles of the oracles of God, and you have come to need milk and not solid food" (Hebrews 5:12 NASB).

Why did the writer expect his readers to be teachers "by this time?" Because it's normal. Yet apparently they were still infants, needing to be pushed in strollers and taught their ABCs even though they had had a great start in the Lord (Hebrews 10:32-34). Something had interrupted their growth. The writer identified their problem as, "you have become dull of hearing" (5:11). Even though they had listened, believed and obeyed back when they first came to Christ, they now had quit listening. As a result they weren't getting any "solid food," and they weren't getting their "senses trained to discern good and evil." They were still sucking on a bottle.

Observe that the writer was not asking whether they had really been saved or whether they had lost their salvation. He was sure they were in the family. But the collection of baby buggies in the pews worried him..

Something was wrong because *faith is designed to grow.* That's the normal Christian life.

II. Growth is not smooth and linear

Children have growth spurts and temper tantrums, and periods of rebellion. The ups and downs are all a part of growing up. It's like love. Do we grow in our love for others in a smooth, linear fashion? Aren't there moments when your love is hotter, and other times when it is cooler? Sometimes you can be actually angry or frustrated with someone you love. Is that *real love* or is that *wanna-be-love?* The truth is that real love is fickle. It comes and goes as it grows, with spurts and tantrums.

Several years ago our eight-year-old grandson gave us the rest of his savings for a Christmas gift, seven dollars and ten cents! That was a tear-jerker because that was all the money he had. In his young way he was saying, "I love you." It was a precious statement. The money didn't pay for the things he had broken over the years, but it expressed his heart at the moment. And we treasured it! It was genuine love, even if the next day he disobeyed us.

In a similar way Christians grow up as they take baby steps in love and faith, sometimes warmer, sometimes cooler. Like Peter, they assure Christ that they are willing to die with Him (Matthew 26:33-35) with a genuine, heartfelt commitment only a couple of hours before they deny they even know Him (Matthew 26:69-75).

What happened to Peter at Jesus' trial? Had he lost his faith or his relationship with Christ? No, it was Peter in the baby buggy, refusing to trust God when facing a new challenge. When Peter met his Lord again in John 21:15-17, the question was, "Simon, do you love Me?" It wasn't, "are you still saved?" Or, "did you ever actually get saved?" The trial of denial helped Peter grow in a way that was painfully bumpy. In fact Jesus prayed for this event when He said to Peter, "I have prayed for you, that your faith may not fail; and you, when once you have turned again, strengthen your brothers" (Luke 22:32 NASB).

Think of the fact that it was probably only fifty-three days later that Peter stood up to preach on the day of Pentecost and saw three thousand people turn to Christ! What happened in between? Did Peter get saved? No, the truth of God's Word got to his brain and straightened him out. He began to trust and obey Christ in a new area.

Love and faith work together. Growth in one is usually connected with growth in the other. Marriage is an example. We tend to think that it's mainly an exercise in love, and it is. But it's also an exercise in *faith*. Someone promises, "I will love and cherish you till death do us part." The other person believes that promise enough to respond with, "I do," and they enter a covenant.

The marriage covenant develops into a relationship only as each partner grows in both love and faith. Trust in each other strengthens love for each other. Faith in the other person brings growth in the relationship. It's not necessarily smooth growth right up the ladder, but husbands and wives love each other more as trust develops.

Growth in the Christian life is similar. As we believe our Savior, respond to His commands, and begin to understand the incredible dimensions of His grace, we love Him in new ways. The process fills us with His presence. Paul prayed for this to happen:

> that He would grant you, according to the riches of His glory, to be strengthened with might through His Spirit in the inner man . . . that you . . . may be able to comprehend . . . the love of Christ which passes knowledge; that

you may be filled with all the fullness of God (Ephesians
3:16-19).

What occurs as we "comprehend . . . the love of Christ" is that we
are "filled with all the fullness of God." That's life!

But what if we fail to respond to God's love and our relationship with
Him stalls? That's what happened to Peter at Jesus' trial, or to Israel in
Exodus 15, or to Jonah. And the question Christ could have asked each
of them is the same question He asked Peter, "do you love Me?" Love is
always displayed by trusting and obeying Him.

If you feel that your love for Christ has not always been consistent,
welcome to the family. That's where we all are. Like Peter we promise
faithfulness to Christ just a couple of hours before we fail him. Growth
in the Christian life includes spurts and tantrums.

III. Refusing to trust and obey interrupts a relationship but doesn't end it

Jonah was a veteran prophet of God who prophesied God's blessing
to Israel in spite of her unfaithfulness (2 Kings 14:23-26). But when God
commanded him to go preach the gospel to the city of Nineveh, he
choked and refused to obey. He had believed and obeyed God for some
time, but now he saw no value in preaching to pagans who might somehow repent and escape the judgment of a gracious God (Jonah 4:2).

Was Jonah an unbeliever? Had he become apostate? No, he was a
faithful prophet of God. But God was using his Nineveh experience to
deliver him from his *racism*. He needed to grow, get over his Israeli na-
tionalism, and meet God in a new way, by understanding that ugly Nineveh was as precious in God's sight as beautiful Israel!

At the same time the issue was not simply racism, the issue was faith, trusting God that every nation, people, and tongue is valuable in His sight. Since God is no respecter of persons, Jonah shouldn't be either (James 2:1).

The entire book of Jonah is the story of how God introduced Himself to Jonah. In Chapter 1 Jonah ran from his assignment, and met God the Creator and Ruler of the winds. Jonah had a "God as Creator" clause in his doctrinal statement. He even explained it to the sailors when he said to them, "I am a Hebrew, and I fear the LORD God of heaven who made the sea and the dry land" (1:9). But his actions called his doctrinal statement into question because he was trying to outrun the One "who made the sea and the dry land!"

In Chapter 2 Jonah spent three days in the wild, smelly, frightening belly of a sea monster, meditating on what he had done, searching his heart, and praying. What did he learn? Here's one thing: "Those who cling to worthless idols forfeit the grace that could be theirs" (2:8 NIV). He was example number one of clinging to a worthless idol, a racist idol that proclaimed Israel better than Nineveh, and forfeited the grace that could have been his if he had obeyed the Creator he claimed to believe and serve.

In Chapter 3, he announced God's promised judgment against Nineveh: "yet forty days, and Nineveh shall be overthrown" (3:4). He apparently repeated the same words over and over to different people. At the same time, under his breath he may have been muttering, "and you deserve all the judgment you will get, you *pagans!*" But God gave him the privilege of watching what might have been the greatest evangelistic response the world had ever seen, because the entire city of perhaps a million people believed God and repented (3:5), from the king (3:6-9) down to the least important person.

Then in Chapter 4, Jonah waited outside the city, hoping for God's promised judgment to arrive. When it didn't come, he became suicidal (4:3, 8) and argued, unable or unwilling to believe in God's immense graciousness.

What happened? This was pretty strong rebellion. Jonah had no intention of obeying. If God wanted to run His world with compassion, Jonah wanted out. He had no concern for nasty Gentiles. Did Jonah lose his salvation? Did he lose his prophet's mantle? No, he was a slow learner when it came to God's love for all His creation. He wasn't listening and obeying when it came to Gentile assignments, because *he didn't understand and trust the heart of God.*

At the same time he was learning. God was reasoning with him in the questions He asked (4:4, 9, 10-11). The questions woke him up to the darkness of his heart, his awful pride, with more interest in a gourd than a million people. The questions also awakened him to the amazing, incredible love of God for *him!* The only reason he was still alive and out of the monster's belly was because of God's love. God simply wanted to do the same thing for the Ninevites that He had done for Jonah. That kind of love was foreign to Jonah's experience, even as a prophet of God.

The book of Jonah gives us a diary of the prophet's growth from faith to faith, and from love to love, despite some serious unbelieving blunders. God loved Ninevites. Jonah did not, until the end of the book.

I find the book of Jonah encouraging when I look back at my own unbelieving blunders and disobedience. Why has God been so gracious to me? Why does He forgive me after I make such stupid choices? It's the work of God introducing Himself, in new, amazing ways, as I, sometimes slowly, trust Him and obey.

So many stories in the Bible are descriptions of people taking similar steps of faith. Abraham became the model of faithfulness through many ups and downs in Genesis 12-25. Jacob didn't seem too promising when he began in Genesis 27. Job started well (Job 1:20-22, 2:10), but in his pain cursed the day he was born (Job 3:3-13) and challenged God (9:13-22). The point is that God is so determined for us to grow up that He "scourges" every one of His sons and daughters (Hebrews 12:6) by pushing us into faith challenges, like trials. Even when we want to jump ship and quit the process, He is faithful and continues His marvelous work in us. What incredible mercy! Praise His name!

IV. Even serious disobedience doesn't end one's relationship with God

Jonah's disobedience was serious. Peter's denial of Jesus was serious. But let's talk about a really bad case of rebellion, the nation of Israel at Kadesh. These people were at the door of the Promised Land, even eating its fruit when they attempted to dump Moses and go back to the slavery of Egypt (Numbers 14:3-4). As a result, God judged them with thirty-eight years of desert wandering until all the people involved in the decision died. What happened to them?

A. The first generation of redeemed from Egypt never entered the Promised Land. What did it mean that Israel never entered the Promised Land? How should we interpret that abrupt turn-around? Did those people lose their salvation? Did they ever have real salvation to begin with? There are at least three common ways of looking at this event.

Some think the thirty-eight years of enforced wandering was evidence that Israel *never really believed in the first place*. It was evidence of head knowledge that had never transferred to heart faith. They would view most of the nation (except for Joshua and Caleb) as unbelievers. However, that would suggest that one could "believe" and obey God at the Passover, go through the Red Sea "by faith" (Hebrews 11:29), experience all the instruction at Mt. Sinai, and yet somehow never come to faith in God.

Others believe that Israel *lost her faith*. She obviously had it at the Passover and the Red Sea, but the trials and difficulties of the journey made it difficult for her to continue believing. She gave up at Kadesh and lost her relationship with God, and never entered the Promised Land.

Still others believe the nation was a *mix of believers and unbelievers*. The accounts from Exodus 12 through Numbers 14 seem to suggest that some of the congregation might not have been genuine believers. There was a "mixed multitude" among them, whatever that meant (Exodus 12:38). They could have been Egyptians or other non-Israelis, who had come along for the ride, hoping for a better life. Or it could have been a loud and noisy unbelieving Israeli population. The presence of the "rabble" in Numbers 11:4 seemed to be a pocket of radicals or unbelievers. It's pretty clear, for example, that Korah and 250 other men weren't part of the believing community (Numbers 16). But then what happened to the good group, those who were real believers? They missed the Promised Land. Did they go to Heaven?

Do you see the difficulty? None of these conclusions really seems to fit the facts. There are at least three ways in which the details don't line up:

(1) Genuine believers didn't make it into the Promised Land. It's clear that Moses, and Aaron, and Miriam knew the Lord. And there were seventy elders upon whom the Holy Spirit had come (Numbers 11:16, 24-25). All of these, along with Joshua and Caleb, seemed to be true believers. They had the Holy Spirit. They followed God, but except for the two, they didn't make it in. You would think that these seventy-three went to Heaven, wouldn't you? And there may have been quite a few other genuine believers in the nation that missed the Promised Land. You mean to tell me that people who didn't enter the Promised Land actually went to Heaven? They died in the wilderness but went to Heaven? That has to be true, because Moses and Aaron didn't enter.

(2) Unbelievers made it into the Promised Land. In a similar but opposite way all those who were under twenty years of age when the fatal decision was made (Numbers 14) entered the Promised Land. Were they all believers? Absolutely not. Was Achan a believer? He and his family died for his disobedience (Joshua 7). And by the time of the judges, the people had turned the Land "flowing with milk and honey" into a land flowing with blood and guts. It's rather obvious that those who followed Joshua into the Promised Land weren't much different than their fathers who had followed Moses. Are we to assume that they were in a place that pictured Heaven? No.

(3) Life in the Promised Land didn't picture Heaven. Why would God make the land of Canaan a picture of Heaven when it was full of fighting and victory mixed in with sin and failure? The truth is that Canaan was never intended to picture Heaven just as crossing the Jordan was not intended to signify death. Instead it was a picture of *the rest that comes from victory* rather than our final rest. God spoke of it as a place of rest (Deuteronomy 3:20; 12:10; 25:19; Joshua 1:13, 15; 11:23; 14:15; 21:44; 22:4; 23:1; Judges 3:11). But the rest became a reality only as the people grew in faith by obeying God's directions, as they did when they initially entered under Joshua.

The nation experienced rest under Joshua (Joshua 1:13, 15; 11:23; 14:15; 21:44; 22:4; 23:1). But it was temporary because genuine rest depended on repeated obedience. Thus Joshua was never able to lead the people into real rest (Hebrews 4:8-11). The only One who can do that is Jesus Christ, who supplies rest as we obey and walk with Him (Matthew 11:29-30).

B. Those that missed the Promised Land became *examples.* One of the best ways to read the Old Testament situation is to listen to the interpretation of the New Testament writers, especially Paul and the writer to the Hebrews. Take, for example, Paul's discussion of what happened back in Numbers 14:3-4. He explains that God established a parallel between those events and the Christian life today so that Israel serves as a warning because her trials and difficulties were similar to ours. Let me quote the entire section:

> Do you not know that those who run in a race all run, but only one receives the prize? Run in such a way that you may win. Everyone who competes in the games exercises self-control in all things. They then do it to receive a perishable wreath, but we an imperishable. Therefore I run in such a way, as not without aim; I box in such a way, as not beating the air; but I discipline my body and make it my slave, so that, after I have preached to others, I myself will not be disqualified. For I do not want you to be unaware, brethren, that our fathers were all under the cloud and all passed through the sea; and all were baptized into Moses in the

cloud and in the sea; and all ate the same spiritual food; and all drank the same spiritual drink, for they were drinking from a spiritual rock which followed them; and the rock was Christ. Nevertheless, with most of them God was not well-pleased; for they were laid low in the wilderness. Now these things happened as examples for us, so that we would not crave evil things as they also craved. Do not be idolaters, as some of them were; as it is written, "THE PEOPLE SAT DOWN TO EAT AND DRINK, AND STOOD UP TO PLAY." Nor let us act immorally, as some of them did, and twenty-three thousand fell in one day. Nor let us try the Lord, as some of them did, and were destroyed by the serpents. Nor grumble, as some of them did, and were destroyed by the destroyer. Now these things happened to them as an example, and they were written for our instruction, upon whom the ends of the ages have come. Therefore let him who thinks he stands take heed that he does not fall. No temptation has overtaken you but such as is common to man; and God is faithful, who will not allow you to be tempted beyond what you are able, but with the temptation will provide the way of escape also, so that you will be able to endure it (1Corinthians 9:24-10:13 NASB).

Paul gives us at least four conclusions from this passage.

(1) Israel shows the difference between being *in the race* and *winning the race*. Paul begins this section by making a distinction between joggers and winners (9:24-27). Israel was in the race because she was redeemed from Egypt and on her way to the Promised Land. She was jogging because she wasn't giving the race her highest priority.

Israel's experience stands as a picture for believers today. The fact that they were "*all* under the cloud and *all* passed through the sea, and *all* were baptized into Moses . . . and *all* ate the same spiritual food, and *all* drank the same spiritual drink means that we need to view the nation *collectively, not individually.* Even the rebels among them (Numbers 11:4) had received immeasurable gifts of Grace. The entire nation was under God's guidance (the cloud), God's protection (in the Red Sea), and God's supply (food and drink).

The challenges Israel faced correspond with the challenges a believer faces today. Paul views Israel as one blessed family because they all went through the Red Sea by faith (Hebrews 11:29), they all experienced God's extraordinary grace, and were all living in hope of the Promised Land, a picture of a believer today.

(2) Israel's failure is a warning to New Testament believers. Israel pictures the results of a *fall.* The application of her example is in verses 12-13: "Therefore let him who thinks he stands take heed that he does not fall. No temptation has overtaken you but such as is common to man." Every believer faces temptations. They are "common to man," and left unchecked, they will cause us to fall and lose the race. The temptations that took Israel down were, idolatry (7), immorality (8), testing the Lord (9), and grumbling (10). These sins may not sound bad to those who have grown up in the twenty-first century, but they brought Israel down. "Grumbling?" How many times have we done that?

The *fall* refers to her fatal mistake in Numbers 14:3-4 when she decided to get rid of Moses' leadership, elect her own leaders, and go back to Egypt. As a result, God judged the entire nation, and everyone over twenty years old, except for Joshua and Caleb, died in the wilderness (Numbers 26:64-65). They were "laid low in the wilderness" (10:5). The word, "laid low" means to "overthrow," to "scatter." God scattered their bodies in the wilderness over a period of thirty-eight years.

God's judgment of Israel stands as a lesson for believers today. We can't view our temptations casually. Their effect on us can likewise be deadly. Israel trusted God to get her out of Egypt, but then yielded to temptations rather than obeying God's word.

(3) Israel's example applies to all believers. Twice Paul states that Israel provides *examples for us* (vv. 6, 11). In fact, they were actually written for "our instruction" (11), because the temptations we face are "common" to those Israel faced more than three thousand years ago.

Everyone needs to "take heed" (12). Even the apostle Paul viewed himself as facing the same danger of falling (9:27). His fear appears in the clause, "I myself will not be disqualified." The word, "disqualified," is the word, "disapproved," "rejected," or "failing to meet the test." It's in the context of winning a race. Paul's fear was that through his sin, or failure to keep his body in check, he would become disapproved, judged and not receive the prize, "laid low," in other words, like Israel was in the wilderness. That's why he had to discipline his body and make it his slave. The body makes a wonderful slave but a horrible master. If the apostle Paul was worried about the danger of falling, we should be too.

Here's the point: *Israel is a picture of a believer* and her experience of judgment from God is a warning to Christians today. She trusted and obeyed at the Passover in Egypt (Exodus 12), at the Red Sea (Exodus 14), and in the wilderness she was "holy to the LORD" (Jeremiah 2:2-3). She was devoted. She was betrothed. She loved and followed her Redeemer by faith.

What happened? She didn't grow in faith by trusting God in her new trials. When facing her first temptation in Exodus 15:23-27, she chose to grumble rather than believe. Instead of walking with God by listening and obeying, she walked after her own desires.

After doing this ten times (Numbers 14:22) she arrived at her great opportunity, the entrance to the Promised Land. Did she believe and obey God this time? No she decided she had enough of walking with God and chose to fully turn away. By that decision she became the prime example of the fact that people with great privileges can fall from the heights of their blessings. They can be "laid low in the wilderness" under God's hand of judgment.

(4) Israel would not live by faith. Israel's example was not of losing her salvation but losing her race (1 Corinthians 9:24-27). It was a *race of faith* (Hebrews 12:1-2). The Promised Land represented rest for race winners like Joshua and Caleb (Numbers 14:24, 30; 32:12; Deuteronomy 1:36). It was Israel's *inheritance*. It was automatically hers *if she had simply continued to trust God*. From the beginning, Canaan was the stated goal of her salvation from Egypt (Exodus 3:8).

In what way is Israel's story a warning to you and me? The last two verses point to the danger. When one "thinks he stands" he is probably overconfident in either his ability or performance. That person needs to, "take heed that he does not fall." "Be warned," Paul says that "Israel is God's example to you of the devastating effects of trusting in your own strength rather than running to God for help."

The truth of 1 Corinthians 10:13 is that in every one of our temptations (a) "God is faithful" no matter what the situation looks like; (b) God will automatically limit the temptation so that it won't overwhelm us no matter how impossible it looks; (c) God will automatically provide a way of escape so that we can successfully endure the temptation. Our job is to trust Him by turning to Him for help (James 1:2-5).

V. Serious disobedience doesn't eliminate one's position with God, but limits one's faith possibilities

After Israel's fateful decision to turn away from the Promised Land, she was still the chosen of God. Her failure to enter the Promised Land didn't erase her salvation from Egypt. She had been permanently freed from Egypt through her initial act of faith. *Failure at step two of faith didn't negate step one of faith.* Even though she wanted to go back to Egypt, she couldn't. It was physically impossible without the blessing of God's food, water and guidance.

But some things had changed. All those over the age of twenty were doomed to die in the wilderness, never to enter the Promised Land, except for Joshua and Caleb. The ten spies who brought a negative report died in a plague (Numbers 14:36-38), and those under twenty suffered for their parents' faithlessness (Numbers 14:33) by having to wait for thirty-eight years before they could enter the Land of Promise.

The worst thing they lost was the chance to walk with God by faith as He led them into giant land and conquered the impenetrable cities one by one. The book of Joshua shows us how God had arranged their Promised Land journey from faith to faith, from one impossible situation to another, so that they would come to know and understand their God in different and delightful ways. Israel had enjoyed the first fourteen months of fellowship with her God (Exodus 12 through Numbers 13), but now had dropped out of God's blessing plan.

She still had the presence of God in the pillar of cloud by day and fire by night. She still had the priesthood, the tabernacle, the sacrificial system. She still enjoyed the manna supply every day, and the protection of God, even during thirty-eight years of wandering.

But there were certain things Israel could have done *the day before* Numbers 14:3-4 that she couldn't do *the day after*. The day before she could have obeyed by stepping out in obedient faith to the Promised Land. But the day after God judged her, Israel's "new" confident desire to "obey" and go into the Land was *disobedience* rather than faith (Numbers 14:39-45). The door to Canaan was now closed.

What remained was a more limited slate of possibilities. Individuals could trust God for their daily needs, trust Him for wisdom, strength, and ability to remain content, but their overall purpose for exiting Egypt fourteen months earlier was no longer on the table. It was replaced with years of hot days, cold nights, sand, and sad memories of what they could have had. Included on Israel's resume was now the fact that she was to be an example of God's *judgment* as well as God's blessing.

When a person rebels enough to come under God's judgment, there are no revealed rules as to what will happen. Samson lost his eyes. David experienced the death of his son among other things after his sin with Bathsheba. Solomon experienced the loss of his kingdom (1 Kings 11:11). Ananias and Sapphira experienced immediate death (Acts 5:5, 10). God dealt with each situation individually. A person can't say, "I'm going to refuse to trust God, and if it doesn't work out, I'll choose God's judgment option number two." We can't predict how God will respond. As someone has said, "you can choose your actions, but you can't choose their consequences."

The bottom line is that the nation of Israel did not lose her salvation pictured by her exodus from Egypt. That was not the issue. What she lost was *her inheritance,* which included the loss of blessings, the loss of watching God perform miracles for her in conquering giant land. That was the inheritance her salvation had provided. She had been saved from

Egypt *in order to be brought into the Promised Land* (Exodus 3:8). But except for Joshua and Caleb, that option disappeared in her rebellion.

She had become like her uncle Esau, who had an inheritance as Isaac's firstborn. But in a fit of hunger, he sold it to Jacob for a bowl of soup (Genesis 25:31-33; Hebrews 12:15-17). He was still Isaac's son, but lost his birthright privilege, even though he tearfully tried to get it back (Hebrews 12:17).

This discussion on Israel's sin helps answer our original question, "can genuine believers quit believing?" The answer is clearly, "yes." What happens to those who refuse to believe God when facing new challenges of faith? What happens if they decide to throw it all away?" God judges them, but that judgment does not erase their position in the family of God. Israel refused to believe, came under the judgment of God, lost the Promised Land, and became an example to us of "choices-not-to-repeat." Yet God was gracious to her as she wandered for forty years and then took her children into the Land.

Can you relate to Israel? Have you grown in Christ by fits and spurts? Be encouraged because your God is amazing. "Oh, the depth of the riches both of the wisdom and knowledge of God! How unsearchable are His judgments and unfathomable His ways!" (Romans 11:33 NASB). And be warned that it isn't a pretty sight when a believer turns away.

Chapter 15

Faith repeated leads to faithfulness

God wants us to develop faithfulness. That may sound like a spiritual statement, but the truth is that the entire world is looking for faithfulness. That's why we look for guarantees that promise reliability. One of the things that propelled the Korean auto maker, Hyundai's rise to fame in 2009 was their offering of a ten-year, one hundred-thousand-mile warranty, which promised, "these cars will be faithful."

Everyone knows what faithfulness is. It's the top rung of life's ladder; it's the quality we are looking for in everybody and everything else. It's the equipment that always works, the systems that always function, from our eyesight to our digestion to our alarm clock. It's friends that are predictable. It's a faithful spouse in marriage. It's a rock-solid, honest business partner.

But where does faithfulness develop? Is it offered as a course in college? Do you get it as you read more books? Why are smarter people not necessarily more faithful? One of God's goals for us is that we become faithful: "Moreover it is required in stewards that one be found faithful" (1 Corinthians 4:2). *How God trains us in faithfulness* is the subject of this chapter.

I. Faithfulness begins with God

He is THE FAITHFUL ONE. That's the only reason we can live on Earth. The sun, the moon, the stars, the seasons, the balance of life in nature and many thousands of other things operate so faithfully that we can enjoy life down here. Imagine if the balance of oxygen and nitrogen in the air we breathed changed and we began gasping for oxygen and suffered from nitrogen poisoning. Imagine if the sun came up late or began wearing down. What we all enjoy about God is His absolute, complete, full faithfulness.

That's one of the oft-repeated descriptions of our God: "Through the LORD's mercies we are not consumed, Because His compassions fail not. His compassions are new every morning; Great is Your faithfulness" (Lamentations 3:22-23). They do not and will not fail. They are fresh every morning. It doesn't matter who you are or what you have done; God's compassions toward you do not change!

That's why Peter could say: "Therefore, those also who suffer according to the will of God shall entrust their souls to a faithful Creator in doing what is right" (1 Peter 4:19 NASB). God is faithful even when we aren't: "If we are faithless, He remains faithful, for He cannot deny Himself" (2 Timothy 2:13 NASB). It's part of His nature.

We sing the song, "Oh to be like Thee." We talk about becoming "More like the Master." Becoming more like God means becoming faithful. He actually wants us to share in His divine nature (2 Peter 1:4), to become transformed into His image (2 Corinthians 3:18), to become sharers of Christ (Hebrews 3:6, 14). These statements in Hebrews are important because Christ is described as "faithful" (3:2).

In fact all through the Bible, as in life, we find this emphasis on faithfulness:

> . . . My servant Moses, He is faithful in all My house"
> (Numbers 12:7).

> Then I will raise up for Myself a faithful priest who shall
> do according to what is in My heart and in My mind. I will
> build him a sure house, and he shall walk before My
> anointed forever (1 Samuel 2:35).

> His lord said to him, "Well done, good and faithful servant;
> you were faithful over a few things, I will make you ruler
> over many things. Enter into the joy of your lord" (Matthew 25:21).

II. God has a course of study that trains us in faithfulness

It's like taking Math in college. There's a syllabus, there's an instructor, expectations, exams and homework. This is where the, shall we say, *shock* comes in the Christian life. When a person first comes to Christ and receives salvation, he or she spends quite a bit of time on cloud nine exploring all the freebies that God has prepared for His children. It's exciting to experience the peace and joy and liberty that salvation brings. God has promised to be with us, to give us wisdom and strength, and to answer our prayers. Bible study is so fresh, like reading a love letter. Can you remember those days, the thrill and joy of being a part of the amazing family of God?

But somewhere in our exploration of the grace of God, we come upon a verse that suggests that our lives might not be all freebies and roses. We come to the realization that God has enrolled us in a course entitled, "Faithfulness 101" and the course description states "In this class you will learn about and experience trials." He didn't ask us whether we wanted to take the course. He didn't even require us to read the course description. We just discovered one day that we had been enrolled, the tuition had already been paid, and our first assignment was in our laps. It may have come in the form of an accident that totaled our car, or a leak in the roof that totaled our oak floor, or a statement by a friend that totaled our confidence. And we wondered where the peace and joy went. And we couldn't find cloud nine where we had been living.

In my case, as I am writing this chapter, my wife of fifty years just departed to be with her Lord. I write in tears, asking questions like: "why did she have to go first?" "Is this the best way to do it?" "We had such a good thing going because God has blessed us in so many ways." "We only retired a couple of years ago and have hardly started our retirement plans, and now this happens." "Why?"

I'm sure that many of you have been there. The apostle James, who wrote the earliest book in the New Testament, began his instruction by talking about these shocks that come into the life of every believer. He was writing to young Christians who had suddenly been "scattered" by persecution that came from a radical Jewish leader named Saul (James 1:1 and Acts 8:1-4). These believers were enjoying the freebies, perhaps thinking that God was always going to give them peace and joy and meet their needs, when suddenly they lost their houses and jobs as they became refugees somewhere out of the country. They discovered, perhaps to their dismay, that they had been enrolled in the "Faithfulness 101" course.

James starts out by giving his readers three quick pieces of advice (actually commands): (a) "count it all joy when you fall into various trials" (1:2); (b) "determine to go through them completely to get all the benefit you can from the experience" (1:4); and (c) "ask God for wisdom as to what to do" (1:5).

Those aren't easy commands. James wants us to ignore our feelings and fears, ignore what we think may happen, and choose to look at the event from God's perspective. Why? Why bother? You feel bad; you've lost cloud nine; it doesn't look like the Christian life is going to deliver what it promised because you've tasted some bitter water. Why not quit?

James' answer is, "don't miss God's point; don't miss the reason why you're in this classroom." "The truth is that God wants to bless you with the *crown of life*, the ultimate kind of life that everyone is looking for (1:12). You'll find it *in this course*, as you do the homework assignments!"

The very reason for all the difficulties in our lives is because God seriously wants us to experience life's *best*. He wants to move us from blessing "A" (salvation) to blessing "B" (sanctification). Blessing "A" is free; that's awesome. Blessing "B" may seem to be a little more expensive but we'll find it just as awesome. In fact that's the way Paul describes it: "For you have been given not only the privilege of trusting in Christ but also the privilege of suffering for him" (Philippians 1:29 NLT).

III. Our Instructor plans that all His students make an "A" in the course

Is it possible for unfaithful people like us to even dream of becoming faithful? I don't see any hope in myself. But Jesus Christ is involved in the project. That's the key. How does He lead us to faithfulness? Has

God ever explained the method? Is there any literature? Well in fact there is a course description. The overall curriculum is captured by the writer of Hebrews:

> It is not to angels that he has subjected the world to come, about which we are speaking. But there is a place where someone has testified: "What is man that you are mindful of him, the son of man that you care for him? You made him a little lower than the angels; you crowned him with glory and honor and put everything under his feet." In putting everything under him, God left nothing that is not subject to him. Yet at present we do not see everything subject to him. But we see Jesus, who was made a little lower than the angels, now crowned with glory and honor because he suffered death, so that by the grace of God he might taste death for everyone. In bringing many sons to glory, it was fitting that God, for whom and through whom everything exists, should make the author of their salvation perfect through suffering. Both the one who makes men holy and those who are made holy are of the same family. So Jesus is not ashamed to call them brothers. He says, "I will declare your name to my brothers; in the presence of the congregation I will sing your praises." And again, "I will put my trust in him." And again he says, "Here am I, and the children God has given me." Since the children have flesh and blood, he too shared in their humanity so that by his death he might destroy him who holds the power of death- - that is, the devil-- and free those who all their lives were held in slavery by their fear of death. For surely it is not angels he helps, but Abraham's descendants. For this reason he had to be made like his brothers in every way, in order that he might become a merciful and faithful high

priest in service to God, and that he might make atonement
for the sins of the people. Because he himself suffered
when he was tempted, he is able to help those who are being tempted. Therefore, holy brothers, who share in the
heavenly calling, fix your thoughts on Jesus, the apostle and
high priest whom we confess. He was faithful to the one
who appointed him, just as Moses was faithful in all God's
house (Hebrews 2:5-3:2 NIV 1978).

Notice the components of the class:

(1) God the Father wants the future earth under the control of humans, not angels (2:5-8b). The syllabus could actually say, "after complet-
ing this course you will be able to rule and reign with Christ." That means
that our life challenges down here are actually training exercises to prepare us for life hereafter.

(2) This course was made necessary by Adam and Eve's failure in the
Garden of Eden. They proved unfaithful and their children have not improved much. That's why we presently don't see much success in human
authority. People aren't doing a decent job of ruling themselves, much
less their world (2:7-8).

(3) The hope is in the fact that Christ is at work repairing the ruin
Adam brought about. He died the death that every person in the world
deserved. At the same time, God the Father made Him "perfect" as a
human leader by completely preparing Him to bring many sons into
glory. The Father trained the Son fully through His sufferings (2:9-10).

(4) Part of His training was to face all the challenges we face with the
same human weaknesses and limitations. Christ was so fully human that
He could genuinely call us "brothers," because He experienced complete
human life with all its difficulties (2:11-17).

(5) Christ is fully equipped to meet every one of our needs in life "because he himself suffered when he was tempted." His experiences on Earth prepared Him so that "he is able to help those who are being tempted." As a result He is the official Apostle and High Priest of our Christian life journey and our Instructor in this course of study (2:17-3:1). Our responsibility is to "fix our thoughts" on Him.

(6) And where does this course lead? It's heading for *faithfulness*. Just like the Old Testament leader, Moses, was faithful, so Jesus, our Leader, is faithful and was "made perfect" to prepare Him for our class. The way we develop faithfulness is identical to the way our Leader developed it, down the road of suffering (3:1-2).

This means that the journey is going to be *hard*. If you feel that you are in overwhelming difficulties right now, welcome to the class. You probably had a test yesterday! God describes this class with the word "chastening" (Hebrews 12:5-11), even saying that He "scourges every son whom He receives" (Hebrews 12:6). The Apostle Paul encouraged young believers by saying, "We must through many tribulations enter the kingdom of God" (Acts 14:22). Some people react strongly to the concept of *hard* and try to immediately drop the course with the comment, "not for me." But wait a minute . . .

IV. The fact that the course is *hard* doesn't mean that other course offerings are easier

Israel thought it would be easier to go back to Egypt. They were looking for a bus that went back to Ramsees. Little did they know. How different God's concept of *hard work* or *suffering* is from ours. We might think it means we'll be burned at the stake or shot by a firing squad, or eaten by piranha in the Amazon. But no, suffering is what you and I are going through right now, trials and temptations and relational situations that we don't know how to handle.

Peter helps us see this when he connects the difficulties his readers were experiencing with the word *suffering*:

casting all your care upon Him, for He cares for you. Be sober, be vigilant; because your adversary the devil walks about like a roaring lion, seeking whom he may devour. Resist him, steadfast in the faith, knowing that the same sufferings are experienced by your brotherhood in the world (1 Peter 5:7-9).

Peter's readers had "cares" and were being attacked by a devil who was trying to "devour" them. He said to "resist him," knowing that all believers experience similar "sufferings." Cares, worries, and difficulties from Satan are "sufferings." You don't have to worry about God making your life a horror movie. You don't have to look for extra pain.

But since the course looks difficult, students try to opt out in order to take another course entitled something like "Easy-Breezy 101" which encourages students to create their own syllabus. It's like the bus back to Egypt.

However, drop-outs are usually surprised to find that such a move doesn't rescue them from suffering. They are still enrolled in trials, temptations and attacks from Satan. In addition, the "easier" course doesn't enjoy the Instructor's fellowship, encouragement and tutelage. Students are on their own. Is that better? In no way.

In the book of Numbers Israel didn't like that the syllabus included fighting giants that were ten and eleven-feet tall. What did they achieve in Easy-Breezy 101? Thirty-eight years of going in circles on choice desert sand. What would you rather do, walk with Joshua and watch God take down eleven-foot giants? or live a dead-end life in the sand until you expire? Faithfulness 101 is the way to go! Sure it's hard, but you have help, Almighty help! And He says, "you can make it; just stick with Me; I'll enable you to make an 'A' in this course."

V. The key is *confidence*

The writer to the Hebrews uses the fathers as an example of what not to do. They were the "class drop-out" models, dreaming of a non-existent bus back to Egypt. Their example is inserted right after the writer says *if we hold fast*. Here's the context:

> Therefore, holy brethren, partakers of the heavenly calling, consider the Apostle and High Priest of our confession, Christ Jesus, who was faithful to Him who appointed Him, as Moses also was faithful in all His house. For this One has been counted worthy of more glory than Moses, inasmuch as He who built the house has more honor than the house. For every house is built by someone, but He who built all things is God. And Moses indeed was faithful in all His house as a servant, for a testimony of those things which would be spoken afterward, but Christ as a Son over His own house, *whose house we are if we hold fast the confidence and the rejoicing of the hope firm to the end. Therefore,* as the Holy Spirit says: "Today, if you will hear His voice, Do not harden your hearts as in the rebellion, In the day of trial in the wilderness, Where your fathers tested Me, tried Me, And saw My works forty years (Hebrews 3:1-9 italics added).

The "therefore" in verse 7 follows the "if" clause in verse 6. What does the author mean by "if we hold fast?" *If* suggests that the readers might not hold fast. It's a warning. Hold fast what? *Confidence and rejoicing of the hope firm to the end.* What does that mean?

In v. 1 the writer calls the readers "holy brethren" and "partakers of the heavenly calling" and talks about "our confession." He views them as believers, as *saved!* Now if they are saved, why do they have to "hold fast?" What is conditional? What could be lost through failure to continue *the confidence and the rejoicing of the hope firm to the end?*

The answer is, *what the fathers lost in 3:7-19.* In the last chapter, we mentioned how the Apostle Paul used the fathers' actions at the door of their opportunity as a warning to believers today (1 Corinthians 10:6, 11), even to himself (9:27). They demonstrated the possibility and danger of a fall (10:12), and the possibility and danger of being "disqualified" (9:27).

So what did it mean that the fathers lost the Promised Land? Some would suggest that they lost their salvation. Others would suggest that they never possessed salvation. The problem is verse 1. How does the writer's confidence of salvation in the first verse connect with a warning of possible loss in v. 6? What could they lose now that they were in the family?

That question would be similar to this question: "what was there for the Prodigal Son to do *the day after* he came home, received a robe, ring and shoes and enjoyed the fatted-calf celebration?" Should he be careful with his robe, ring and shoes *lest he lose them?* Or should he be careful to use his robe, ring and shoes wisely *to prove that he genuinely received them?*

Do you see how those thoughts don't really fit the Prodigal's situation? It wasn't that he needed to hold onto his relationship with his father lest he lose it, or to prove that he actually had it. Rather the question for him was, "will you take what you have been given and develop it in such a way that you will run this farm with faithfulness to the eternal joy of your father?" "Will you be faithful in what you have been given?"

The issue in Hebrews is similar. The readers had a great beginning and successfully endured difficult times of persecution (10:32-34). The major question in the book is not "will you protect your robe, ring and shoes so that you can stay in the family and not lose your salvation." Neither is it, "will you protect your robe, ring and shoes to prove that you really are in the family?"

Instead the issue is *faithfulness*. "Will you run your race with endurance?" (12:1-2), "will you refrain from throwing away your confidence which enables you to endure?" (10:35-36), or "will you hold fast the beginning of your confidence firm to the end?" (3:6, 14).

That's the point of the father-failure story (3:7-4:16). The fathers had faith; otherwise they would have still been in Egypt on the other side of the Red Sea (11:29). But when it came to new experiences that presented them with the challenge of believing God and growing in faith, they refused. And they turned away at their big opportunity to enter the Promised Land, petrified by giants because they had lost sight of the power, grace and mercy of their awesome God.

Thus the command in 3:1 is for these believers to "consider the Apostle and High Priest of our confession, Christ Jesus, who was faithful to Him who appointed Him, as Moses also was faithful in all His house." The Greek word for "consider" means to focus one's mind on Christ, to fasten one's mind down in order to observe Him closely. The word is used in Acts 7:31 to picture Moses studying the burning bush. He was amazed at the sight and came closer to examine it. The word is used in James 1:23 to picture a man studying his natural, unpainted, unimproved, early-morning face in a mirror. In a similar way we are to study Christ "who was faithful to Him who appointed Him, as Moses also was faithful in all His house" (3:2).

The *if* clause ("if we hold fast the confidence and the rejoicing of the hope firm to the end") presents the importance of staying in the class. Success in class depends on confidence. It depends on holding fast to the *hope*. Hope, remember, is the end zone in football. Every play in the game is played in hope of the end zone. Hope represents graduation from college, or a grade in the class. Every test you take and paper you write is done in light of the hope ("I am going to make an 'A' in this class). Hope was the Promised Land for the nation of Israel.

That's exactly where the readers were, in the middle of the football game, or just before a mid-term exam in class. It was comparable to Israel in Numbers 1-13. They were leaving Mt. Sinai, heading for the Promised Land with the *hope* in view of conquering the CHAPHJ (that's code for the Canaanites and the Hittites and the Amorites and the Perizzites and the Hivites and the Jebusites – Exodus 3:8).

What did they need to reach the end zone by defeating the CHAPHJ? More men in the military? More equipment? No, what they needed was *confidence to believe God's promise of victory and launch out in faith*. Why did they not enter the Promised Land? Confidence: that's all it was! It had nothing to do with ten-foot giants or impenetrable city walls. It was simply holding on to their confidence.

Football teams talk about "showing up for the game" even though all their players are present. They talk about the "momentum" shifting from one team to the other. It's all confidence language.

Israel was at that stage of faith where they were close but not yet in the end zone. They were in the red zone only nine yards away from the goal. Except that all of a sudden the opposing team now seemed to have 400 pound, ten foot linemen crouched against them. What do the readers need? The same thing the fathers needed; the same thing a student enrolled in a difficult class needs; the same thing all the people listed in Hebrews 11 needed: confidence to take another step of faith, to go into the exam room and start answering questions, or to "count it all joy" when facing an impossible difficulty.

This means that being a *holy brethren* (3:1) is not the end of the story. Life as a believer involves training exercises that bring difficulties and challenges because holy brethren are predestined for holiness and glory (Ephesians 1:4-5). Should we fail in the difficulty, it would not affect our status as "holy brethren," but it would greatly affect the beautiful plan God has to make the holy brethren *faithful.*

The danger is that like Israel, we will throw away our confidence and endurance (Hebrews 10:35-36) and "draw back" (10:38) and try to get out of the class or get out of the game or give up on the challenges God places before us.

But we don't have to! Just because the fathers flunked the course because they quit doesn't mean that the children are destined to be chips off the old blocks. We can endure by studying Jesus and holding fast to our confidence in His Word.

VI. Yes there are those who graduate with an "A"

You may think that the task is impossible: "it's too hard; this Instructor is overbearing; the trials are too difficult; nobody can make it through." The truth is, *everybody can make it through!* All you have to do is hang onto your confidence enough to show up for class and do the homework. The Christian life is not something for spiritual giants, it's the *opposite;* it's for weak people like you and me who will *connect themselves to the Spiritual Giant, Jesus Christ.* He is completely equipped to lead us to success!

Success is defined as graduation. We see it in this passage:

> For they indeed [our earthly fathers] for a few days chastened us as seemed best to them, but He for our profit, that we may be partakers of His holiness. Now no chastening seems to be joyful for the present, but painful; nevertheless, afterward it yields the peaceable fruit of righteousness to those who have been trained by it (Hebrews 12:10-11).

Notice, "afterward." That's graduation. Imagine "partakers of His holiness!" Does that sound impossible? Imagine "the peaceable fruit of righteousness!" Beyond all expectation! Notice who finds these two gems: "those who have been trained by it." It doesn't say "spiritual giants with loads of faith." It's simply those who listen in class and stay up with the homework.

There are several big words that coalesce up here at the top of life's ladder. "Faithfulness" is connected with "holiness" is connected with "righteousness" is connected with "blessing" (James 1:12), and the "crown of life" is connected with "perfect and complete" (James 1:4). This is where the smile of God appears, the *blessing* of the Beatitudes, the "this one will be blessed" of James 1:25.

It's the hope of Hebrews 11. The first two verses say, "Now faith is the assurance of things hoped for, the conviction of things not seen. For by it the men of old gained approval." Then we see a list of people throughout the chapter who "gained approval" from God through faith (Hebrews 11:39-40 NASB), and experienced the smile of God.

The point is that God wants us to gain approval through our faith. That's why Chapter 12 encourages us to "run with endurance the race that is set before us." That's why Chapter 6 encourages us to join those who have inherited the promises by imitating their faith (Hebrews 6:12).

VII. Those who graduate with an "A" do it by repeated responses of faith

Hebrews 12:11 tells us that chastening (that's the faithfulness 101 class) "yields the peaceable fruit of righteousness to those who have been trained by it." What does "to those who have been trained by it" mean? It simply means that they have learned to believe and obey God *again and again.* That's why Hebrews 11 compares it to running a race. A marathon is a repetitive experience, putting one foot in front of another, time and time again. But it's also a repetitive experience of ignoring your body's tiredness and desire to quit. That's what faith is, ignoring the circumstances and your tiredness, to believe God again.

Have you ever been there? Taking one more simple step of faith? Forgiving your neighbor one more time? Receiving back your rebellious teen one more time? Trusting God to meet today's need without complaining? That's running the race. That's faith and *patience"* (6:12).

The word, "endurance" or "patience" parallels the concept of "confidence" or "confession" or "hope" that the author of Hebrews mentions several times (3:6, 14; 4:14; 6:18; 10:23, 25-26). Endurance is simply *trusting God's Word again, obeying God's Word again.* Every day Noah would go back to work believing that rain was coming, even though the possibility may have seemed less and less probable. He ran the race of faith with patience – and won!

VIII. Running a marathon depends on *practice*

In reality the Christian life is often like *training* to run a race. It's like the Olympics. Athletes will train for four years hoping to win a ten-second race in the one-hundred-meter event and receive a gold medal. Faithfulness is not connected with the ten-second run as much as the previous four years of training.

In a similar way we train: "everyone who competes in the games exercises self-control in all things. They then do it to receive a perishable wreath, but we an imperishable" (1 Corinthians 9:25 NASB). "Self-control" describes what we do in practice. Success is measured in our training.

Successful athletes usually love practice. *It's almost as if the tournament race is not the important thing.* The race is only the *fruit* of the important thing. The important thing happened day after day, hour after hot hour, aching knee and blistered toe after aching knee and blistered toe. Practice was where the faithfulness came in.

Suppose we took someone who had grown up as a couch potato and somehow got him into the Marine Corps Marathon, a twenty-six mile race through Washington, DC. His muscles have atrophied, he is full of Burger King french fries, but he has watched marathon runners on YouTube. He starts running at 8 a.m. on a Sunday at Arlington Cemetery.

What do you think our boy needs? He's got the gear on, the nice air ride tennis shoes, sharp looking running shorts and the tee shirt. He even has a number on his back. He's official. What else does he need?

Well he probably could take some encouragement. So we could station different people every five feet on both sides of the road, shouting encouraging words. And he probably would need water fairly quickly, so we would have people stationed with gallon jugs every 100 yards.

And suppose we did everything to help him make it through the 26 miles. What would happen? There's no hope. He's never done it before; he's never practiced; he's never gotten off the couch. His heart rate has never been elevated. He needs more than encouragement and water. He would have a heart attack before he finished. We could say to him, "Stick it out; don't quit; victory depends on just putting one foot in front of the other." The problem is that victory also depends on practice, being toughened up, and getting experience in the running environment.

Can you connect this with your life? A big trial comes into your life, and you need to pray. Have you practiced? Do you feel comfortable enough in God's presence to say anything more than the "now I lay me down to sleep" prayer or the "bless me and everyone else" prayer? How do you get ready for the big trial? Practice drawing near by drawing near.

Take another scenario. A big problem comes up. You need someone's help. Do you have anyone you can turn to? Is there anyone you have practiced being honest with? Someone to whom you have already shared what's actually going on in your life?

Here's the point – people who aren't in training don't do very well in a race. They can talk about it, sing about it, they can even really want it, but to do it, they need to get up and *practice*. They need to *deny* themselves. They need to *take up the cross* and do something hard. Read the Bible, seriously, not just casually. Memorize a chapter. Read a theology book. Join a prayer meeting, a small group. Take a college credit course in Old Testament Survey.

God wants to teach us to *love practice*. To run effectively in an Ironman race, one has to become a training junkie. As I write this paragraph, Noel Mulkey, who is training for the Ironman World Championship in Hawaii later in 2021, said, "I look forward to waking up every day and training."[71] What a great picture of the Christian life! God wants us in training, learning, practicing, taking on challenges. Memorizing your Bible is training, prayer is training, using your spiritual gift to help others is training, giving away a significant amount of your money is training. God wants us to *love it, do it with joy, full of confidence*. That's faithfulness.

And that's the goal of it all, for unfaithful sinners to become like their God! To become "partakers of the divine nature" (2 Peter 1:4), "partakers of His holiness" (Hebrews 12:10) and enjoy the "peaceable fruit of righteousness" (Hebrews 12:11) and the "crown of life" (James 1:12). You don't think it can happen to you? God does! He's got you enrolled in the course! Go after that privilege with all your heart. And, as Jesus said, "Rejoice and be exceedingly glad, for great is your reward in heaven!" (Matthew 5:12).

Chapter 16

The majestic glory of God's plan of faith

The *sine qua non* (the must have) of our relationship with God is faith. Without faith it is impossible to please Him. This means that everything in our spiritual lives begins and continues by faith. Our relationship with God rises or falls on the basis of our trust in Him. Thus understanding what that responsibility is, and understanding what faith is, is of great importance. Let me summarize what we have claimed or discussed in this brief discourse:

1. The unity of the act – Faith is always listening, believing and obeying

It's one act. Believing depends on listening. You can't believe in a promise you haven't heard. Calling on the name of the Lord depends on believing that His promise of salvation is true. Even though faith has three aspects, they are one act, one event. When someone says to you, "loan me $100 and I will pay you back tomorrow," the fact that you hand over the money says that you have gone through these three aspects. You wouldn't have handed her the money if you didn't hear what was asked or didn't believe what was promised. In a similar way we walk with Christ by listening to Him, believing His Word, and obeying it in every situation that we find ourselves.

We can know we are saved by this one act of "calling on the name of the Lord." Jesus promised that anyone who hears His word and believes on the One who sent Him *has* eternal life and *will not come* into condemnation, but already *has passed from death to life* (John 5:24). It's true that a changed life gives evidence of the presence of the Holy Spirit. It's true that we should expect a new believer to live differently, but like the Philippian jailer, one can believe on the Lord Jesus Christ, know he is saved, and be baptized all in one night (Acts 16:25-34) –and have an amazing story to tell all the prisoners the next day at work!

The fact that there are three parts in the process of faith does not deny the truth that it is one act. Any other step by itself, like believing without obeying, may not be real faith.

The three-step act is often compacted into the word, "obey." "By faith Abraham obeyed when he was called to go out to the place which he would receive as an inheritance" (Hebrews 11:8). "By faith Abraham, when he was tested, offered up Isaac" (Hebrews 11:17). "By faith Moses, when he became of age, refused to be called the son of Pharaoh's daughter" (Heb. 11:24). "By faith he forsook Egypt" (Heb. 11:27). "By faith he kept the Passover and the sprinkling of blood" (Heb. 11:28). In each situation faith was exact obedience to what God commanded.

The same is true in living by faith: "My brethren, count it all joy when you fall into various trials" (James 1:2). Counting it joy is an act of faith. It shows that the person has heard God's command, believed it and is obeying.

2. The object of the act – Faith responds to the Word of Christ

Everyone has faith of some sort, but it is most often placed in the wrong thing or person. People believe themselves. They believe the testimonies of their peers. They believe the lie of Satan or his false prophets. Each time the object of their faith is revealed by the word they obey. When they follow their rationalizations, or trust their peers, or swallow the lie of the false prophets, it may be some kind of "faith" at work, but it's worthless faith because it's placed in the wrong person. Saving faith comes from listening to the "word of Christ" (Rom. 10:17 NASB). "Just have faith" is a ridiculous bumper sticker because it doesn't point to an object. Just have faith in whom? Or what?

Jeremiah found his people to be believers – in the wrong object:

> Behold, you are trusting in deceptive words to no avail (7:8 NASB).

> "And now, because you have done all these things," declares the LORD, "and I spoke to you, rising up early and speaking, but you did not hear, and I called you but you did not answer, therefore, I will do to the house which is called by My name, in which you trust, and to the place which I gave you and your fathers, as I did to Shiloh. I will cast you out of My sight, as I have cast out all your brothers, all the offspring of Ephraim" (7:13-15 NASB).

Much faith. Wrong object.

3. The energy of the act – Faith is active, not passive

The notion that faith is a gift encourages a person to passively wait for it or to ponder how to get God to give it to us. The directions in Scripture go in the opposite direction, encouraging us to engage our will to trust and obey. Lack of faith is normally not spoken of as the lack of a gift, but the lack of a *will to believe*. The command is to *believe*, and the promise is that *whoever* believes will receive eternal life (John 3:16, 18). The condemnation in John 3:18 comes, not simply because people are sinners, nor that they have yet to receive a gift, but that they haven't *believed*.

Our relationship with God goes no further than our interest and our response. Jesus Christ offers us His presence, His grace, His love, His forgiveness, blessings. But Isaiah 55 says to "come, buy and eat" (55:1). The people who meet God are *those who come*. No others. The word "come" involves energy, movement.

Jesus said, "Come to me, all who labor and are heavy laden, and I will give you rest" (Matt. 11:28). It was an invitation to those who realized the weight of their sin and wanted out. The responsibility was on them to make the first move. When they got up and came, He gave them the gift of rest.

The notion that people can't believe because they are dead in trespasses and sins, is false. Unbelievers believe all kinds of things. Like Adam and Eve (Gen. 3:3-6), or Cain (Gen. 4:6-7), or Israel (Psalm 95:7-11), they can listen and believe Satan as easily as they listen to and believe God. Unbelievers *are* dead in trespasses and sins. They are hopeless and helpless apart from God's grace. But dead people can *listen* (John 5:25) and believe (Romans 10:17).

4. The beginning of the act – the source of faith is listening

Faith always begins with listening to God's Word. His promises are everywhere. Peter claims that God has given "precious and magnificent promises, so that by them you may become partakers of the divine nature, having escaped the corruption that is in the world by lust" (2 Peter 1:4 NASB).

The faith of the woman at the well began with this promise: "if you knew the gift of God, and who it is who says to you, 'Give Me a drink,' you would have asked Him, and He would have given you living water" (John 4:10).

In a similar way all faith begins with hearing a message, even misguided faith: "If you send me $10 seed money, God will bless you 100 fold and turn it into $1000." "You can eat the apple and become like God, knowing good and evil." Even Satan seeks to create faith by getting us to listen to his word.

Because of this fact, one of the most consistently emphasized but under-recognized responsibilities presented in the Bible is the responsibility to listen to God's Word. It's the Great Shema in Deuteronomy 6. It's the often-repeated, "he who has ears to hear, let him hear" of Jesus. It's Paul's announcement to Jewish leaders after they had rejected the gospel: "Therefore let it be known to you that this salvation of God has been sent to the Gentiles; they will also listen" (Acts 28:28 NASB). "So faith comes from hearing, and hearing by the word of Christ" (Romans 10:17 NASB).

Listening is critical, yet it is rarely taught in schools or colleges today. We need to teach it to ourselves and our families. Our relationship with God (and others) begins with (and continues with) listening.

5. The completed nature of the act – Faith obeys at a moment in time

Faith is an act of obedience in a moment of time. Israel believed and obeyed God when they put blood on the doorposts of their houses (Ex. 12:28). They believed God again when they chose to follow Moses into the Red Sea (Heb. 11:29). But they grumbled rather than believing God when they came to Marah (Ex. 15:23-24). They could have believed Him, rejoiced in what they knew about His supply, and watched Him answer their prayers.

The notion that faith has to "continue" to be genuine is misleading. It gives the picture of us "propping it up" or holding on to it long enough for it to become genuine. Some have the idea that faith is a continuous thing that never wavers. That you trust once, and then you never doubt. That those who doubt (or persist in doubt), have lost their faith (or never had it).

But God doesn't intend that we wait until the end of our lives (believing all the time) before we know that we are truly saved by faith. John wrote that we might know (1 John 5:13-14) that we have eternal life. So much in the Christian life depends on the assurance that we *are children of God*. Most of the epistles were written to saints. Not only *were* they saints, but they needed to *know that they were saints*.

The apostle Paul repeatedly addresses his readers as saints, repeatedly assumes that they have been sealed by the Spirit and are in the family of God. Salvation is not a process but an *event*, like birth. Sanctification is a *process* of growth and development.

Romans 1:17 states that the righteousness of God is revealed in us *from faith to faith*. That's the process. "The righteous shall live by faith." Faith repeated is the means of growing in righteousness.

6. The permanency of the act – refusal to believe in a new area doesn't change the position that genuine faith originally brought

When Israel refused to believe and obey God at the waters of Marah (Ex. 15:23-24), she didn't go back to Egypt. She was still rescued from bondage. Esau lost his birthright and couldn't get it back (Hebrews 12:17), but he was still Isaac's son. Israel lost the Promised Land, but they were still the people of God. A believer can come under the chastening, discipline, even judgment of God. God can even take them home early, in order to protect them from being condemned with the unbelieving world (1 Corinthians 11:29-32). Although sin and lack of faith brought the Corinthians under the judgment of God (11:30), it didn't change the original position of sonship to which faith had brought them.

The nation of Israel, in its rebellion and disobedience in refusing to enter the Promised Land is an example to Christians today. Paul argues on one hand in 1 Corinthians 9:24-10:13 that she is an example of losing privileges, opportunities, her inheritance in the Land, while maintaining on the other hand that they were all blessed by the cloud and the Sea and

Moses' baptism, and the spiritual food and drink. They all drank from the spiritual blessings of the Rock, Christ.

Then he says, "no temptation has overtaken you but such as is common to man," implying that what caused Israel to fall is temptation similar to that which we face. He applies this thought to his Christian audience with, "Therefore let him who thinks he stands take heed that he does not fall" (10:12-13 NASB). Israel fell and lost her potential, lost the amazing plans God had laid out for her, but didn't lose her position as the redeemed-from-the-bondage-of-Egypt people.

7. The simplicity of the act – walking by faith is listening to, believing and obeying God in different situations

The word, "walk" is a metaphor for making decisions, choosing what to do. At countless numbers of times in our lives it comes down to, "who are you going to listen to and obey?" Yourself? Your peers? The world? Or God's Word? So often the choices that life presents us are choices of faith.

People often view faith as something needed in big, impossible situations, like trusting God for large amounts of money, or a cancer cure. That concept encourages us to relegate faith to the special times when we need a miracle. But Hebrews 11:6 sounds like God intends faith to be an everyday part of our lives. The fact that we cannot please him apart from faith suggests that every choice we make needs to be a choice of faith.

For example, James 1:2 says: "count it all joy when you fall into various trials." Obedience to that command is an act of faith. In verse 4 he says that we should determine to go through the trial so patience can complete its work. Obedience to that command is an act of faith. In verse 5 he directs us to ask God for wisdom, another act of faith.

Walking by faith is very practical. It's letting God's words guide my choices in life. They tell me to forgive. I forgive by faith. They tell me to speak the truth at all times. I speak truth by faith.

8. The goal of the act – growth, holiness and maturity result from believing and obeying God repeatedly

God's Word is comprehensive. It has promises, commands, and guidance for every situation we face in life. It may take a believer some time before he or she will actually forgive someone who has really hurt them. But when they do forgive by faith because God said to do it, they grow in faith.

Similarly we may hesitate at casting our cares on Christ (1 Peter 5:7), or at praying instead of worrying (Philippians 4:6-7), or at bridling our tongues (James 3). But growth in faith comes as we choose to listen to and obey God's Word. As we do that we run the race of faith (Hebrews 12:1-11) and develop faithfulness.

So there it is; faith is *the reach of an empty hand.* By that reach we become a part of God's amazing GRACE plan. He gives the gifts; He meets the needs and repairs the damage, all in response to people who trust and obey His Word. We should live in total gratitude for the incredible opportunities we have.

I conclude with this beautiful summary of God's grace plan captured in a hymn written by John H. Sammis (1846-1919):

> When we walk with the Lord, in the light of His word
> What a glory He sheds on our way.
> When we do His good will, He abides with us still, and with
> all who will trust and obey.
>
> Trust and obey, for there's no other way, to be happy in
> Jesus, but to trust and obey.
>
> But we never can prove the delights of His love
> Until all on the altar we lay;
> For the favor He shows and the joy He bestows
> Are for them who will trust and obey.
>
> Trust and obey, for there's no other way, to be happy in
> Jesus, but to trust and obey.

Amen!

About the Author

James Samuel Schuppe was born and raised in a Christian family in the Washington area. His father worked for the Post Office Department. He trusted Christ as Savior in 1949 when a neighbor took four or five kids on the block to a meeting he was holding at a church in Washington, DC. He entered the Washington Bible College in 1959 and then the Capital Bible Seminary in 1963, graduating in 1966. He then was offered a full-time position as instructor in Speech at the Washington Bible College for the fall of 1966 and taught there for twenty-three years. In 1984 he entered a PhD program in *Rhetoric and Public Communication* at the University of Maryland and holds a PhD ABD (all but dissertation).

Jim and the former Martha Hearn were married in June 1970 at her father's church in Rossville, Georgia. They have been blessed with six children, fifteen grandchildren, and three great-grandchildren. In 1989 the family moved to Lynchburg, Virginia, where Jim taught at Liberty University for seven years. For a short time he served as interim pastor of Grace Church in Roanoke, Virginia.

The family moved to Bowie, Maryland, in 1996 when he became pastor of Belcroft Bible Church, where he served for sixteen years, retiring in 2012. Martha went to be with her Lord after a very short bout with bone cancer. It was only discovered in December 2020 and was at stage 4 then. She passed away at 7:15 on Sunday morning May 2, 2021 and will be greatly missed. Jim now lives in Shepherdstown, West Virginia, and enjoys country life in "almost heaven." In addition to teaching and preaching, he enjoys family life, music, sports (with specialties in ping-pong and racquetball), carpentry and auto mechanics (Hondas only).

Bibliography

Augsburger, David W. *Caring Enough to Hear and Be Heard.* https//www.goodreads.com/quotes/tag/listening?page=3.

Arndt, William F. and F. Wilbur Gingrich. *A Greek-English Lexicon of the New Testament.* Chicago: University of Chicago Press, 1957.

Barclay, William. *A New Testament Wordbook.* New York: Harper & Brothers, no date.

_____. *A Spiritual Autobiography.* Grand Rapids: Eerdmans, 1975.

_____. *The Letters of James and Peter.* Philadelphia: Westminster Press, 1960.

Berkouwer, G. C. *Divine Election,* Grand Rapids: Eerdsmans, 1960.

Bing, Charles. "The Condition for Salvation in John's Gospel." In *Journal of the Grace Evangelical Society.* Volume 9, Spring 1996.

_____. "The Cost of Discipleship." In *Journal of the Grace Evangelical Society.* Volume 6, Spring 1993.

Boice, James Montgomery. *Christ's Call to Discipleship.* Chicago: Moody Press, 1986.

Brothers, Joyce. https//www.brainyquote.com/authors/joyce_brothers_122637.

Bruce, F. F. *Commentary on the Book of the Acts.* Grand Rapids: Eerdsmans Publishing, 1968.

_____. *The Epistle to the Galatians.* In "The New International Greek Testament Commentary." Grand Rapids: Eerdmans, 1998.

Byers, AviYah. www.melohagoyim.org/index.php/faq-s/26-what-is-the-shema.

Calvin, John. *Calvin's Commentary on the Bible.*

https//www.studylight.org/commentaries/cal/james-2.html.

Chafer, Lewis Sperry. Grace. Grand Rapids: Kregel Publications, 1995.

Cockerill, Gareth Lee. "A Wesleyan Armian View" in *Four views on the warning passages in Hebrews*, Herbert W. Bateman IV General editor. Grand Rapids: Kregel, 2007.

Cole, Stephen J. Sermon on July 21, 2013.

Copeland, Kenneth. *Authority of the Believer II*. Fort Worth: Kenneth Copeland Ministries. Audiotape #01-0302, 1987.

_____. *Forces of the Recreated Human Spirit*. Fort Worth: Kenneth Copeland Ministries, 1982.

_____. *The Force of Faith*. Fort Worth: KCP Publications, 1989.

_____. *The Laws of Prosperity*. Fort Worth: Kenneth Copeland Publications, 1974.

_____. *The Power of the Tongue*. Fort Worth: KCP Publications, 1980.

_____. "Spirit, Soul and Body." Fort Worth: Kenneth Copeland Ministries. Audiotape #01-0601, 1985.

_____. "What Happened from the Cross to the Throne." Fort Worth: Kenneth Copeland Ministries. Audiotape #00-0303.

Denny, James. *The Second Epistle to the Corinthians*. In "The Expositor's Bible." London: Hodder & Stoughton, 1894.

Epoch Inspired Staff. "From Heroin Addict to World-Class Athlete. The Epoch Times. Wednesday, August 18, 2021.

Geisler, Norman L. *Systematic Theology*. Minneapolis: Bethany House, 2011.

Geldenhuys, Norval. *Commentary on the Gospel of Luke*. Grand Rapids: Eerdmans, 1960.

Grudem, Wayne. *Systematic Theology*. Grand Rapids: Zondervan, 1994.

Hodges, Zane. *Absolutely Free!* Grand Rapids: Zondervan, 1989.

_____. *Romans, Deliverance from Wrath*. Corinth: Grace Evangelical Society, 2013.

_____. *The Gospel Under Siege*. Dallas: Redencion Viva, 1982.

_____. "The New Puritanism Part 2." In *Journal of the Grace Evangelical Society*. Volume 6, Autumn 1993.

Lenski, R. C. H. *The Interpretation of The Epistle to the Hebrews and The Epistle of James*. Columbus: The Wartburg Press, 1946.

Lloyd-Jones, D. Martin. *Romans*. Edinburgh: The Banner of Truth Trust, 1985.

Luther, Martin. *A Commentary on Saint Paul's Epistle to the Galatian*s. Philadelphia: John Highlands, 1891.

MacArthur, John F. Jr. *The Gospel According to Jesus*. Grand Rapids: Zondervan Publishing House, 1988.

_____ *Faith Works*. Dallas: Word Publishing, 1993.

Moo, Douglas. *The Epistle to the Romans*. Grand Rapids: Eerdmans, 1996.

Motyer, J. A. *The Tests of Faith*. London: Inter-Varsity Press, 1970.

Mueller, Marc T. "Lordship/Salvation Syllabus," Grace Community Church, 1985.

Oesterley, W. E. *The General Epistle of James*. In "The Expositor's Greek Testament." Grand Rapids: Eerdmans Publishing, 1961.

Oxford English Reference Dictionary. New York: Oxford University Press, 2002.

Peck, Scott. https://www.goodreads.com/quotes/tag/listening?page=2.

Piper, John. *Desiring God: Meditations of a Christian Hedonist*. New York: Doubleday Religious Publishing Group, 1996.

Plummer, Alfred. *The General Epistles of St. James and St. Jude*. New York: A. C. Armstrong, 1905.

Ryrie, Charles C. *So Great Salvation*. Wheaton: Scripture Press Publications, 1989.

Sproul, R. C. *What is Faith?* Sanford, FL: Reformation Trust Publishing, 2010.

Thayer, Joseph Henry, translator. *Greek-English Lexicon of the New Testament.* Grand Rapids: Zondervan Publishing, 1962.

Thoreau, Henry David. https//www. brainyquote.com/authors/henry-david-thoreau-quotes_2.

Trench, Richard C. *Notes on the Parables of our Lord.* New York: Fleming H. Revell, 1953.

Warfield, Benjamin B. *Biblical and Theological Studies.* Philadelphia PA: Presbyterian and Reformed Publishing Co, 1952.

Webster-dictionary.org/definition/work.

Wright, Marianne, editor. *The Gospel in George MacDonald.* Walden, NY: Plough Publishing House, 2016.

Wuest, Kenneth. *Romans in the Greek New Testament.* Grand Rapids: Eerdmans, 1955.

_____. *Hebrews in the Greek New Testament.* Grand Rapids: Eerdmans, 1947.

Wynkoop, Mildred Bangs. *A Theology of Love: The Dynamic of Wesleyanism.* Kansas City: Beacon Hill Press of Kansas City, 1972.

Notes

1   Barclay, William, *A Spiritual Autobiography*, 36).

2   Denny, James, *The Second Epistle to the Corinthians*, 215.

3   *Oxford English Reference Dictionary*, 129.

4   Thayer, *Greek-English Lexicon of the New Testament*, 248.

5   Ibid.

6   *Oxford English Reference Dictionary*, 1665.

7   Moo, *The Epistle to the Romans*, 666.

8   Hodges, *Romans, Deliverance from Wrath*, 310.

9   Cranfield, *Romans, a shorter commentary*, 263.

10 Byers, AviYah, www.melohagoyim.org/?page_id=190.

11 Trench, *Notes on the Parables of our Lord*, 71.

12 Peck, goodreads.com.

13 Thoreau, brainyquote.com.

14 Brothers, Joyce, brainyquote.com.

15 Augsburger, *Caring Enough to Hear and Be Heard*, goodreads.com.

16 Geldenhuys, *Commentary on the Gospel of Luke*, 245.

17 Thayer, *Greek-English Lexicon of the New Testament*, 322.

18 Ibid, 2.

19 Ibid, 339.

20 Piper, *Confessions of a Christian Hedonist*, 50.

21 Calvin, *Calvin's Commentary* on 2 Peter 3:9.

22 Calvin, *Calvin's Commentary* on John 3:16.

23 Grudem, *Systematic Theology*, 684-5.

24 Sproul, *What is Faith?* 64.

25 Ibid.

26 *Oxford English Reference Dictionary*, 129.

27 Warfield, B. B. 426 of *Biblical and Theological Studies*, 1952 Presbyterian and Reformed Publishing Co, Phil. Pa).

28 Berkouwer, *Divine Election*, 32f.

29 Ibid, 26, 144.

30 MacArthur, *Faith Works*, 69.

31 Sproul, *What is Faith?* 49.

32 Ibid, 50.

33 Ibid.

34 Ibid, 51.

35 Geisler, *Systematic Theology*, 1015.

36 Hodges, "The New Puritanism Part 2," *Journal of the Grace Evangelical Society*, 29.

37 Ibid.

38 Bing, "The Condition for Salvation in John's Gospel," *Journal of the Grace Evangelical Society*, 31. See also Zane Hodges in *The Gospel Under Seige*, 44-45.

39 Ibid.

40 Ibid.

41 Ibid, 34.

42 Wright, Marianne, editor, *The Gospel in George MacDonald*, 3-4.

43 Copeland, *The Force of Faith*, 10.

44 Copeland, *Forces of the Recreated Human Spirit*, 8.

45 Copeland, *The Laws of Prosperity*, 18-19.

46 Copeland, *Spirit, Soul and Body*.

47 Copeland, *Authority of the Believer II*.

48 Copeland, "The Power of the Tongue," 8.

49 Copeland, "What Happened from the Cross to the Throne."

50 Lenski, R. C. H. *The Interpretation of the Epistle to the Hebrews*, 374-375.

51 *Oxford English Reference Dictionary*, 129.

52 Thayer, *Greek-English Lexicon of the New Testament*, 512.

53 Ardnt & Gingrich, 666.

54 Thayer, 511.

55 Ibid, 666.

56 MacArthur, *The Gospel According to Jesus*, 21.

57 Mueller, "Lordship/Salvation Syllabus," Grace Community Church, 20. Quoted from Ryrie *So Great Salvation*, 71.

58 Boice, *Christ's Call to Discipleship*, 16.

59 Quoted from Hodges in "The New Puritanism Part 2," 29.

60 Lloyd-Jones, *Romans*, 146 supplied this thought and has an excellent discussion of the issue on pages 143-154.

61 Ibid, 147.

62 Chafer, *Grace*, 308-309.

63 Cole, sermon on July 21, 2013.

64 Hodges, *Absolutely Free!* 74.

65 MacArthur, *Faith Works*, 70.

66 Luther, *A Commentary on Saint Paul's Epistle to the Galatians*, 212.

67 Luther, 214.

68 Ibid.

69 Wuest, *Romans in the Greek New Testament*, 210.

70 Wynkoop, *A Theology of Love: The Dynamic of Wesleyanism*, 332

71 Epoch Inspired Staff, "From Heroin Addict to World-Class Athlete, B3.